Experiencing the Classical World

Edited by Phil Perkins

This publication forms part of an Open University course A219 *Exploring the Classical World*. Details of this and other Open University courses can be obtained from the Student Registration and Enquiry Service, The Open University, PO Box 197, Milton Keynes, MK7 6BJ, United Kingdom: tel. +44 (0)870 333 4340, email general-enquiries@open.ac.uk

Alternatively, you may visit the Open University website at http://www.open.ac.uk where you can learn more about the wide range of courses and packs offered at all levels by The Open University.

To purchase a selection of Open University course materials visit http://www.ouw.co.uk, or contact Open University Worldwide, Michael Young Building, Walton Hall, Milton Keynes MK7 6AA, United Kingdom for a brochure. tel. +44 (0)1908 858785; fax +44 (0)1908 858787; email ouwenq@open.ac.uk

The Open University
Walton Hall, Milton Keynes
MK7 6AA

First published 2006. Second edition 2009

Copyright © 2006, 2009 The Open University

All rights reserved. No part of this publication may be reproduced, stored in a retrieval system, transmitted or utilised in any form or by any means, electronic, mechanical, photocopying, recording or otherwise, without written permission from the publisher or a licence from the Copyright Licensing Agency Ltd. Details of such licences (for reprographic reproduction) may be obtained from the Copyright Licensing Agency Ltd of 90 Tottenham Court Road, London W1T 4LP.

Open University course materials may also be made available in electronic formats for use by students of the University. All rights, including copyright and related rights and database rights, in electronic course materials and their contents are owned by or licensed to The Open University, or otherwise used by The Open University as permitted by applicable law.

In using electronic course materials and their contents you agree that your use will be solely for the purposes of following an Open University course of study or otherwise as licensed by The Open University or its assigns.

Except as permitted above you undertake not to copy, store in any medium (including electronic storage or use in a website), distribute, transmit or retransmit, broadcast, modify or show in public such electronic materials in whole or in part without the prior written consent of The Open University or in accordance with the Copyright, Designs and Patents Act 1988.

Edited and designed by The Open University.

Typeset by The Open University.

Printed and bound in the United Kingdom by The Alden Group, Oxford.

ISBN 978 0 7492 2546 9

2.1

B/a219_essays_e2i1_n9780749225469

CONTENTS

Introduction *Phil Perkins*		5
Essay One	People, worlds and time *Phil Perkins*	21
Essay Two	The Homeric poems: ancient and modern perspectives *Chris Emlyn-Jones*	47
Essay Three	Sing Muse: authorial voices in early Greek poetry *Naoko Yamagata*	69
Essay Four	Self and society in Classical Athens *James Robson*	86
Essay Five	Performance, competition and democracy in Athenian culture *Lorna Hardwick*	111
Essay Six	Roman reputations: famous figures and false impressions in the late republic *Paula James*	133
Essay Seven	Seneca: a philosophy of living *Carolyn Price*	153
Essay Eight	The Roman child *Valerie Hope*	172
Essay Nine	The voice of a Roman audience *Valerie Hope*	193
Glossary		213
Index		232
Acknowledgements		244

Introduction

Phil Perkins

Some books aim to tell you something: a book called *A History of the Classical World* might reasonably be expected to tell you what happened in the Classical world and when it happened. It might have a strong, authoritative narrative voice of the author telling you how it was – a reliable voice guiding you through unfamiliar territory. Other books might aim to show you something: *The Remains of the Classical World* would, hopefully, contain a number of images of what has survived from the Classical world and ancient written words that can still be read, in either the original or translated into a modern language. Such a book might present items from the Classical world as speaking for themselves and expect the reader to understand what they were saying. Another kind of book might be entitled *Finding out about the Classical World* and this might investigate how it is possible to know about the Classical world and consider the approaches and methodologies needed to understand what such voices from the past might be saying. So what is to be expected from a book entitled *Experiencing the Classical World*? Different people will have different expectations, but picking apart the words in the title should help to investigate how expectations might be shaped.

'Experiencing' is a slippery word. Who is doing the experiencing? Is this book about us, in the present, experiencing something from the past? Or is it about people from the past experiencing the world that they lived in? The slippery answer is that it is a bit of both. The only way to meet anything from the past is by experiencing it in the present. This experience might be travelling to visit an archaeological site where the physical remains from the past survive in the present. Yet how can we understand and interpret the experience? Prejudices, education, interests and emotions – in short, previous experience – all help to shape responses to the past. A schoolchild who visits a Roman museum and becomes fascinated by a fine-toothed bone comb in a glass case, may think 'head lice!' and after initial horror, empathise with a child who lived in the past, by relating the object with his or her own personal experience. The humble head louse (*pediculus humanus capitis* in Latin) speaks across the centuries. The survival of a fine-toothed hair comb enables a contemporary person to infer that people in the past suffered itching caused by parasitical insects and so know of something that a person in the past experienced.

An alternative way of meeting head lice from the past is to hear voices from the past telling of how people in the Classical world related to the parasites. Herodotus, one of the first historians in ancient Greece, describes how in Egypt 'The priests shave their bodies all over every other day to guard against the presence of lice, or anything else equally unpleasant, while they are about their religious duties' (Herodotus, *Histories* 2.37). Another survival from the past is to be found in an encyclopaedia written by Pliny the Elder who was killed in the same eruption of Mt Vesuvius that destroyed Pompeii. He wrote 'Nits are removed by dog fat, snakes taken in food like eels, or by the cast slough of snakes taken in drink' (NH XXIX. xxxv) or else lice are treated by 'taking the shed skin of a snake in drink' or salted whey (NH XXX.xlix.144). He also recommended the application of powdered seeds of the staphis (*delphinium staphisagria*), preferably mixed with a special pine resin, to kill body and head lice (NH XXIII.xiii.18).

Both provide remedies and an indication of attitudes towards lice in different parts of the Classical world at different times. However, in the first case lice are not Herodotus' main concern, he is describing in an authoritative way the rituals of Egyptian priests, whereas in the second Pliny is describing plants and animals and their medicinal uses. The first is an indirect, incidental observation whereas the second is a direct account of how to produce a remedy.

So it is possible to hear voices from the past, providing information for the present, but just as with any other information provider it is just as well to be critical and sceptical about the information they provide. How did Herodotus know about the rituals of Egyptian priests? Was his information accurate, and is that really why they shaved? How did Pliny know about remedies, and did they actually work? Both present their information as if it were reliable, but how is it possible to check on these pieces of ancient wisdom? Ideally, some other ancient testimony corroborating the information would help to establish the ultimate truth of the claims, but very often a piece of information or fact has only survived in the writings of one author and so independent verification is often lacking. Alternatively, in the case of Pliny's remedies, it might be possible, if unwise, to attempt some experiments to test whether or not his remedies actually worked, or consider any usefully insecticidal properties of the ingredients he suggests. Yet the truth about whether or not the rituals existed or the remedies worked is not the only critical line of enquiry that may be explored.

Regardless of their veracity, the accounts both tell us about ancient attitudes towards lice. Herodotus, at least, and probably the Egyptian priests too, considered them to be an unpleasant pollution of the body. The accounts incidentally also tell us about attitudes towards the body and religious rituals. Pliny's remedies also provide a cure, without even needing to express the desirability of exterminating the parasites. It is taken for granted that lice can be cured – just like any of the other diseases he discusses – through the application or ingestion of a preparation of natural ingredients. What Pliny is deliberately passing on is the matter-of-fact knowledge of how to treat the undesirable malady.

Although we can read what voices from the past tell us we cannot hear them directly. The words have survived through a process of copying from ancient manuscripts and the editing of the surviving manuscripts into a reliable printed volume. These words have then been translated from ancient Greek and Latin into a modern language. Translation is not a neutral, clinical process of replacing a word from one language with a word from another. It is a more complex process aimed at translating not just meaning, but also expression, character and style from one language to another. In the Herodotus extract the word 'unpleasant' is used to translate the Greek, but the original Greek word can also carry the meaning of 'impure' and so support the idea that the priests needed to purify themselves. Once the ancient Greek and Latin languages have been learned there is still an effective translation into a modern language that takes place in order for a modern person to comprehend the ancient language. Gifted linguists or bilingual individuals may be able to 'think' in other languages, but individuals with such skills in ancient languages are exceptionally rare. Translating languages therefore modifies the way that we can experience the Classical world, by assimilating the concepts and expressions from the ancient world with appropriate concepts and expressions from the modern world. Just as an example, compare a 1918 translation of the epic poem *Aeneid* written by Virgil in 19 BCE of a tender reconciliation scene between the king and the queen of the gods 'Cease now, I pray, and bend to our entreaties, that such great grief may not consume thee in silence, nor to me may bitter cares so oft return from thy sweet lips' (Virgil, *Aeneid XII*.800–2; in Rushton Fairclough, 1918, p.355) with a more recent translation 'The time has come at last for you to cease and give way to our entreaties. Do not let this great sorrow gnaw at your heart in silence, and do not make me listen to grief and resentment for ever streaming from your sweet lips'(Vergil, *Aeneid XII*.800–2; in West, 2003, p.286). Both are faithful to the original Latin, but express the emotions and meaning using very different idiom and vocabulary. How we can experience the Classical world is mediated not only by the passage of time but also by how the past is presented to us, in this case as translated into another language and into prose.

A discussion of lice may seem to be an unusual place to start a book about the Classical world, as indeed it is, but it provides a counterpoint to the more traditional conceptions about the study of the Classical world. Traditionally, the Classical world has been a world of epic battles, gladiators, emperors and slaves; vases, fine sculpture and lofty architecture; poetry, history and drama; gods and goddesses. Some of the earliest surviving western poetry, Homer's *Iliad*, takes the lives and passions of heroic warriors as its principal theme. The ancient biographer Suetonius writes about the achievements and misdemeanours of the first Roman emperors. Museums contain beautiful objects, collected together as the finest examples of their type, illustrating an ideal form of art with the potential to inspire contemporary artists. The emotion and passion of a love-struck Roman poet such as Catullus may be a model of expression and strike a chord in a modern heart. A Greek tragedy performed on a modern stage can still have the power to encapsulate human emotions and fallibility. Such traditional stereotypical views do not do justice to either the richness and complexity of the Classical world or the variety and subtlety of the investigations and interpretations that can be made while experiencing the Classical world. If this is the case, how did such stereotypes arise and why do they still persist?

A whole book could be written to answer these two questions, but here a few paragraphs will have to suffice. Stereotypes do not emerge from nowhere: where there is smoke there must be at least some fire, and the place to look for it is where Classical scholars have focused most of their attention. Study of the Classical world, since the European renaissance, has focused upon five principal areas: (1) criticism of ancient Greek and Latin texts and study of the ancient languages; (2) the reconstruction of a narrative history of the ancient world; (3) developing an understanding of ancient philosophy; (4) studying the physical remains of the ancient world (Classical archaeology); and (5) studying ancient art history. It is these five topics that dominated study of the Classical world up until the middle of the twentieth century at least. Textual criticism (1) started in fifteenth-century Italy and has as its aims the analysis of ancient texts, trying to establish edited versions of texts that are as close as is possible to the originals and to study the language, written records and literature of the Classical world. As well as establishing a standard text in the ancient language, textual studies also often produce translations of ancient works into modern languages. The writing of a translation simultaneously makes clear the meaning of the original language, since it needs to be understood before it can be translated, and also communicates the meaning and content of the ancient text in a modern language, making it accessible to people who are not expert in the original language. The range of texts that have survived is extremely wide – there is poetry, drama, history, biography, novels, epitaphs, records, commemorations, letters and even graffiti.

The study of ancient history (2) aims to distil facts from the texts that have survived from the past and to arrange and interpret them in order to provide an account of what happened in the past. As such it requires a high degree of accuracy and precision so that it is possible to assert that a certain event occurred and to provide the supporting evidence for the occurrence in the form of a reference to an ancient text. These carefully researched sources then need to be interpreted and fitted into their historical background in order to understand historical processes and write a modern narrative of ancient history. Ancient philosophy (3), the study of what Greeks and Romans wrote about how they thought and how they understood the world, has been studied for a variety of motives: to understand the ancient world itself, to explore a world view – so, for example, in the Middle Ages, St Thomas Aquinas developed his own theological conclusions based on the thought of the ancient Greek, Aristotle; or to understand the history and development of contemporary philosophy.

Although some remains of the past, particularly buildings, survive and have been in use continuously, interest in antiquities (4) became a pursuit of the wealthy from the sixteenth century onwards. Following the discovery of Herculaneum and Pompeii in the eighteenth century, visiting Classical ruins as a part of a Grand Tour became an essential part of a gentleman's education. Artefacts collected and purchased in Greece and Italy became the core of the collections of many of the museums in Europe and America. The remains of ancient buildings which were found on archaeological sites and surviving descriptions in ancient texts provided a springboard for new designs by architects. Ancient styles of architecture inspired new buildings with columns and pediments, imitating the ancient orders of architecture. Archaeology and art history (5) are closely related, with perhaps a traditional division drawn between on one side, architecture alongside crafts and on the other, statuary, painting and the minor arts. Ancient art has been studied both in its own right, providing examples of high achievement in the visual arts but also as a source of inspiration for artists such as David, or designers such as Josiah Wedgewood.

These five areas of study – literature, history, philosophy, architecture and art – form the core of traditional studies of the Classical world. Through the nineteenth and earlier twentieth centuries, these topics formed an essential part of a gentleman's education. Study of the literature and remains of the ancient world were seen as an excellent preparation for the (male) children of the ruling classes of Britain, Europe and America to perpetuate their hegemony and extend their rule around the world. A study of Roman or Greek politics provided the basis for a career in government. Heroic Classical warriors provided models of behaviour for aspiring soldiers. In short, the study of the classics became closely aligned with the ruling élite.

Models from the Classical world also became accepted as ideals of their kind. So advice provided by Marcus Tullius Cicero, an orator, politician and philosopher from the Roman republican period, provided a basis for moral and political attitudes and expression. Classical Greek or Roman marble statues provided a model of male and female beauty to be both admired and imitated. The poetry of Homer or Virgil provided the best examples of epic poetry, which have not been surpassed. As a result, 'Classical' in English has come to mean both something that is ideal or pure, and also something that is an example of 'the best' of its kind. However, this is not a new idea, the notion of 'Classical' meaning 'the best' was even used by an ancient author Aulus Gellius writing in the second century CE. He considers whether the word 'sand' (*harena*) could be expressed as a plural 'sands' (*harenae*) since it is constituted by many grains of sand and whether the plural word '*quadrigae*' meaning 'four-horse chariot' could occur in the singular as '*quadriga*' since even if the horses are plural the chariot is singular. The question is resolved by saying that it would only be necessary to ask if 'any orator or poet, provided he be of that earlier band – that is to say, any Classical (*classicus*) or authoritative writer, not one of the common herd (*proletarius*) – has used *quadriga* or *harenae*' (Aulus Gellius, *Attic Nights XIX*.viii.15; in Rolfe, 1982, pp.377). '*Classis*' in Latin, the noun from which the adjective '*classicus*' derives, means a social class, particularly the upper class, and so could perhaps be translated as 'first-class' but readily translates as 'Classical' since the meaning of the word in English coincides with the meaning of '*classicus*' in Latin. Aulus Gellius considers that the best Latin can be found in authors that he calls 'Classical', even in his own time. All of this might seem like pointless nit-picking, but it is the kind of erudite, refined discussion that has shaped the traditional attitude to Classics as the study of all that is best. Furthermore, the voice of Aulus Gellius speaking to us from the second century CE provides ancient support for this attitude.

It is this meaning of Classical that has become attached to Greek and Roman social, political and cultural development between the sixth century BCE and the fifth century CE. During this period, many of the positive cultural values such as heroism, democracy, liberty and rationality first emerged in the western world and so the period is seen in an idealised way. This is particularly true when the Classical period is fitted in to a larger scheme of western history, where it is preceded by uncivilised prehistory and followed by barbaric Dark Ages. However, these periods are themselves defined with reference to the Classical period: prehistory lacks the civilisation and history, barbarism lacks all that is good about the Classical world. At the same time all the negative aspects of the Classical world – slavery, high mortality, chronic warfare, despotism and oppression – are ignored. So 'Classical' is used selectively to describe periods, and also applied to cultures in other parts of the world where a particular stage of development may be seen as 'the best'. For example, in central America, the Classic period of the Lowland Maya civilisation (CE *c*.200–*c*.900) sees the development of writing, political sophistication, monumental architecture and cities, all of which is followed by a collapse in socio-political complexity and population levels. Meanwhile, in India the term 'Classical' meaning 'the best' is applied to art, literature and philosophy from the first millennium CE. All of these other 'Classical' civilisations have their own equally important place in the development of world culture, but this book will restrict itself to the Classical Mediterranean world of Greece and Rome.

The combination of the history of Greco-Roman Classical studies along with the notion that the Classical past provided perfect ideals and the 'best things' is one of the reasons why Classical Studies is often held to be an élitist subject, a study of élitist topics by students drawn from a social élite. Over the past centuries, the Greek, and especially the Latin, languages have been associated with controlling power and social élites. In the Christian West, Latin has been the language of spiritual power and religion in the Roman church and Latin the language of medieval states and their culture. Latin was taken by scientists as a universal language to classify the natural world, including the louse. Doctors, academics and lawyers expressed significant parts of their professional activities using Latin. As a result, by the twentieth century CE, Latin, and the Classical world, were firmly associated with the social and political élite of the western world. However, this is an image that modern Classical Studies is eager to escape from. Indeed, many researchers into the Classical world now try to redress this imbalance and study topics that are consciously non-élite. Furthermore, Classical Studies does not now simply consider the Classical world as an example of human perfection in order to emulate and imitate it – as it once did. Rather it aims to employ a critical methodology that develops a critical understanding of both the ancient past and the present. There is no longer the automatic assumption that Classical is 'the best', Classical is now a more neutral term describing a long and varied episode of human cultural development that had, and has, a significant influence over subsequent cultural practices, across large portions of the globe.

Modern Classical Studies – a name adopted in order to differentiate the study from simply 'Classics' which often implies a focus upon textual subjects – has also markedly increased its range of coverage, new topics such as comparative literature, anthropology, sociology, gender studies or human geography, for example, have now been added to the traditional range of topics that formerly comprised Classical Studies. These have brought with them a wider variety of approaches and methodologies. This enlarged scope means that the discipline of Classical Studies now incorporates a diversity of sub-disciplines – all united by the fact that they may be studied as an aspect of the Classical world. This wide scope for Classical Studies presents both opportunities and challenges. The inclusiveness means that any aspect of human experience in the Classical world becomes a part of Classical Studies. What is more, the inspiration and examples that the Classical world provides for later cultures and societies, for example the renaissance period or indeed the modern world, can also become an aspect of Classical Studies. This potentially vast range of topics presents a challenge. How is it possible to explore all the different facets of the Classical world?

A traditional solution to this problem has been to subdivide the Classical world geographically and culturally into a study of Greece and Rome, thus giving a primary role to the ancient spatial distribution of the Greek and Latin languages across the Mediterranean region as a means of dividing up the Classical past. Time may also be used to approximately separate out a first millennium BCE when Greek cultural influence predominated from a first millennium CE dominated by Roman culture. Further sub-divisions come easily, with a more refined division of space or time, and also with the possibilities of separating out different spheres of cultural activity, for example language and literature, philosophy, art and archaeology. Following this logic, Classical Studies becomes a portfolio of specialised studies of restricted topics in great depth. Specialised study is fascinating and rewarding but it requires a high degree of training and experience in order to advance the frontiers of knowledge about the Classical world. Most of the contents of this book depend upon such specialist studies of one sort or another. They are the building blocks of a more generalised understanding of the Classical world. However, our knowledge and understanding of the Classical world are not simply the sum of these specialised parts. The stimulating and exciting challenge is to fit together the results of specialist studies in sub-disciplines so that they provide a wider view of the Classical world that adds up to a greater whole. This challenge has always been a part of Classical Studies, but now that the subject is drawing from an ever wider range of sub-disciplines, Classical Studies is becoming an extremely flexible interdisciplinary subject.

But what precisely is an interdisciplinary subject? An easy answer is to characterise it as one combining a variety of sub-disciplines – history, literature, art history, archaeology, language, for example. But what makes interdisciplinary work exciting is not only the range of different topics involved, but how they are combined, and how the combination provides new insights. A short case study can serve to illustrate some of the possibilities of an interdisciplinary approach.

Introduction

The assassination of Julius Caesar is perhaps the best known single event in the history of the Roman republic. Caesar took too much personal control of political power in the republic, behaved like a king, was too popular with the people, and threatened to deprive the ruling élite of its power. The events are recorded by several ancient historians as either an historical episode or a part of Caesar's biography, and the background to the assassination have been thoroughly investigated by generations of scholars (see Essay Six). This case study is not going to add to those, but it will ask an interdisciplinary question and begin to explore some interdisciplinary answers. The question is where was Caesar assassinated, and what was the significance of that place? A number of ancient authors identify where Caesar was killed, it was a meeting place of the governing body of Rome, the senate, called the Hall of Pompey (the *curia pompei*) (e.g. Suetonius, *Julius Caesar* 80). This hall lay at the eastern end of an open square (*porticus*) surrounded by columns and a covered walkway at the opposite end of which was the stage building of the first stone theatre in Rome, also built by Pompey after his triumphal return from conquering much of the eastern Mediterranean region in 62 BCE (Gros, 1999). Vitruvius, a Roman writer on architecture, says the *porticus* was constructed to provide shelter for the theatre audience in bad weather (*On Architecture* 5.9.1), but this functional explanation of the building is not completely satisfactory since it is the first of its type in Italy, and may well have been influenced by buildings Pompey had seen in Asia Minor while conquering the East. This would mean that the design of the building could also be seen as an result of cultural interaction between Rome and Asia. The *porticus* was a popular place to walk in the city of Rome; several poets describe it, including Martial, who says it contained two groves of trees, presumably providing shade, and it was larger than the Roman forum – the large square in the traditional centre of the city. Some of the theatre survives beneath modern buildings, and some walls and floors where you may be shown stains claimed to be the blood of Caesar are visible in the restaurants on the Via del Biscione. The *porticus* is not visible but its shape is known in detail since it survives on the *Forma Urbis Marmorea*, a plan of the city of Rome carved in marble and set on a wall near the centre of the city in the late second century CE. Only a small part of the plan has survived in fragments, but some of the fragments show the theatre, *porticus*, pergolas and some of the temples to the East that have been excavated in the Largo Argentina (Figure 1). They also show the back wall of the *curia pompei*, which, according to Suetonius in his biography of Julius Caesar, was walled up and not used again by order of the senate after the assassination (*Julius Caesar* 88), and a statue of Pompey that had been there was moved to elsewhere in the *porticus*.

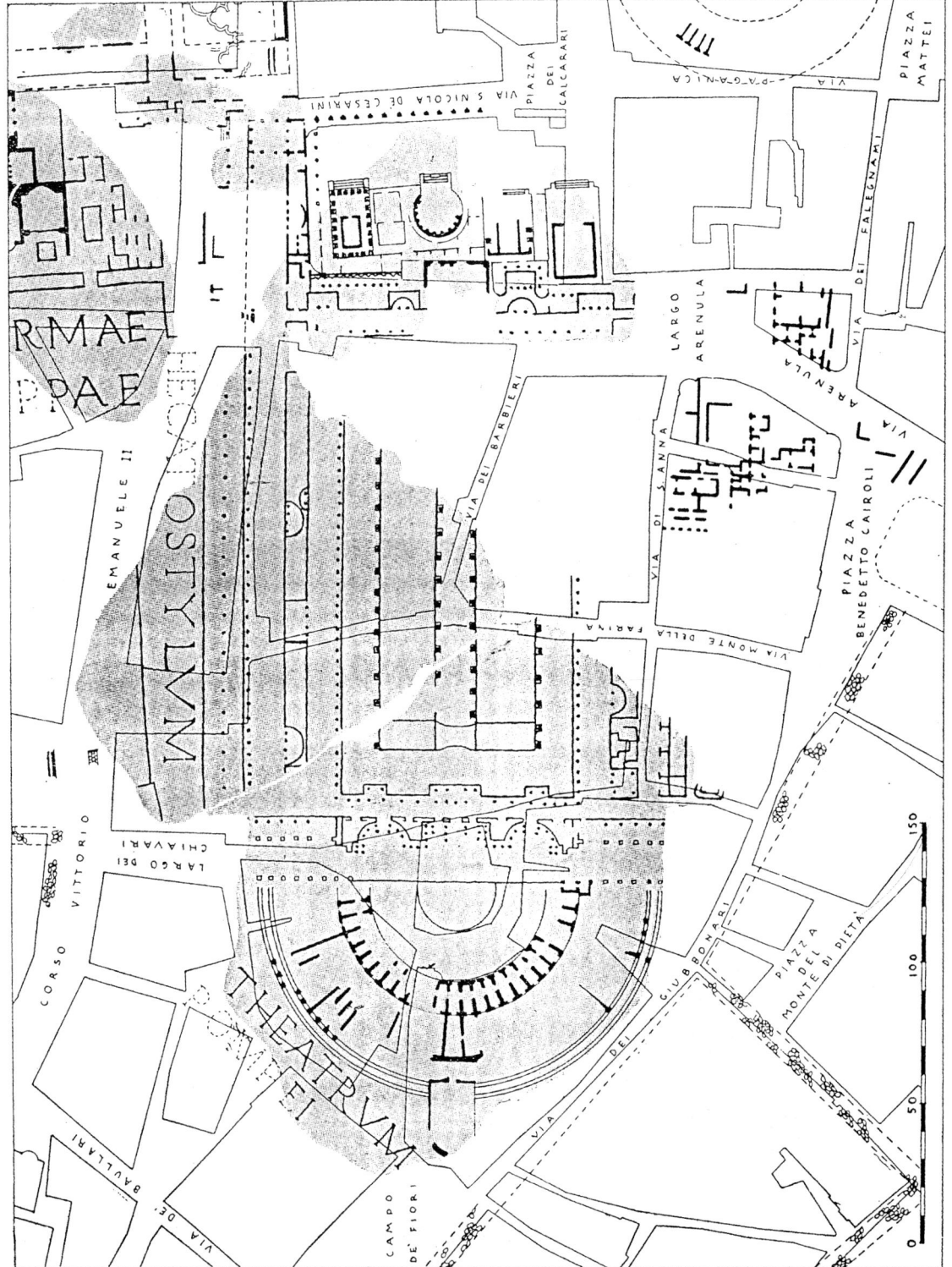

Figure 1 Plan of the streets of Rome overlaid with fragments of the *Forma Urbis Marmorea* showing the *curia pompei* next to the circular temple on the right. (Reproduced from Steinby, E.M. (ed.) (1993) *Lexicon Topographicum Urbis Romae*, vol.1, Figure 123a.)

The place was deliberately chosen by the deadly conspirators and held an irony, since Pompey the Great (*Gnaeus Pompeius Magnus* to give him his Latin name) had been the greatest rival of Caesar and according to some authors (e.g. Plutarch, *Life of Caesar* 66) Caesar even fell at the feet of the statue of Pompey, or at least was pushed there (Figure 2). So the place of assassination of Caesar contained a political irony, even more so when put in an historical context since Pompey had also been stabbed to death, to please Caesar, four years earlier, after he had been defeated in battle. So it is possible to combine the historical descriptions of the murder, other literary references to the building and archaeological discoveries in Rome to gather a relatively detailed picture of the scene of the crime and its political significance, each of the sub-disciplines adding more information and combining to produce a more complex understanding of the place and its significance. Bringing more disciplines to bear – art history, epigraphy, mythology and literature – deepens the understanding further.

A detailed examination of the ancient texts mentioning the *porticus* and a study of some inscriptions found there, have enabled an Italian scholar,

Figure 2 Statue of Pompey from the *porticus* of Pompey now in the Palazzo Spada, Rome, *c*.55 BCE. (The head is a modern replacement.) Photo: © *c*.1890 Alinari Archives – Anderson Archives, Florence.

Filippo Coarelli, to identify some of the statues that stood in the gardens of the *porticus* (Coarelli, 1972). These findings have been interpreted by a French scholar, Gilles Sauron, to provide an interesting and credible explanation of the ideas behind the choices that were made about which statues to place in the gardens, and how these related to Pompey's public persona (Sauron, 1987). Ancient written sources tell us that the best artists were used (Pliny, *Natural History* 7.34) and that the statues were carefully arranged for Pompey by Atticus, a friend and financial adviser of Cicero, so we know for sure that there was some rationale behind the arrangement. All the known statues are of famous mythical and historical women and they may be divided into three categories – lovers or prostitutes (*hetairai*), poets and those famed for their extraordinary couplings and offspring. This seems an odd collection of women, but Sauron saw a connection between them and their patron goddesses: for the lovers, Venus, obviously enough; for the poets Minerva (or the Greek Athena); and for the super-fertile women, Juno, the queen of the gods. These three goddesses competed in a beauty contest for a golden apple, which became a cause of the Trojan Wars. Venus won. At the highest part of the Theatre of Pompey, a temple dedicated to Venus 'Victrix', 'the victorious', was built by Pompey to honour Venus, who was also his patron goddess. The pieces of the puzzle begin to fit together, and it becomes possible to see the arrangement of the statues as reflecting Venus' victory in the beauty contest, and this echoes Pompey's recent military victories in the East. In passing it is interesting to wonder how in Classical Rome it was possible for differently gendered victors to be so easily equated with one another. Could victory in a (male-judged) beauty contest be paralleled with victory in war in the modern world?

A further element of Sauron's interpretation involves the statue of Pompey: he is sculpted naked, with a cloak over his shoulder and a sword-belt across his chest – the traditional appearance of a hero – and he holds an orb, representing the cosmos in his hand. Therefore, while he is a spectacularly successful victorious general (*imperator*) he is also represented as a hero, and almost a god, in the presence of Venus .This mythological and religious association opens another possible strand of interpretation for the *porticus*. In Greek and Roman myth and legend, one famous and daring exploit of gods (e.g. Dionysis) and superheroes (e.g. Hercules, Orpheus, Aeneas and Odysseus) was visiting the underworld and conversing with the dead. In a famous passage of Homer's *Odyssey*, Book 11, its hero, Odysseus, travels to the ends of the earth and conjures the spirits of the dead, first Elpenor one of his companions (Figure 3), and then the seer Teiresias who foretells his future, and then his own mother who gives him news of his family. Following this, the hero meets a throng of fantastic women, the wives and daughters of princes, lovers and mothers of gods. The early part of the scene is represented on a vase (Figure 3) made in Athens in the middle of the fifth century, at the same time as the Parthenon, and Odysseus appears dressed as a hero – naked, with a cloak, sword-belt and his distinctive hat. Four hundred years later, another hero, Pompey, is

Figure 3 *Pelike* (storage jar), the Lykaon Painter, Greek, Classical period, *c.*440 BCE. Place of manufacture: Greece, Attica, Athens. Ceramic, Red-figure. Height: 47.4 cm, diameter: 34.3 cm. Museum of Fine Arts, Boston. The vase depicts Odysseus conjuring the spirit of Elpenor as Hermes (right) looks on. (Note the hero's costume is similar to Pompey's in Figure 2.)

represented in the same manner at one end of a *porticus* filled with statuary. The parallel is not precise, but Pompey before a host of extraordinary women, in a divinely charged setting, clearly evokes the image of Odysseus before the spirits of women who founded great human and divine dynasties. Could it be that placing Pompey in this context is drawing attention not only to his heroic status but also to his ambitions to found a ruling dynasty? Another insight is that in this mythic context the *porticus* becomes an entrance to the underworld, populated by its potent spirits. These infernal associations would have provided a further ironic twist to the choice of place to assassinate Julius Caesar.

So this case study, tracing links from a historical and political event to a context investigated through archaeology, architecture, art, epigraphy, mythology, religion and literature provides a demonstration of how it is possible to enrich the understanding of a single episode through interdisciplinary investigations. Inevitably it will never be possible to reconstruct all aspects of the Classical world and experience its original variety and richness. However, a broad interdisciplinary approach can help to build an appreciation of its texture and complexity and to go beyond events and facts and work towards the interpretation and understanding of their significance.

Interdisciplinary study does not have a fixed methodology, there is no correct way to combine the results of different specialist studies. Equally, there can be no fixed set of sub-disciplines to bring to bear upon a particular topic. Often the relevance of a sub-discipline will be dictated by the nature of the surviving evidence. Statues require artistic analysis, and buildings architectural analysis. But other avenues should not be excluded, in our case study literature and mythology provide a key to understanding that was not immediately apparent or obviously relevant to the surviving evidence. For this reason it is necessary to look for interrelationships and be open to the fact that one field may inform another.

This book both exemplifies and explores the interdisciplinary nature of the subject. None of the following essays combine all possible sub-disciplines to bear upon a single question or topic, but they do draw from different disciplines to explore the ancient world. The different essays explore different aspects of how we in the modern world can hear the voices of individuals – or indeed groups – from the ancient past and what those voices can tell us about experiencing the Classical past.

This final part of the introduction will highlight, very briefly, the interdisciplinary approaches of each of the essays, concentrating on describing their methodology rather than summarising their content. In the first essay some basic issues are discussed, drawing widely from different sub-disciplines to focus upon concepts of time and how they were, and are, used to structure and characterise cultural change. The second essay by Chris Emlyn-Jones considers the extent to which our knowledge, specifically in this case of the Homeric world, is shaped by the surviving evidence and how the approaches of different sub-disciplines produce different, and not easily reconcilable, conclusions. Naoko Yamagata brings different literary approaches to the study of poetry in order to critically investigate whether Homer and other early poets have individual voices. The theme of the individual in the past is extended to the individual in society by James Robson in his investigation of fifth-century BCE Athens that draws from literary, linguistic, cultural and sociological approaches. All of these sub-disciplines are drawn together to analyse Athenian voices. A different range of sub-disciplines – theatre, ideology, history and politics – are brought to bear on Athens by Lorna Hardwick who provides a complementary analysis of Athenian culture, politics and society.

Moving to Rome, but staying with a highly competitive society, Paula James brings literary, poetic analysis to bear upon the question of how the voices we hear from the past shape our perception of it. Carolyn Price uses philosophical and literary approaches to analyse a very individual voice from the past and investigates the tension between ancient words and deeds. In contrast, Valerie Hope investigates a far less vocal group, analysing the perception of children through literary and sociological approaches. The final essay, also by Valerie Hope, considers a collective voice using historical, sociological and literary approaches.

Together the essays investigate a wide range of experiences of ancient individuals and groups, paying attention to how we interpret and experience their voices using interdisciplinary approaches. This introduction started by suggesting that some books aim to tell you something, this book hopes to introduce you to some ways of experiencing the Classical world.

Bibliography
Ancient sources
Aulus Gellius, *Attic Nights*, in Rolfe, J.C. (trans.) (1982) Aulus Gellius: *The Attic Nights of Aulus Gellius*, vol.3, London: Heinemann.

Herodotus, *Histories*, in de Sélincourt, A. and Marincola, J. (trans.) (2003) Herodotus: *The Histories*, Harmondsworth: Penguin.

Homer, *Iliad*, in Lattimore, R. (trans.) (1951) *The Iliad of Homer*, Chicago and London: University of Chicago Press.

Homer, *Odyssey*, in Lattimore, R. (trans.) (1965) *The Odyssey of Homer*, New York: Harper Perennial.

Pliny, *Natural History*, in Rackham, H. (trans.) (1938–63) Pliny the Elder: *Natural History*, London: Heinemann.

Plutarch, *Life of Caesar*, in Perrin, B. (trans.) (1914–26) Plutarch: *Plutarch's Lives*, London: Heinemann.

Suetonius, Julius Caesar, in Graves, R (trans.) (1957) Suetonius: *The Twelve Caesars*, Harmondsworth: Penguin.

Virgil, *Aeneid*, in Rushton Fairclough, H. (trans.) (1918) Virgil: *Aeneid VII–XII, The Minor Poems*, London: Heinemann.

Virgil, *Aeneid*, in West, D. (trans.) (2003) Vergil: *The Aeneid*, Harmondsworth: Penguin.

Vitruvius, *On Architecture*, in Granger, F. (trans.) (1970) Vitruvius: *On Architecture*, London: Heinemann.

Modern scholarship

Coarelli, F. (1972) 'Il complesso pompeiano del Campo Marzio e la sua decorazione scultorea', *Rendiconti della Pontificia accademia Romana di archeologia* , ser.III, vol.XLIV, pp.99–122.

Gros, P.(1999) 'Porticus Pompei', in Steinby, M. (ed.) *Lexicon Topographicum Urbis Romae*, vol.4, P–S, Rome: Edizioni Quasar, pp.148–9.

Sauron, G. (1987) 'Le complexe pompéies du champ de Mars: nouveauté urbanistique à finalité idéologique', in *L'Urbs: Espace urbain et histoire (Ier siècle av. J.-C. – IIIe siècle ap. J.-C*, Collections de L'École française de Rome, 98, pp.457–73.

Essay One

People, worlds and time

Phil Perkins

Introduction

The Classical world is a world in the past. It is a part of global history. Geographically is it easy enough to define broadly where the Classical world was located – it was the parts of Africa, Asia and Europe that surround the Mediterranean Sea. But saying when, in the past, the Classical world may be found is not so simple. The most straightforward way of doing so is by counting time. In years, the ancient world may be placed between about 2,800 and 1,500 years ago. But how is it possible to be so specific about saying when the ancient world happened when it was so long ago? The answer is that Classical Studies, as an academic subject, has chosen boundaries for itself. Anything before 814 BC, the date of the earliest 'reliable' historical date in the area around the Mediterranean Sea, is a part of prehistory – the massively long part of the human past that was lived without written historical records. Everything after that date is a part of recorded history (see Essay Two).

If such great significance is to be placed upon a single year it demands some closer examination. The date of 814 BC has been recorded for the foundation of the city of Carthage in the modern state of Tunisia. The date is given by a Greek-speaking writer named Timaeus from the city of Taormina in Sicily in his history of that island that was written over 500 years after the foundation of Carthage. He used earlier lists of kings in Phoenicia (modern Lebanon), which have not survived, to fix the date of the founding of Carthage at 38 years before the first Olympic Games, a set of ancient athletic contests first held in 776 BCE (Lancel, 1997, p.22).

Using written records in this way to divide up time needs some explanation. Why should the presence or absence of written words recording an event play such a powerful role? The clearest answer to this question is that the written word that has survived from the ancient world gives us a voice from the past. We can say that Timaeus *says* that the city of Carthage was founded in 814 BC. His voice gains authority through the fact that he lived closer to the time itself and had sources of evidence not available to us. Other historians living in ancient times relied on his work to write their own histories. In modern times, scholars who have studied the question in great detail have found good reasons to believe that Timaeus was providing a reliable piece of information free from prejudice or wilful misrepresentation, and this reinforces its credibility.

This voice from the past, and the others like it that have survived through to the present by being written down, form the raw materials from which ancient history is written by modern historians. The use of the earliest reliably dated event to mark the very beginning of the ancient world underlines the traditional emphasis placed by historians of the ancient world on the word as the most important source of knowledge about what happened in the ancient world. The date of 814 BC may be considered reliable for historical reasons, but independent corroboration has not yet been found for this: the earliest dated archaeological finds made at Carthage, up to now, date to about 50 years later, in the middle of the eighth century BC (Lancel, 1997, pp.25–34). This lack of supporting evidence does not necessarily prove that the historical date is not believable. All that can be said is that evidence to support the date has not yet been found.

At the other end of Classical Studies the boundary is harder to draw, but in the western Mediterranean the ousting of the last Roman emperor, Romulus Augustulus, in AD 476 is commonly taken as the end of the Roman period. This too is a reliably dated event given to us by an anonymous voice known as the Anonymus Valesii, writing in a fragmentary chronicle of the period (Anonymus Valesii, viii; in König, 1987, p.38). However, in the eastern Mediterranean, emperors continued to reign. Voices from the past, preserved in writing, tell us that later figures in Byzantium, such as the emperor Justinian (lived AD 527–65), who controlled parts of the western empire and was titled 'Emperor of the Romans' (Procopius, *History of the Wars* 1.1), continued to consider themselves as maintaining the traditions and civilisation of the ancient world. The end of the ancient world, or the Classical world as it is often termed to differentiate it from ancient periods in other parts of the world such as India or China, is often taken to have happened when Islamic peoples conquered the southern and eastern shores of the Mediterranean in the seventh century AD, thus marking the beginning of the Middle Ages. Yet if we follow the Classical world through into the Byzantine empire, the end of the ancient world may be placed even later, in 1453, with the Ottoman conquest of Constantinople, which in the west of Europe is nearer in date to the end of the Middle Ages.

Wherever precisely markers are placed at the beginning and end of the Classical world, a long period still remains to be studied in between. How can such a long period of time, at least 1,300 years, be divided into manageable, meaningful and useful shorter periods that can be studied and understood? Making such divisions is essential, since once this has been done it becomes possible to investigate processes of change within the ancient world by comparing one period with its predecessor or successor.

Essay One People, worlds and time

The aim of this essay is to investigate methods used for the dividing up of the past and also to ask why the past is divided up into different periods, how it has been done and what effect that has upon our understanding of the ancient world.

The organisation of time

Perhaps the most obvious way to divide up the past is to measure time, as we have already done, using 'years ago'. This may be convenient but it is not very precise. 'Two thousand years ago' said in 2005 is not the same as 'Two thousand years ago' said in the year 2015 – it is different by ten years. Using a system derived from observations of the rotation of the earth around the sun to calculate the length of a year has the advantage of being related to the unchanging rhythm of the natural world. Indeed, it might seem an ideal system: it is very regular and it is independent of human events and cultural changes (provided it is measured accurately). Furthermore, it is a system that has been in use from before the start of the Classical world, and the calendar adjusted by Julius Caesar in antiquity (in 46 BC) was in use in western Europe until the eighteenth century AD and is still used in Russia. However, even if we can measure the length of a year and count the passing of individual years, it is still necessary to define a year zero, be it the present, from which we can count back (as in years ago), or in the distant past, from which we can count forward. But this is where the problems start.

Up to this point in this essay, in discussing how the Classical world was delimited, a year zero has been assumed using a system of identifying years as BC or AD (but it should be noted that in the BC/AD system there is actually no year zero since the measurement of time passes directly from 1 BC to AD 1). This system of referring to years is familiar to some, but is itself controversial. It has been argued that it is inaccurate since it uses the date of the birth of Christ as a fixed point before or after which things can be measured to have happened, yet the historical fact of the date of that reported birth is disputed by many on two different grounds, both the accuracy of the actual date and the historicity of such an event. Others object to the system because it is too culturally specific and the division of world history into years fixed upon the date of birth of a figure key to a particular religious faith is inappropriate for other people with different faiths – who use their own, different, culturally specific systems. Attempts to remove the cultural significance of the system by replacing BC (before Christ) with BCE (before the common era) and AD (*anno Domini*, Latin for 'the year of our Lord') with CE (common era) are hardly more satisfactory in that they still use the same religiously defined date as a year zero. Neither the BC/AD system nor its derivative, the BCE/CE system, were used in antiquity. The former was invented in the fifth century CE and the latter in the twentieth century CE. However, we will for convenience be using the BCE/CE system throughout the essays in this book from here on.

The ancient Romans had a similar system, which used the traditional date of the founding of the city of Rome, 753 BCE, as a year zero. In this system of reckoning, the year 2006 would be 2759 AUC (*ab urbe condita*, Latin for 'from the founding of the city'). This system was commonly used in history books written before the early twentieth century CE, but it has now fallen out of fashion. Furthermore, it does not seem that the system was widely used in ancient times and the actual date of founding of the city was debated in antiquity and still is. Another system that used significant events in the past as fixed points was employed in the Ancient Greek world. This divided the passing solar years into groups of four years, the beginning of which were celebrated by the Olympic Games. Thus, CE 2008 would be the start of the 696th Olympiad. Yet another ancient system reckoned time in years after the Trojan War, thought to have ended in 1183–1182 BCE.

So in antiquity, as now, there was a variety of reckoning systems in use but no consensus about a universal system. A more common system was one that was not absolute, in that it did not work from a fixed zero, but instead identified each year by referring to the names of those holding certain offices of state in that year: the two ruling consuls (chief magistrates) in Rome, the archons in Athens or the ruling magistrates in other cities, each of which maintained its own system of identifying years. Thereby, time was defined locally by referring to individuals in authority, and making the marking of time a part of public and political life in each independent city. In this system, in Rome, the year CE 15, for example, was referred to as the year when Drusus Caesar and Gaius Norbanus Flaccus were consuls. It is the surviving lists of consuls that provide the possibility of matching the years in the two systems: that is, the one defined by year zero and the other by named officials (Figure 1.1). Later on, years might also be identified by referring to anniversaries of the accession of a new emperor. For example, CE 122 could be referred to as the fifth year of the emperor Hadrian.

This form of time measurement, being precise about years, provides a means of describing how long ago events happened and the amount of time that elapsed between different events happening. It also makes it possible to put events in the past into a chronological order. This is time used to gauge the past and it is an important basis for constructing history, or cultural development, since once observations of events or situations, judged to be important, have been put into a sequence it becomes possible to investigate change and causes and effects. This chronological time is important for students of the past but there are other uses for time and other ways of dividing the human past.

Essay One People, worlds and time

Figure 1.1 Inscription of the Capitoline Annals, with the list of the names of the magistrates of the Republican period; found in the Roman forum. First century BCE. Capitoline Museums, Palazzo dei Conservatori Museum, Rome. Photo: Alinari Archives 1985–1995.

The cosmos and time

Even before the time of the Greeks and Romans, the length of the solar year was known to be approximately 365¼ days, and calendars were devised at different times and places to divide the year into a number of days and months. Some calendars attempted the difficult task of combining the length of the lunar month (29½ days) with the solar year to form a coherent system. Roman calendars have survived which map the days and the months against public business and religious festivals and these were used to record and predict the time-dependent aspects of the ancient social world. Within each day the time between sunrise and sunset was divided into twelve equal parts, as were the hours of darkness. This was a geometric and rational organisation of time that was easily measurable with a sundial by dividing the part of the sundial where the shadow is cast into twelve parts, but it led to hours of different lengths at different times of year as the length of time between sunrise and sunset varied with the seasons.

The passing of the months and seasons was also related to the apparent movements of the stars, and in one of the earliest surviving pieces of Greek poetry, *Works and Days* by Hesiod (*c.*700 BCE), the timing of farm work appropriate to each season is related to the rising of various constellations, for example:

> As soon as mighty Orion rises above the horizon
> exhort your slaves to thresh Demeter's holy grain
> in a windy, well-rounded threshing floor.
>
> (Hesiod, *Works and Days* 597–9; in Athanassakis, 1983, p.82)

The passing and measuring of time was therefore intimately associated with the natural world and the cosmos with its cyclical rhythms (Figure 1.2). In the middle of the fourth century BCE, the same close relationship between time and the cosmos was rationalised and put in theological terms by Plato:

> For before the heavens came into being there were no days or nights or months or years, but he [god] devised and brought them into being at the same time that the heavens were put together ... the sun and moon and the five planets as they are called came into being to define and preserve the measures of time.
>
> (Plato, *Timaeus* 38; in Lee, 1977, pp.51–2)

This creation of time and the cosmos clearly parallels the Old Testament account of the creation.

The role of divinities in measuring and regulating time is visualised by the Roman poet Ovid (43 BCE– CE 18) in the second book of his *Metamorphoses*, where he tells the story of Phaethon, the son of Phoebus, god of the sun, who took over driving the chariot of the sun for a day – with disastrous results:

> He went at once into his father's presence, but stood some way off: for he could not bear his light too close. The sun, dressed in a purple robe, was sitting on a throne bright with shining emeralds. On his right hand and on his left stood Day, Month, Year, the Generations and the Hours, all ranged at equal intervals. Young Spring was there, his head encircled with a flowery garland, and Summer, lightly clad,

Essay One People, worlds and time

Figure 1.2 Floor mosaic showing Aeon (god of eternal time), or the spirit (*genius*) of the year, surrounded by (from left anti-clockwise) the Sun, Spring, Summer, Moon, Autumn and Winter, each in a roundel set in a circular composition, from El Djem, second half of the third century CE, El Djem Museum, Tunisia. Photo: Akg-images, London/Gilles Mermet.

crowned with a wreath of corn ears; Autumn too, stained purple with treading out of the vintage, and icy Winter, with white and shaggy locks.

(Ovid, *Metamorphoses* 2.22–30; in Innes, 1976, p.50)

The personifications to either side of the sun god are carefully arranged: the *Dies*, *Mensis*, *Annus* (Day, Month, Year), the natural temporal divisions, followed by artificial divisions, the *Saeculi* and *Horae* (Generations and Hours) (Zissos and Gildenhard, 1999, p.33). It has even been suggested by Andrew Zissos and Ingo Gildenhard that the arrangement of the Hours at equal intervals to either side of the sun reflects the arrangement of a Roman sundial with twelve even intervals to either side of the shadow of the sun at midday.

Ovid used words to create his images, but physical representations of time were also popular. Roman mosaics decorating the floors of the residences of the Roman élite commonly feature themes related to time, particularly personifications of the seasons. Such personifications became standardised, often as female figures, with flowers to represent Spring, ears of corn to represent Summer, grapes for Autumn and olives for Winter (Figure 1.2). The days of the week, each of which was sacred to a god or goddess, also occasionally appeared on mosaics, as did the signs of the zodiac. Time was ordered and unchanging, it had a regular, cyclical

Figure 1.3 Silver statuette of the goddess Tutela (Fortune) by an altar with an offering dish, with busts of Apollo and Diana in a pair of cornucopiae in one arm, Castor and Pollux on her wings and deities of the days of the week, Saturn, Sol, Luna, Mars, Mercury, Jupiter and Venus above. Found at Mâcon, France, c.CE 260, British Museum, London, Silver 33. Photo: © Copyright The Trustees of the British Museum.

structure. This order was often represented in geometric compositions, such as mosaics featuring the seasons arranged in a circular composition.

Thus, time was divided, measured, rationalised, mythologised and visualised in Graeco-Roman thinking, life and art (Figure 1.3).

People and time

Human lifespan was meshed into this ordering of time: it was used as a measure of the passing of time. For example, Herodotus (484–430 BCE) describes the Heraclid dynasty in Lydia as reigning for 22 generations, equating this to a period of 505 years, and so giving an average life of nearly 23 years to each generation (Herodotus, *Histories* 1.7). But an ordered cosmos could also be mapped against the individual's life in order to understand the future through the calculation of horoscopes. The tradition of ancient horoscopes came from the earlier civilisations of Babylon and Egypt, and the influence of these systems can be seen in modern descriptions of stars as constellations and also, indirectly, in contemporary astrology (Figure 1.4).

The telling of fortunes in ancient times depended upon the positions of the celestial bodies at the moment of birth. For this reason, if no other, it was important to be able to measure time precisely enough to allow the use of astronomical tables, built up through centuries of observation and calculation, to establish the positions of the stars and planets at the moment

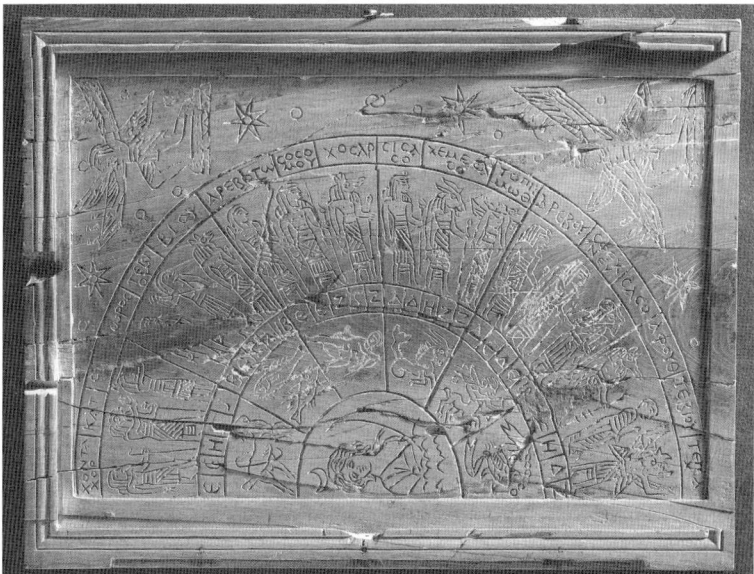

Figure 1.4 Egyptian wooden horoscope plaque, showing Luna in the centre, the signs of the zodiac in the inner ring and further out the houses represented by Egyptian divinities, with stars around the edge. From a Roman sanctuary, Grand, Vosges, France, second century CE, Musée départemental d'art ancien et contemporain à Epinal. © Musée départamentale d'art ancien et contemporain, Epina. Photo: Bernard Prudhomme.

of birth. Although astrology does not play a significant role in standard histories of the ancient world, it does seem to have been widely practised, at all levels in society (Figure 1.5):

> At Apollonia, Augustus [the future emperor] and Agrippa together visited the house of Theogenes the astrologer, and climbed upstairs to his observatory; they both wished to consult him about their future careers. Agrippa went first and was prophesised such almost incredibly good fortune that Augustus expected a far less encouraging response, and felt ashamed to disclose the time of his birth. Yet when at last, after a deal of hesitation, he grudgingly supplied the information for which both were pressing him, Theogenes rose and flung himself at his feet; and this gave Augustus so implicit a faith in the destiny awaiting him that he even ventured to publish his horoscope, and struck a silver coin stamped with Capricorn, the sign under which he had been born.
>
> (Suetonius, *Augustus* 94; in Graves, 1979, p.93)

The taking of a horoscope is a demonstration of faith in fate and predestination, the moment of birth being vital for defining an individual's future. It is also a demonstration of faith in an astrologer. Time is vital for gauging the future by means of the time of birth and hence the position of the celestial bodies, but the knowledge and skills required to interpret these were those of the astrologer. Astrology provided not only a knowledge of fate, but also the power to manipulate that fate. A second-century CE manual of astrology sums up this power:

Figure 1.5 Silver coin (denarius) of Augustus, showing on the obverse Augustus with a laurel crown and on the reverse his birth sign, Capricorn, holding a globe and rudder symbolising steering of the empire, 27–24 BCE, British Museum, London. Photo: by courtesy of the Trustees of the British Museum.

> if future happenings to men are not known, or if they are known and
> the remedies are not applied, they will by all means follow the course
> of primary nature; but if they are recognized ahead of time and
> remedies are provided, again quite in accord with nature and fate,
> they either do not occur at all or are rendered less severe.
>
> (Ptolomy, *Tetrabiblos* 1.3.13; in Robbins, 1980, pp.27–9)

Thus, a knowledge of time and its relationship to nature might yield control over the future.

Periodisation

Time, past or future, can thus be measured in various ways, both absolute and relative, for a variety of purposes. History, the study of past time, traditionally divides time into broad areas, such as modern times, medieval times, ancient times, even prehistoric times, but why do students of the past need to divide up history? At a simple level the answer is that periodisation – dividing things into periods – makes the practice of history easier. It makes it easier to talk about the past, it 'enables the drawing of lines and to be able to say some common thread unites a block of human lived experience, also that this block is different from the preceding or following ones' (Morris, 1997, p.96). For example, if something or someone can be identified as belonging to the Archaic period, that on its own enables us to situate it or them in history with respect to other periods, such as the preceding Orientalising period or the following Classical or Hellenistic periods (see Table 1.1). It is also often possible to identify common features of artefacts or societies that can be characterised as Archaic (for example) and to draw boundaries for a period when such features begin and cease to be found.

Table 1.1 Table of periods

Greece	Iron Age/Dark Age		Archaic period		Classical period		Hellenistic period
				Orientalising period			
Italy	Bronze Age	Iron Age		Orientalising period	Archaic period	Classical period	Hellenistic period
Central Europe	Bronze Age			Iron Age			
					Hallstatt D period	La Tene period	
Years BCE	1,000	900	800	700	600	500	400	300

(Sources: Barker and Rasmussen, 1998, p.6; Champion *et al.*, 1984, p.271; Whitley, 2001, p.62)

There is, however, a need to be careful about precision – that is, how closely we can be sure of a date assigned to something in the past. In some cases ancient historians can be sure of a date, for example the eruption of Mount Vesuvius, known from surviving eyewitness accounts to have started on 24 August CE 79. But in many other cases such certainty is not possible and various techniques are used to express uncertainty. For instance, a historian may write 'In about BCE' or 'Between X BCE and Y BCE' or commonly the abbreviation *c*. of the Latin word *circa* is used, meaning 'about'. Another area where dates can be less than precise is when the dates of birth and death of an individual from the past are not known but some information about when the person lived is available. In these cases, the Latin term *floruit* ('flourished') is used to indicate that the individual is known to have been alive at a certain date but that any more precision is not possible. There are no hard-and-fast rules to dictate how a particular level of uncertainty should be expressed, and it will often be necessary to dig deeper to find out just how certain of a date historians actually are. So there are problems with precision in dating events, and perhaps even greater problems in dating artefacts from the past where it may be difficult to assign a date in calendar years to an object. In some cases it is necessary to ask how we can be sure that we have placed an object, a text or an event even in the correct period.

Some periods appear to be very precisely defined – for example, the Hellenistic period is usually taken to begin in the year 323 BCE, the year of the death of Alexander the Great. This was no doubt a key event for the history of the Macedonian kingdom that Alexander ruled, yet why that should become the borderline between two historical periods goes beyond the effects of an individual's death upon his contemporaries. It is the result of generalisations made later by historians who have taken the individual event and used it retrospectively as some kind of marker of change, indicating that something that was 'typical' before the event becomes different after the event. The problem with this kind of definition of periods is that the closer one looks the more difficult it is to see differences between periods. With a time perspective of 2,500 years, and a knowledge of what came before and after, it becomes easier to see large-scale differences. Yet these large-scale changes in history which are visible to later historians are most likely to have been much less visible to contemporaries.

So who defines boundaries between periods and how is it done? Are they ancient or modern? Are they relevant to ancient people or just to modern students? Did ancient people conceive of themselves as belonging to a particular time and were they aware of the fact that they belonged to part of a broader sequence of cultural development and historical change? A first question is, did ancient people think that they were part of a process of change, be it progress or decline? The answer, for once, is relatively straightforward: yes they did. Provided that is, and there is almost always a proviso in the study of the ancient past, the 'ancient people' we are asking questions of are those who were aware of their own contemporary élite culture, since theirs is the only point of view that has survived.

Hindsight and periods

In *Works and Days*, Hesiod tells the story of a myth of human development through five races of men. Each race described is characterised: the first is the race of Gold, the next Silver, then Bronze, Heroes and Iron, with Hesiod's contemporaries being of the race of Iron (*Works and Days* 106–201). This myth was used by Hesiod to symbolise moral and material decline rather than to explain humankind's technological, social and cultural development (Dodds, 1973, pp.1–5), and the myth recurs in later Roman poetry and philosophy – for example, in Lucretius' (lived 98–55 BCE) work *The Nature of the Universe*. However, it re-emerges in the early nineteenth century CE, when it influenced the development of the 'Three Age' system that archaeologists still use to divide prehistory into Stone Age, Bronze Age and Iron Age (Trigger, 1989, pp.60–1, 75–6). Perhaps surprisingly, the modern division of early Greek history places the boundary between the end of the Iron Age (the Geometric period) and the Orientalising period at precisely the same time, and so, in modern terminology, Hesiod unwittingly lived at the end of the Iron Age, which he himself mythologised as the time of the race of Iron. This immediately raises again an important question, which must be addressed before progressing: how precisely are boundaries between periods drawn? In Hesiod's work, the sequence of stages is driven by the gods of Olympus, who replace one race with the next, each characterised poetically by its moral character, predilection to violence or carefree life. In modern archaeology it is identification of the materials that were used for tool technology that divides the periods, although one does not necessarily entirely replace its predecessor, so, for example, bronze tools were still used in the Iron Age. These two forms of periodisation divide the past of human kind into different periods using different criteria to define the periods (the moral and the technological).

Making periods

In other areas of human culture, scholarship has developed criteria for assigning artefacts to different periods, for example in the study of Greek sculpture. Figures 1.6 and 1.7 show two sculptures of a nude male. The first is from the Archaic period (*c*.800–*c*.480 BCE) and the second is from the Classical period (*c*.480–323 BCE). (The Classical period is a shorter period within the whole period that Classical Studies covers.) The Archaic characteristics of the so-called 'Apollo of Tenea' include the upright, rigid pose, with apparently taut muscles; one leg in advance of the other but with the weight shared between them; the straight arms; the anatomy and musculature not being quite natural; the patterned, stylised hair; the pointed nose and chin; the almond-shaped eyes; and the fixed grin. This type of statue is specifically called a *kouros* and is similar to earlier statues from Pharaonic Egypt.

Compared to this the Classical characteristics of the *Doryphoros* ('spear-bearer', who would originally have had a spear in his left hand and resting on his shoulder, but this is now missing) include the more relaxed pose, with the muscles of the left leg and right arm relaxed and the weight on the right leg; the torso curving and the head turned; overall the axis of the body sinuous rather than upright; the anatomy apparently more natural (e.g. the ribs), even if the musculature is exaggerated; the hair and the more naturalistic facial features. These differences are the clearest indication of the Archaic qualities of the one and the Classical qualities of the other. These formal characteristics may be used to assign the sculptures to the Archaic and Classical periods, and so, incidentally, to date them approximately.

These and other defining characteristics have been developed and refined by scholars through the comparison of many statues and other representations of the human form – for example on painted pottery where, very generally, Attic Black-figure and earlier Red-figure painting is Archaic and later Red-figure Classical. The combination of recognisable characteristics comes to define a style of visual culture for each period, thus the Apollo of Tenea can be said to be in the Archaic style and the *Doryphorus* in the Classical style.

This characterisation and structuring of ancient sculpture is not entirely a creation of modern scholars inventing and imposing a system onto ancient art. Polyclitus (c.460–410 BCE) is known to have written a book titled 'The Canon' (from the Greek word *kanon* meaning 'rule' or 'standard'). Only a few short passages have survived, but it outlined a system of ideal proportions for the human body expressed in mathematical ratios between the fingers and toes and other parts of the body. The 'Canon' also discusses the nuances that are part of the creative expression of the artist, as well as the more technical aspects of representation. It is generally believed that Polyclitus embodied the ideas in the book in a statue, which is thought to be the *Doryphorus*, and that the statue subsequently became the stereotyped model of the perfect male form in Greek and Roman art. It has even been suggested that the statue represents the perfect Greek warrior, Achilles, and so another range of idealisations could be brought to the statue. There is, however, no sure identification of the figure in the statue. The original bronze statue has not survived but

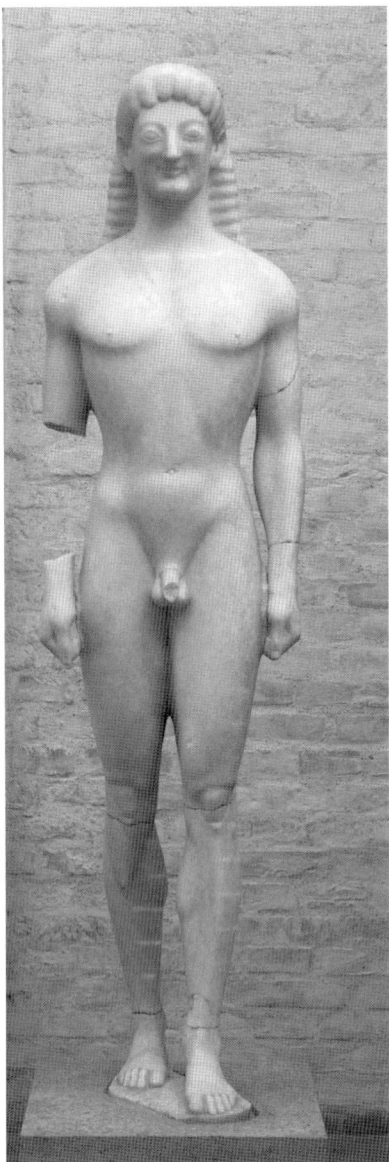

Figure 1.6 'Apollo of Tenea', from Attiki near Corinth, c.560 BCE, Staatliche Antikensammlungen und Glyptotek, Munich.

over 50 whole or part stone copies are known, including the one shown in Figure 1.7.

Scholarship during the nineteenth and twentieth centuries CE has largely unified the periodisation of different sub-disciplines of Classical Studies so that it is possible now to characterise literature, political systems, history and society, to list a few examples, as being Archaic or Classical.

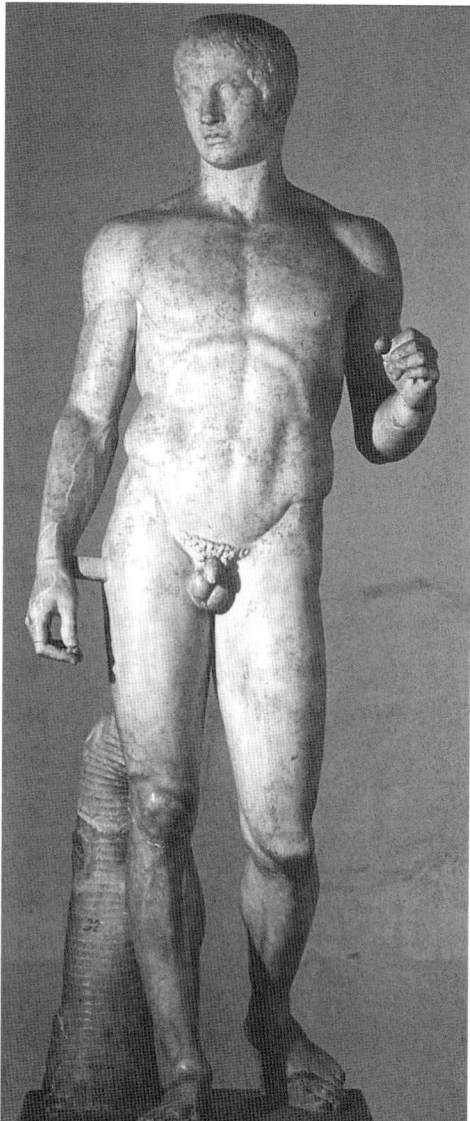

Figure 1.7 Roman copy of the *Doryphoros* (spear-bearer) of Polyclitus, original *c.*440 BCE, copy from Herculaneum, National Archaeological Museum, Naples. Note that the tree supporting the right leg is a feature of the copy that would not have been part of the original statue.

This is not to say that the same formal characteristics define both statuary and politics alike. Rather, the statuary defined as Classical can be said to date from a period with boundaries set (*c.*480–323 BCE) and the known political system from that same period – democracy – can also be seen to have a set of characteristics – liberty, citizenship, freedom of speech, for example – that can be said to define the Classical period. The Archaic period, on the other hand, is characterised by a different political system – tyranny – typified by monarchy and personal monopoly of political power. This possibility of characterising elements of a period is the unifying 'common thread' specified by Morris, quoted above (Morris, 1997, p.96).

Of course, the boundaries between the Archaic and Classical periods (or any others) are not sharply discernible. The *Doryphorus* may be canonical in that he can be taken as emblematic, or even quintessentially Classical, but other statues may not share so many Classical features and may even have both Classical and Archaic features. This can be seen in Figure 1.8, where the rigid pose is more Archaic yet the naturalistic tendencies in the face and the musculature are more Classical. Furthermore, changes in statuary are not systematically matched by changes in politics. The dating of the transition from one period to the next cannot be precisely confined to a single year, yet historically recorded events, held to be significant, are often used as markers of the transition from one period to the next. So 480 BCE – the date of the sack of Athens by the Persians, a well-recorded and traumatic episode in the city's history – marks the boundary between the Archaic and the Classical periods. This event itself caused the destruction of old Archaic buildings on the Athenian Acropolis that were subsequently replaced with new buildings constructed in the Classical style, which helps to reinforce the distinction between the periods. However, stylistic changes in different genres and media were not tightly synchronised, the historical marker date does not precisely match the transition in all areas of culture. Statuary and pottery, for example, had developed towards Classical styles before this time. The boundaries between periods are therefore somewhat fuzzy, and it is not possible to be overprecise or always certain about the date of a transition or the assignation of an artefact to a period. The degree of uncertainty will vary from case to case but that is not an insurmountable problem: it is a feature of working with imperfect evidence from the ancient world. After all, Classical Studies is not a precise science.

The characterisation of periods has often taken on something of a moral tone, in that the ideal, perfect form of the *Doryphorus*, or the happy state of living in a well-regulated democracy and other idealised aspects of human culture have often been intellectually combined in order to set up the Classical period as an ideal of perfection, a time when everything in human history was at its best. The preceding period, the Archaic, has been characterised as primitive, partially formed and imperfect, and so the name Archaic – a modern term meaning old, out-of-date and primitive – has been applied to the period. Transition into the Classical period is a bettering of everything. Following the perfection of the Classical period, the

Hellenistic period is decadent, impure and over-embellished. This characterisation is deeply rooted in western culture. For example, in contemporary English referring to something as a 'Classical example of ...' is drawing upon the same cultural stereotyping. Such definition of the Classical period is not simply a modern phenomenon. Romans idealised Classical Greek art: Cicero (106–43 BCE) calls the work of Polyclitus 'completely perfect' compared to earlier works that were 'too rigid' (Cicero, *Brutus* 18.70), and in the time of the emperor Augustus, Classical, Attic, artistic style was much in vogue. In later centuries up to modern times, the ancient world was not always very finely divided into discrete periods and

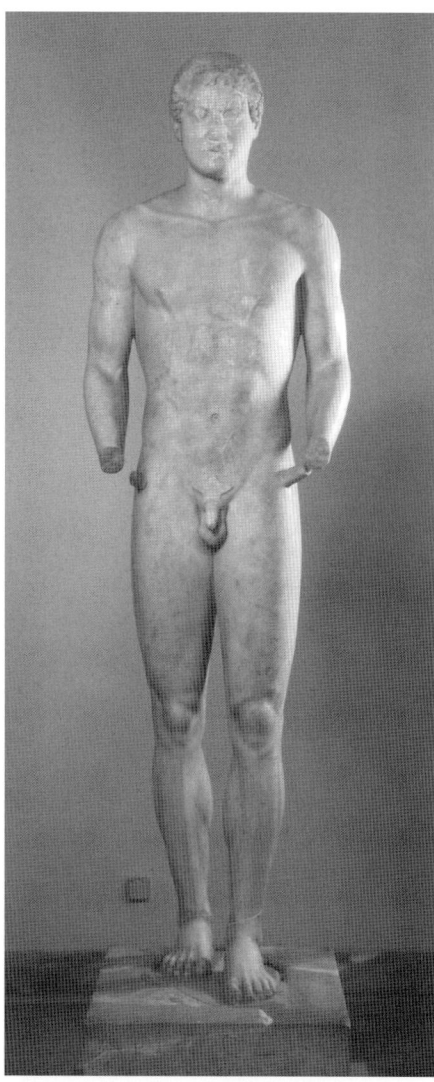

Figure 1.8 *Kouros* of Aristodikos, c.510–500 BCE, Athens National Museum.

the term 'Classical' was often extended to cover the whole of Graeco-Roman antiquity, hence the term 'Classical Studies'.

Although assigning an artefact or other cultural product to a period may carry the risk of weighing it down with unwanted baggage, it is a key stage in developing a context for that item. Context, in its broadest meaning, is identifying the other things that belong together with an item, including both the physical circumstances of its finding or preservation and the cultural circumstances of its creation. So, for an artefact found on an archaeological excavation, that means the location where it was found, the soil it was found in and all the other artefacts that were found in the same soil. It also means the broader cultural context of the society that produced the artefact (and here artefact is being used in its broadest possible meaning of anything produced by humans using skills, so it includes literature and art as well as objects). For a Latin poem the context is both the manuscript upon which it was written, with the means by which it was transmitted, by copying to the present; the cultural world within which it was written; the social, educational and economic background of its author; and all of the other cultural factors that shaped the creativity of the author. A further aspect of context is the historical context: that is, both the events and circumstances contemporary with the production of the artefact and the times preceding and following its production that may have influenced, or been influenced by, its production.

A context can thus be considered as all of the many and various elements that belong in the same period as an artefact. A period is therefore a descriptor that can be used to identify and to some extent characterise a context. Once boundaries have been defined for a period – and, as has been discussed, boundaries are fluid, negotiable and debated – it becomes possible to place an artefact with respect to some other artefacts from a preceding or subsequent period. Once things are placed in a historical sequence it is then possible to consider two different forms of enquiry. The first is a central plank of any historical enquiry and that is the study of change through time – identifying and explaining how and why things change or develop from one period to the next. This form of study is often termed 'diachronic', as for example in the short investigation into Greek statuary above (although there was no attempt there to explain why it changed). The second form of enquiry is how and why things are different in separate places at the same point in time, often called 'synchronic'. The first can be considered as a 'vertical' study in that it examines the same place through time and the second can be considered as a 'horizontal' study in that it examines the same time across different places. Thinking this way it becomes possible to study change and difference in the Classical world in an interesting variety of ways. Change can be studied in the same place from period to period, for example change between the Archaic and Classical period in Athens. Alternatively, the Classical period in Athens can be compared with the Classical period in Sparta, that is, the same period but in different places. Another possibility is to study a particular point in time, noting that one place, say Athens, can be identified as Classical, while at the same time another place, say Rome, can be identified as Archaic. This discussion is getting rather abstract and so a short case study will both anchor these points to evidence from the ancient world and return to the central focus of this chapter – people and periods.

A person in periods
In midwinter CE 1953, in the Modern period, the French archaeologists M. Moisson and R. Joffroy opened a tomb beneath a mound near the village of Vix in Burgundy, central France (Joffroy, 1954). Nobody had seen the contents of that tomb for nearly 2,500 years since the Hallstatt D period (*c*.625–475 BCE) in the Iron Age. The tomb contained the body of a female aged about 35 years with bad teeth. She was buried on a chariot-like wagon, with three necklaces of gold, bronze and amber with semi-precious stones, brooches, bracelets and an anklet, as well as an Archaic-period Greek bronze *crater* (wine-mixing bowl) 1.64 metres high, weighing 209 kilograms, with a capacity of 1,100 litres, made in Sparta or its colony Taranto (Figures 1.9 and 1.10), and two Archaic ceramic vases made in Athens, one decorated with Black-figure scenes of battle between Greek male warriors and female Amazon warriors. Along with these were various other metal vessels, some made in Etruria, Italy. The wheels of the wagon had been removed and placed against the side of the burial chamber. All in all this was a particularly rich burial containing some exceptional items that can be used to date the deposition to *c*.500 BCE (Mohen, 1997, pp.119–21). The nature of this burial and the finds made raise a host of lines of interest to research and analyse, but here the focus will be kept upon periods. (A plan of the burial is reproduced in Champion *et al.*, 1984, p.284 and in Hornblower and Spawforth, 1998, p.298.)

First of all, the discovery was made in the Modern period, an unfortunate title to choose for a period, since the middle of the twentieth century CE no longer seems very modern. It is important to consider the historical context of the discovery: the 1950s were early days for scientific archaeology and the bones in the deposition were not well preserved, but if such a discovery were to be made now a whole range of new techniques, such as analysis of DNA, might be applied to the human remains. At the time, the best available techniques were used, and the study of the skull revealed dental abscesses on the right side of the jaws and indications of an infected wound on the back of the head. From measurements of the skull, it was suggested that the female was a Nordic individual. This finding reflects the emphasis placed upon establishing race and nationality through skeletal remains that was current in the middle of the twentieth century CE.

The context of the deposition is labelled as Hallstatt D, which is a smaller division of the Iron Age that started in *c*.725 BCE in central Europe. Hallstatt is the name of a large cemetery site in Austria, the finds from which were used to first differentiate the Bronze Age from the Iron Age in central Europe. In contrast, the items in the tomb that were made in Greece and Italy were produced in the Archaic period in those areas. Thus, as well as being transported from the Mediterranean to central Europe, they were also transposed from one period to another, and from one context to another. Now, of course, the items reside in yet another context – a modern museum in France. This case study illustrates how, from an intellectual perspective, artefacts may simultaneously belong to different periods without difficulty. If the perspective is shifted to that of the ancient individuals, a further range of interpretative possibilities arises.

The name of the female buried at Vix with such exceptional artefacts is unknown, yet something of her context can be discovered by considering

Figure 1.9   Vix *crater*, from Chatillon-sur-Seine, France, *c*.500 BCE. Photo: MSM-France.

EXPERIENCING THE CLASSICAL WORLD

Figure 1.10 Vix *crater*, detail showing Gorgon handle and procession of hoplites and chariots, from Chatillon-sur-Seine, France, *c*.500 BCE. Photo: MSM-France.

what she was buried with, and the finds made at other nearby sites dating to the same period. Modern Vix is a village that lies close to Mont Lassois, the site of a large, defended Iron Age settlement (an *oppidum* or hill-fort). Evidence from here and elsewhere, which it is not necessary to discuss in detail in this essay, indicates that society at this time was very hierarchical, with a small élite controlling power and resources. The exceptional nature of the burial at Vix suggests that the female buried there was a member of that élite. Her status is represented by the artefacts buried with her (it is not important for this discussion whether the artefacts actually belonged to her in her lifetime, or were buried with her by others to signify the importance of her burial). Part of representing her status was the burial of artefacts with origins alien to her own context – from Greece and Italy. Presumably they acquired a value in excess of their intrinsic worth through their exotic origin. In this way Archaic Mediterranean vessels play a role in the Hallstatt D period of the Iron Age of central Europe. From a distance of

2,500 years we cannot be sure precisely how the artefacts represented that status. It could be their alien nature; their sheer size (for the *crater*); the value of the metals; their decoration, evoking aristocratic values with warriors, chariots and battle; their mythological content – Gorgons and Amazons; or their function as vessels all used for the ritual and social consumption of wine (in the Greek world at least). The relative importance of these factors to Iron Age individuals is a matter for intellectual debate, and it may be that several or all of the factors played some role in establishing and legitimising the female's status. In order to facilitate such debate, terms such as 'Archaic', 'Iron Age' or 'Hallstatt D' are used flexibly to signify chronological periods and cultural contexts as well as characterising the artefacts themselves.

Periods and the Classical world

Periods are thus useful in both analysing and discussing the past. Periods are not, however, simply blocks of time that can be pinned down with a starting date and an end date, using whichever means of measuring time – ancient or modern – is appropriate. Periods can be related to calendar years, enabling them to be placed in time with respect to one another and their duration to be gauged, but they also have geographical and cultural aspects. Once established they powerfully shape how the past is conceptualised: one period happens before or after another, something changes from one to the next, one period may influence another, as we have seen.

Where the lines are drawn between periods is a complex and debatable process, both when dealing with details, for example between the Archaic and Classical periods in Greece, or on the larger scale with the beginning and end of the Classical world. Different criteria may also be used to explore the boundaries of periods: changes in visual representation; social development; political change; the death of a great man; the invasion of a foreign power; or a combination of some of these may be used as criteria to define the boundaries of periods. These choices about how to define the boundaries themselves influence the nature of the periods. A periodisation of history using solely political criteria may not be especially effective in the analysis of art, while a history arranged by poetry may not facilitate the study of ancient warfare. Ideally, the boundaries are drawn in a flexible manner that facilitates analysis and discussion using a suitable combination of criteria. The drawing of lines is not only influenced by empirical evidence and scholarly debate, but also by the interplay of the divisions in intellectual, educational and cultural life. Classical Studies sets its own boundaries that differentiate the periods it studies from those studied by Prehistoric Archaeology at one end and History at the other, and these disciplines in turn set their own boundaries.

Further reading

Rather surprisingly, ancient historians and archaeologists do not frequently discuss time, although Kristen Lippincott, *The Story of Time* (1999) provides a broad world perspective. Periodisation is rarely introduced as a facet of methodology, but Ian Morris, 'Periodisation and the heroes: inventing a Dark Age' (1997) gives an insight into periods and the practice of ancient history. Archaeology is more forthcoming on chronology and dating: see James Whitley, *The Archaeology of Ancient Greece* (2001) for a chapter on the topic, or Colin Renfrew and Paul Bahn, *Archaeology: Theories, Methods and Practice* (2000, Chapter 4) for a textbook discussion of dating. The concept of progress in antiquity is not often discussed in anything other than technological terms, but Ludwig Edelstein, *The Idea of Progress in Classical Antiquity* (1967) is an exception (although now out of print).

We are in more familiar territory in the study of Greek art. John Boardman, *The Oxford History of Classical Art* (1993) provides a thorough and well-illustrated account, while John Boardman, *Greek Art* (1973) and Robert Cook, *Greek Art: Its Development, Character and Influence* (1972) both give reliable and non-controversial introductions to the development of Greek art.

For a broad discussion of the archaeology of Europe in prehistoric times, which overlaps with much of the period covered by Classical Studies, Timothy Champion *et al.*, *Prehistoric Europe* (1984) gives a well-organised and wide-ranging synthesis.

Bibliography

Ancient sources

Anonymus Valesii in König, I. (trans.) (1987) *Origo Constantini*, Trier: Trierer historische Forschungen.

Cicero, *Brutus* in Hendrickson, G.L. and Hubbell, H.M. (trans.) (1939) Cicero: *Brutus; Orator*, London: Heinemann.

Herodotus, *Histories* in de Sélincourt, A. and Marincola, J. (trans.) (2003) Herodotus: *The Histories*, Harmondsworth: Penguin.

Hesiod, *Works and Days* in Athanassakis, A.N. (trans.) (1983) Hesiod: *Theogony, Works and Days, Shield*, Baltimore and London: Johns Hopkins University Press.

Lucretius, *The Nature of the Universe* in Lathan, R.E. (trans.) (1951) Lucretius: *The Nature of the Universe*, Harmondsworth: Penguin.

Ovid, *Metamorphoses* in Innes, M.M. (trans.) (1976) *The Metamorphoses of Ovid*, Harmondsworth: Penguin.

Plato, *Timaeus and Critias* in Lee, D. (trans.) (1977) Plato: *Timaeus and Critias*, Harmondsworth: Penguin.

Procopius, *History of the Wars* in Dewing, H.B. (trans.) (1979) *Procopius: History of the Wars*, London: Heinemann.

Ptolomy, *Tetrabiblos* in Robbins, F.E. (trans.) (1980) *Ptolomy: Tetrabiblos*, London: Heinemann.

Suetonius, *Augustus* in Graves, R. (trans.) (1979) Suetonius: *The Twelve Caesars*, Harmondsworth: Penguin.

Modern scholarship

Barker, G. and Rasmussen, T. (1998) *The Etruscans*, Oxford: Blackwell.

Boardman, J. (1973) *Greek Art*, London: Thames & Hudson.

Boardman, J. (ed.) (1993) *The Oxford History of Classical Art*, Oxford: Oxford University Press.

Champion, T., Gamble, C., Shennan, S. and Whittle, A. (1984) *Prehistoric Europe*, London: Academic Press.

Cook, R.M. (1972) *Greek Art: Its Development, Character and Influence*, Harmondsworth: Penguin.

Dodds, E.R. (1973) *The Ancient Concept of Progress and Other Essays on Greek Literature and Belief*, Oxford: Oxford University Press.

Edelstein, L. (1967) *The Idea of Progress in Classical Antiquity*, Baltimore: Johns Hopkins University Press.

Hornblower, S. and Spawforth, A. (1998) *The Oxford Companion to Classical Civilization*, Oxford: Oxford University Press.

Joffroy, R. (1954) 'Le trésor de Vix (Côte d'Or)', *Monuments et mémoirs Piot*, vol.48, no.1.

Lancel, S. (1997) *Carthage: A History*, Oxford: Blackwell.

Lippincott, K. (1999) *The Story of Time*, London: Merrell Holberton.

Mohen, J-P. (1997) 'Le tombe principesche della Borgogna' in S. Moscati (ed.) *I Celti*, Milan: Bompiani, pp.116–22.

Morris, I. (1997) 'Periodisation and the heroes: inventing a Dark Age' in M. Golden and P. Toohey (eds) *Inventing Ancient Culture*, London: Routledge, pp.96–131.

Renfrew, C. and Bahn, P. (2000) *Archaeology: Theories, Methods and Practice*, London: Thames & Hudson.

Trigger, B.G. (1989) *A History of Archaeological Thought*, Cambridge: Cambridge University Press.

Whitley, J. (2001) *The Archaeology of Ancient Greece*, Cambridge: Cambridge University Press.

Zissos, A. and Gildenhard, I. (1999) 'Problems of time in *Metamorphoses* 2' in P. Hardie, A. Barchiesi and S. Hinds (eds) *Ovidian Transformations: Essays in the Metamorphoses and its Reception*, Cambridge: Cambridge Philological Society, pp.31–47.

Essay Two

The Homeric poems: ancient and modern perspectives

Chris Emlyn-Jones

Cultural authority: how the Greeks and the Romans regarded Homer

> Now, since I am not going back to the beloved land of my fathers,
> since I was no light of safety to Patroklos, nor to my other
> companions, who in their numbers went down before glorious Hektor
> ...
> Now I shall go, to overtake that killer of a dear life,
> Hektor; then I will accept my own death, at whatever
> time Zeus wishes to bring it about, and the other immortals.
>
> (Homer, *Iliad* 18.101–3, 114–16; in Lattimore, 1951, p.378)

Thus, at a climactic moment in the epic poem the *Iliad*, the Greek hero Achilles chooses to avenge the killing of his dear friend Patroclus by the Trojan Hector and himself face almost certain death rather than survive in dishonourable inactivity. Achilles is expressing here, in characteristically extreme form, a code of values that motivates all of Homer's heroes, indeed without which they cannot maintain their status as heroes: death rather than dishonour and a compulsion towards self-assertion in physical combat and in debate – 'excellence' (*aretē*), which ensures the respect of their fellow warriors as well as 'fame' (*kleos*) among the generations to come.

In purely physical terms, even for the late eighth-century BCE audiences in the presence of whom the *Iliad* and the *Odyssey* were being created, the world depicted by Homer was already a far-distant memory. But the massive *c*.25,000 verses of the poems survived to represent for the Greeks their greatest and most enduring model for the way a man's life ought to be lived, even when transmuted away from the battlefield. For example, Socrates, a philosopher on trial for his life at Athens in 399 BCE for unorthodox moral and political views, still reaches back three centuries to Homer's Achilles as a paradigm for his own actions, and quotes from that hero's speech (see above) to express his need to choose death rather than recant his beliefs (Plato, *Apology* 28b–d). The more orthodox citizens of fifth-century BCE Athens may have had as little tolerance for the eccentric extremes of a Socrates as they would have had for the violent individualism of an Achilles, but the basic requirements of a Homeric hero – 'excellence' in words and deeds – remained as an essential aspiration for success in the main areas of life where men gained distinction: politics and war.

Figure 2.1 Zeus and Hera, metope from east of temple of Hera at Selinous, Sicily, c.460 BCE, limestone, height 162 cm, Museo Nazionale Archeologico, Palermo. (Photo: akg-images, London/Nimatallah)

Essay Two The Homeric poems: ancient and modern perspectives

It was not, however, only a code of ethics that Homer bequeathed to Greece and the ancient world generally, but a theology too: the gods and goddesses of Greece and Rome, with their human 'anthropomorphic' manner and appearance, were to a large degree modelled, not only in literature but in art (Figure 2.1), on Homer's Zeus, Hera, Poseidon, Apollo, Athena etc. The legendary stories were also recreated, and critically treated, in popular drama; the depiction on the fifth-century BCE Athenian tragic stage of Greek heroes became the focus of creative and individualised presentation by Aeschylus, Sophocles and Euripides of events and personalities from the world of the Trojan War and its aftermath. On this stage room was made also for an exploration of the feelings and experiences of Homer's female characters, such as Helen and Andromache (Hector's wife), and how their world presented a challenge to the dominant value of male 'excellence'. Moving on to the Roman empire, the Roman poet Virgil (70–19 BCE), in his *Aeneid*, an epic poem on the destruction of Troy and the escape of the Trojan hero Aeneas to found the Roman race, 'imitated' (in the special sense of recreating in Latin Homer's style and metre) the myth and story-patterns of the original in order to represent a distinctively Romanised version of Homeric 'excellence', *virtus* (Latin for 'bravery' or (male) 'virtue').

Some visible monuments served the Greeks and Romans as a reminder of their remarkable heritage: at ancient Mycenae in the Argolid, south-west of Athens, traditionally the home of Agamemnon, leader of the Greek forces at Troy, there was veneration of what were imagined to be the tombs of well-known heroic figures. Later ages marvelled at the enormous blocks of stone that made up the fortifications of the citadel, calling them 'Cyclopean' because their size was such that surely only legendary giants such as the Cyclopes could have built with them (Figure 2.2). The site of what was popularly believed to be Homer's Troy, along with the alleged tombs of Achilles and Hector (who in the legend were killed at Troy), were visited by the Persian king Xerxes (early fifth century BCE) and the Macedonian conqueror Alexander the Great (late fourth century BCE) in the course of their military campaigns of conquest across the Dardanelles, westwards and eastwards, respectively. Both of these leaders, in order to put a necessary emphasis on their military prestige, could do no better than recall the memory of Achilles and pay homage to Homer's Troy. The enhancement of status worked both ways: although already by the time of the Greek Classical period (fifth to fourth centuries BCE) a small and unimportant place in political and military terms, Troy continued to derive considerable celebrity from its association with Achilles, Agamemnon and the other heroes. For example, in the period of the philhellenic Hadrian (Roman emperor CE 117–38), the inhabitants of Alexandria Troas (a

Figure 2.2 The Lion Gate at Mycenae, 1350–1300 BCE, archaeological site, Mycenae, Greece. (Photo: akg-images, London/Erich Lessing)

Essay Two The Homeric poems: ancient and modern perspectives

Roman city popularly identified as Homer's Troy) managed to procure funds for a new water supply, thereby incurring the disapproval of local Roman governors, who wrote to the emperor that 'it was a scandal that the tribute [money paid to Rome by subject cities] received from five hundred cities should be spent on the fountain of one city' (Philostratus, *Lives of the Sophists* 548; in Wright, 1921, p.143). In the early Roman empire the city also enjoyed considerable fame as an early example of a 'heritage site': visitors well versed in the poems of Homer, as all educated Greeks and Romans were, could walk on the highest battlements of the remains of Troy and imagine that they were treading in the steps of King Priam, Hector or Helen of Troy, as described in the *Iliad*. For these 'tourists' Homer's works had in some respects perhaps the same kind of status as the Arthurian legend has had at some periods for the English, except that the Greeks and the Romans were the heirs of a much more authoritative and pervasive tradition and, certainly up to the early Roman empire, a more obvious point of physical contact.

This iconic status enjoyed by Homer in the ancient world has its own problems for the modern student who attempts to go behind the façade, as it were, and with different priorities from those of the ancients. In one sense – how the Greeks and Romans regarded the poems – we know almost too much about Homer; in another – for example, how the poems were composed, how they relate to the events about which they tell and to the period in which they were composed – we know only too little. These are the questions we will now be looking at in this essay.

The Greek perspective: Homer and the heroic past

The Greeks did not know anything for certain (as we still do not) about the identity of Homer, nor could they agree about exactly where he came from, although the predominant Greek dialect in which the poems were composed suggests the middle of the west coast of Asia Minor. A number of places competed for the prestige of having produced him, Smyrna and Chios (an island just off the Asia Minor coast) perhaps having the best claim (Graziosi, 2002).

With regard to the events with which the poems are concerned, the Greeks thought of Homer, and other less significant contemporaries, as reporting more or less accurately a real world of cities, individuals and deeds, which constituted their own past. At the same time, they were clear that there was a distinction between the period *in which* the poems were composed and that of the events *about which* they told. They could perceive that the Homeric heroes were men greater and stronger than themselves, not only from the evidence of the Cyclopean walls at, for example, Mycenae (see above), but also from the internal evidence of the poems. In

Lion Gate

an attack on the Greeks, warriors such as the Trojan Hector could snatch up a stone that could barely be hoisted by two men onto a wagon, 'such as men are now' (*Iliad* 12.445–9; in Lattimore, 1951, p.270). The fact that the god Zeus made the stone light for Hector (450) does not detract from the feat of strength. Rather, it illustrates a major difference between Homer's world (the 'now' of the poem) and the extraordinary heroic past in which Olympian gods came to the aid of their mortal favourites in direct ways, and also associated, joked and conversed with them in human shape, as, for example, the goddess Athena does with Achilles and Odysseus (*Iliad* 1 and *Odyssey* 13). Some prominent heroes were intimately connected with deities. For example, Achilles' mother, Thetis, a sea-nymph, a lesser divinity, intercedes with Zeus (in *Iliad* 1) and so provides the main impetus for the action of the poem. The Greeks believed that far back in the past was an age when gods walked the earth and there existed not only mortals who enjoyed divine favour but even heroes who attained divine status on Olympus, such as the demi-god Heracles (Hercules), worshipped in later ages by the Romans as well as the Greeks.

So, clear distinctions are made between the heroic past and the present in which the poems are created. The poet claims that his unique authority for accurate knowledge of this past comes to him through one or more of the heavenly Muses, the goddesses of poetry and other arts. This is an authority he calls on at the beginning of both the *Iliad* and the *Odyssey*: 'Sing, goddess, the anger of Peleus' son, Achilleus' (*Iliad* 1.1; in Lattimore, 1951, p.59); 'Tell me, Muse, of the man of many ways' (*Odyssey* 1.1; in Lattimore, 1965, p.27). When about to embark on a particularly detailed recreation of the past, the account of the composition of the Greek forces at Troy, the 'Catalogue of Ships', the poet asks for special guidance: 'Now speak to me [or 'for me', or 'through me' – the Greek may mean any of these], Muses who have dwellings on Olympus – for you are goddesses: you are present and you know all things, but we have heard only the report of it and know nothing' (*Iliad* 2.484–6; my translation). Whether the Muses speak to the poet directly or through him to the audience, Homer claims a privileged insight into the past, based upon his status as the mouthpiece of these divine beings. (For further discussion of the function of the Homeric Muse, see Essay Three.)

Modern approaches: Homer and the Trojan War

Without the insight and certainty afforded by the Muses' assistance, but with other more scientific techniques of investigation, modern scholarship has been concerned with how far we can aim at greater precision than the Greeks in locating the Homeric past – the world in which the poems are set. For any event earlier than *c*.650 BCE, later Greek historians could rely

Essay Two The Homeric poems: ancient and modern perspectives

on no systematic historical records, and so, if one excludes the works of the poets themselves, were dependent on information derived from oral (unwritten) traditions and calculations of genealogies (successive generations of well-known individuals from the past). While such historians made a number of calculations or inspired guesses about the date of the Trojan War, these were, by their very nature, speculative. Events recorded in this way were prehistoric in a very specific sense of the word, that is, they did not fall within the period illuminated by written records, which form the basis of history. The ancients did not dig up their past, and in later antiquity even the physical point of contact with Homer was lost: changes in the landscape turned the area around Troy into a fever-ridden swamp, and the city the ancients believed to be Troy disappeared from sight under the ground.

No further progress was made until the nineteenth century CE, when, under the influence of the European Romantic movement, attention was directed particularly towards Greek antiquity. The Greeks, early in the century engaged in a war of liberation against the centuries-long domination of the Turkish empire, caught the imagination of, among others, English poets such as Byron and Shelley, steeped as they were from school and university in Classical, and particularly ancient Greek, culture. It was also during this century that modern archaeology effectively emerged as a new tool of investigation of the past, and was specifically directed towards Greece and Homer. In the 1870s, Heinrich Schliemann (1822–90), a wealthy German businessman, directed an obsession with Homer towards trying to rediscover the physical reality of the poems by digging. He was convinced that under a Turkish hill called Hissarlik, overlooking a wide plain and the narrow channel of the Dardanelles, he would find the city of the Trojan King Priam, which Agamemnon and the Greeks had attacked, as Homer related. As he dug through the archaeological layers of the site, Schliemann discovered near the bottom a strikingly rich hoard of precious metal objects, which he assumed were from Homer's city and which he called 'Priam's treasure'. Excavations at Mycenae unearthed what appeared to him to be a strikingly similar culture, with equally rich gold objects ('Mycenae rich in gold': *Iliad* 11.46; my translation), including an imposing death-mask which he thought was that of Agamemnon himself (Figure 2.3). It seemed possible that the historical reality of the poems, which was axiomatic for the ancient Greeks, but about which, outside Homer's works and other legendary material, they knew next to nothing, was being revealed.

Subsequent improved methods of archaeological investigation showed this hypothesis to be, to say the least, premature. Schliemann and his successors were successful in unearthing a pre-Classical civilisation in the

Figure 2.3 'Agamemnon', gold death-mask, from the fifth shaft grave at Mycenae, sixteenth century BCE, National Archaeological Museum, Athens. (Photo: akg-images, London/Erich Lessing)

Aegean area dated to the second half of the third and the second millennium BCE (the 'Bronze Age', c.2500–1100 BCE), but constructing from any part of this vast period a plausible context for a war as described by Homer proved much more intractable. As Schliemann himself began to realise at the end of his life, careful stratification of the site, that is, separating out the successive layers of settlement on the basis of designs on pottery (*the* major survival from prehistoric sites) and other indicators, showed that his valuable finds at Troy and Mycenae had to date from much earlier than any likely occasion for a war between the Greeks and the inhabitants of Troy.

It is remarkable how long the precise details of Homer's dramatic scenario, the historical truth of which had been a largely unquestioned assumption for Schliemann, still held sway among professional archaeologists. Excavations at Troy in the 1930s led by the American Carl Blegen were still dominated by the imperative of trying to match the archaeological evidence with the topography and events of Homer's *Iliad*. The fact that Blegen felt compelled to reject a large and imposing settlement (conventionally known as Troy VI, which flourished at the end of the second millennium BCE; Figure 2.4), apparently destroyed by earthquake, in favour of its much less imposing successor (Troy VIIa), stemmed largely from his apparently unargued conviction that he had to square the archaeological evidence with Homer, whose account fitted much better with the evidence revealed by Troy VIIa – a long siege of the city, followed by a destruction of the citadel by fire (Blegen, 1963).

Underlying the increasingly evident doubts in the post-Second World War period concerning Blegen's attempt to bring Troy and Homer together was a major problem of method: trying to relate two totally different types of evidence. Trojan archaeology has yielded much concrete evidence about the physical site, including evidence of Mycenean pottery, but has revealed nothing about named individuals or their lives; on the other hand, Homeric poetry, dealing with specific named individuals and situations, was set in no identifiable historical context. The two types of evidence were also widely separated in date. In the last 30 years, a great deal has been discovered about the topography and uniquely long settlement history of Hissarlik,

Figure 2.4   Walls of Troy VI, *c.*1300 BCE. (Photo: Deutsches Archäologisches Institut, Athens, negative no. Troja 545)

with use made of the most modern scientific technologies. Under the direction of the German prehistorian Manfred Korfmann, such research has deployed, for example, equipment that can detect without digging underground structures such as defensive walls. This has revealed that Troy was a much larger city than previously suspected, in fact one of the largest settlements in west Asia Minor, ideally situated for lucrative trade at a strategic crossing-point between Europe and Asia (Korfmann and Mannsperger, 1998). The written archives of the Hittite empire to the east suggest that Troy may have had connections with the Greek world towards the end of the second millennium BCE. Evidence of burnt layers and scattered masonry indicate that successive Trojan settlements frequently met a violent end, either by fire or earthquake, and one of these might well have been the result of conflict of some kind with the Greeks, perhaps about trade. But evidence for a dispute over Helen, let alone the presence of, for example, Agamemnon or Menelaus, is lacking. The general conclusion seems to be that the more Troy has become regarded as an important city in its own right, the less is its significance dependent on a specific association with Homer.

The creation of the Homeric poems

If we turn our attention from Troy to the period when the *Iliad* and the *Odyssey* were composed, we are confronted with a situation that is in effect the reverse: unlike Troy, Homer presents a massive amount of poetic evidence but no historical context. The Greeks had little idea of precisely when, and under what circumstances, the poems were created. As we have seen, they realised that the poems were composed much later than the events they related, but for the Greeks, Homer, like Troy, was still prehistoric, in the sense, defined above, that the poems emerged before the time when historical records could give them any kind of context.

As with archaeology so with the Homeric text, the first significant shift in perspective since the ancient world came in the nineteenth century CE. Up to that time there had almost never been any doubt that 'Homer' was the uniquely great individual creative genius of the *Iliad* and the *Odyssey*. In 1795, F.A. Wolf, a German scholar, in his *Prolegomena ad Homerum* ('Preface to Homer') (Wolf, 1985), cast doubt on the idea of Homer as a literary poet who wrote his poems down. This hypothesis was partly a result of scholarly research into the comparatively late introduction of alphabetic writing into early Greece in the eighth century BCE (with letters borrowed from a script used by Phoenician trading neighbours); if Homer preceded this development, what written medium could he have used? This speculation was coupled with an awareness, deriving from linguistic analysis, of the poems' apparent inconsistencies in dialect and style and a looseness of narrative structure, which suggested that more than one hand, even more than one period, were involved in their creation.

In addition, external influences were at work from beyond the Classical scholarly world that gave support to this hypothesis. The popular nationalist movements that spread across Europe in the nineteenth century caused nations to reach back into their cultural pasts to find epics that celebrated the early heroic struggles of their peoples. These poems, often the apparent amalgamation or expansion of diverse short poems, or 'lays', seemed to suggest a striking model for Homer: in the case of the Finnish Kalevala, for example, the putting together of lays into a national epic was being accomplished under the editorship of a contemporary scholar. Perhaps Homer's poems might be the result of the editing of pre-existing ancient Greek poems that had begun life as 'folk poetry', composed orally, on the themes of the Trojan War and the homecomings of the Greek heroes, principally Odysseus. Was the genius of Homer perhaps the genius of the 'folk' from whom the poetry came? The historical facts as known and interpreted at the time even suggested a possible 'editor' in the Athenian ruler Pisistratus (middle of the sixth century BCE), who was said to have organised recitations of the Homeric poems at the Panathenaic festival (the principal religious festival at Athens), having rhapsodes (reciters of the poems) take it in turns to go through them in order. This hypothesis also gained strength from its apparent suitability as an explanation for another striking characteristic of the poems, the fact that the *Iliad* and the *Odyssey* seem to have emerged at about this time (middle of the sixth century BCE) as *the* canonical Homeric epics, from a 'penumbra' of poetic material (surviving for us only in fragments and later versions) covering the remainder of the Troy legend (the 'Trojan Cycle') and stories connected with other cities such as Mycenae and Thebes. It was therefore plausible to view the two Homeric epics as the carefully edited survivors (perhaps because considered the best) of what was originally a vast quantity of Greek 'folk poetry', which throughout most of its existence was composed orally. This also furnished a convenient explanation for why the Homeric poems emerged, apparently fully formed, without precursors: far from being a beginning, they were in fact an end – the final product of an unwritten tradition, which by its very nature could leave no enduring traces of itself behind.

This development of the Wolf hypothesis illustrates a further factor that we need to consider when looking at scholarly perspectives that are, ostensibly, objectively arrived at: the strengths and weaknesses of contemporary cultural influences on the scholars themselves. The apparently exact fit between what nations, especially Germany, were experiencing politically and culturally in the nineteenth century, and their scholarly model for Homer may have initially blinded them to three serious problems that became increasingly apparent as the century wore on: first, the complexity of the 'patchwork' of lays out of which the poems were said to be formed, about the details of which no two investigators could agree; secondly, the rather shadowy place left for a creative poet, 'Homer', somehow sandwiched between primitive lays on the one hand and editorial activity on the other; finally, and most significantly, the dramatic cohesion and artistic quality of the poems themselves, a factor that led some nineteenth-century critics, particularly in Britain and North America, to fly in the face of the evidence in simply asserting that poems of the quality of the *Iliad* and the *Odyssey* could surely not be the result of mere editorial activity.

This tension between appreciation and analysis of the artistic qualities of the poems and hypotheses about how they might have been created went on into the twentieth century. An American scholar, Milman Parry (1902–35), working simultaneously from fieldwork study of modern oral epic poets in the Balkans and close stylistic analysis of the text of Homer, attempted to bring into harmony the hypothesis that Homer was oral poetry with an explanation of the coherence and quality of the poems. 'Oral composition' (hitherto a vague concept defined negatively, by the – supposedly restrictive – absence of writing) was shown to be far from restrictive. In fact, it was a highly skilled form of improvisation, in which the poet created a story in front of an audience by using an inherited traditional verse language; the quality of the poem was indicated by the originality of the treatment of themes, the skill at weaving these into an extended story and the detailed handling of the traditional diction (Parry, 1971; Finnegan, 1977).

An obvious example of the flexibility of themes is, in the *Iliad*, the arming of heroes and subsequent combat, which can extend from the clashing of minor figures, disposed of in as little as half a dozen lines, to the dramatic climax of the duel between Hector and Achilles, which takes up most of *Iliad* 22 (*c*.500 lines). The most obvious examples of traditional 'formulae' are phrases that repeatedly begin and end speech, such as (Telemachos and Athena at Ithaca): 'Then the thoughtful Telemachos said to her in answer'; 'Then in turn the goddess gray-eyed Athene answered him' (*Odyssey* 1.213, 221; in Lattimore, 1965, pp.32–3). But, as Parry and his successors (chiefly in Britain and North America) have demonstrated, analysis of Homeric language goes much further than identifying simple phrases and epithets such as 'godlike Achilles', 'crafty Odysseus', 'circumspect Penelope', and even beyond recognising traditional themes such as the donning of armour; Homeric verse is analysable more or less in its entirety as a traditional but highly flexible idiom, mastery of which allows the highly skilled poet to improvise (i.e. compose on the hoof) using inherited elements in an original way (Lord, 2001).

This hypothesis has the advantage of apparently solving a number of the problems we have outlined so far: Wolf's 'lays' become more precisely defined as earlier stages of an oral tradition in which stories telling of events in the past (which might well go back to the late Bronze Age and a hypothetical Trojan War) were handed on via a rich and continually developing poetic idiom preserved by a specialised class of highly skilled poets, or 'bards' (*aoidoi*). The diversity of reference to material objects, social and cultural institutions, dialect and individual linguistic forms naturally reflected the long, historically and geographically diverse gestation of this tradition (Sherratt, 1992). The stories were therefore not 'stitched' together, as Wolf and his successors supposed, but recreated new every time (Clark, 2004).

Homer in the ancient and modern world

What motivated poets to compose poems about the Trojan War? Here we may be helped by the content of the poems themselves. In *Iliad* 9 (186–91), visiting heroes come upon Achilles passing his self-enforced idleness (he has refused to fight for Agamemnon) by singing to the lyre of the 'famous deeds of men' (*klea andrōn*) (*Iliad* 9.189; my translation). The world created by Homer is (with one or two minor and questionable exceptions) a world without writing, and, in the absence of a permanent record, the need to find a way to preserve individual fame beyond death becomes correspondingly urgent. If we think of Achilles as the 'gentleman amateur' bard (his chief occupation was undoubtedly fighting), the *Odyssey* provides evidence of what appear to be professionals. In Book 1, a bard, Phemius, apparently attached to the household of Odysseus, entertains the suitors of Penelope after supper with a song of the homecomings of the Achaeans (Greeks) from Troy, an example of a theme that is developed with increasing complexity in the plot of the *Odyssey* itself: the return of Odysseus, and the sufferings he had to endure before he reached home and safety. Elsewhere in the *Odyssey* (8.499–520), at the court of the Phaeacians, another bard, Demodocus, sings, in the presence of Odysseus himself (up to this point incognito), the story of his devising of the wooden horse, and how this stratagem tricked the Trojans into giving up their city.

We cannot assume that in presenting these scenes of entertainment after supper in noble households the poet of the *Odyssey* was necessarily reflecting the circumstances of his own performance. The centuries following the collapse of the Bronze Age palaces at Mycenae and elsewhere were a period of material poverty in Greece (traditionally known as the Dark Ages). If the story of the Trojan War and its aftermath was transmitted through these centuries, the performer would more likely have been an itinerant bard, singing for his supper and a bed for the night in isolated village meeting-places, rather than a court minstrel.

In looking at this sparse contextual evidence for Homeric transmission and performance, probably the most discussed question in recent scholarship is this: where within the Greek oral tradition are we to place the *Iliad* and the *Odyssey*? Their style and dramatic finesse tend to draw attention away from the fact that they cover a very small part of the whole Trojan story. The *Iliad* covers 50 days from a ten-year war and stops well short of the fall of Troy (there is no Trojan Horse, except in the report of Demodocus' *Odyssey* recital, and brief reminiscences elsewhere). The *Odyssey* tells of the return of only one hero, and not, from the evidence of the *Iliad*, the absolute front-ranker. That the emergence of these two poems as canonical in the Greek world was a gradual process is indicated by evidence of illustrated scenes on pottery and other visual media, which were as likely as not to reflect scenes from non-Homeric parts of the Trojan War story and other legends (Figure 2.5). From internal evidence, we can detect the incorporation of many non-Trojan elements into the *Iliad* and the *Odyssey*: to take just two examples from many, stories about the conflict between the Greek cities of Argos and Thebes associated with the Argive hero Diomedes in *Iliad* 4, or the reminiscences in the adventures of Odysseus in *Odyssey* 9–12 of the legend of Jason and the Argonauts.

Alongside Homer, with less, but still considerable, status for the Greeks, was Hesiod, a poet from Boeotia, to the north of Attica, whose two complete poems, the *Theogony* and the *Works and Days*, spoke about the world of the gods and humans, presenting a universal cosmology, possibly in conscious competition with Homer's less systematic world-view (see Clay, 2003). We also have a number of 'Homeric Hymns' to the gods, which reveal many aspects of the relationships of gods and mortals that do not feature in Homer. From here, in the *Hymn to Delian Apollo* (169–73), we receive our most vivid vignette of a supreme poet 'a blind man he is, and dwells/On rugged Chios' (172; in Crudden, 2001, p.29), popularly identified with Homer. All these poems were composed in the metre and style of the Homeric poems. The Greeks were also familiar with a number of other named epic poets, whose works survive only in fragments, and whose complete stories we know about from prose summaries composed in the later Roman empire. The vast range and vitality of Greek legendary material not in the two Homeric poems becomes clear when it (from our point of view) 'surfaces' in the diverse stories that formed the basis of much sixth- and fifth-century BCE lyric poetry and drama: to take just two examples from many, *Helen*, a play by Euripides about the Egyptian adventures of Helen (taking the non-Homeric version of the legend that not

Essay Two The Homeric poems: ancient and modern perspectives

Figure 2.5 Attributed to the Timiades painter, Black-figure Tyrrhenian (Italian) amphora depicting the sacrifice of Polyxena, daughter of Priam and Hecuba, made in Athens, second quarter of sixth century BCE, British Museum, London. © Copyright The Trustees of the British Museum.

Helen but a phantom looking like her went to Troy), or *Philoctetes*, the dramatisation by Sophocles of the fate of the Greek bowman hero Philoctetes, suffering from a mortal wound in his leg and left marooned on an island by his comrades, a story only briefly outlined in Homer (*Iliad* 2.716–25).

Focusing on all this other material brings more urgency to the question of why and how the *Iliad* and the *Odyssey* gained their authoritative status and so their complete survival amid so much that has perished. For the Greeks of the Classical period, this question, when asked at all, was framed simply in terms of Homer's literary and dramatic quality, his 'genius'. The tragedian Aeschylus (*c*.525–456 BCE) was said to have described his plays as 'slices from the banquet of Homer' (Athenaeus, *Deipnosophists* 8.347; in Gulick, 1930, vol.4, p.75); the philosopher Aristotle (384–322 BCE), in *Poetics* 23, describes Homer as 'divinely inspired' (Heath, 1996, p.38) in the ability to construct a coherent dramatic plot out of a single incident within a series of events (the anger of Achilles; the return of Odysseus), as opposed to the other less talented poets of the Trojan Cycle, who tried to cram in too many stories, and so destroyed dramatic unity. So, for the Greeks, the Homeric poems survived because they were, quite simply, the best. Their plots, and the descriptions and actions of their compelling and multi-faceted characters, took over the imagination of later centuries. Translated into terms that we might also use, they can be seen as the dynamic culmination of a particularly rich tradition of oral poetry.

This explanation does not, however, entirely dispose of the 'why and how' question. The linguistic evidence of the poems themselves tends to place their composition at roughly the end of the eighth century BCE, which has thrown up the question – why then? What factors influenced the fixing, as it were, of something so apparently fluid?

Specifics are hard to come by. We can, however, point to some generally important developments in Greek society at about this time: the first appearance of alphabetic writing (in the form of words and sentences scratched on pots; Figure 2.6), and archaeological evidence for the expansion of trade within the Aegean area and beyond. It is possible, although we cannot do more than conjecture, that the introduction of the alphabet was behind the fixing of the poems in roughly their later shape. Even more important may be the fact that Greek settlements appear to have been going through a period of swift economic and social change, in which the power of traditional kings and aristocracies was being challenged – a stage on the way to the Greek 'city state' (*polis*), which was to become the standard social and political unit of the Greek world (Morris, 1986; 2000).

This perspective tends to move us away from considering the *Iliad* and the *Odyssey* as artistic monoliths, somehow above and beyond all specific social influences, and towards a focus on the way in which they might reflect the instabilities and tensions of their times. The individualistic 'excellence' exhibited so notably, as we saw at the beginning of this essay, by Achilles, had its negative, destructive side. The *Iliad* gives us an insight

Figure 2.6 Nestor's Cup, large wine bowl from Pithecusae, with inscription incised upon it, *c*.725 BCE. (Photo: Sansaini, German Archaeological Institute, Rome, negative no. 54.1050)

into the weaknesses of heroes as leaders of their people and the inherent instability of the social code by which they operate: examples are the actions of Agamemnon and Achilles in *Iliad* 1, which, in their different ways, cause their followers to perish, or the irresolution of Hector in *Iliad* 22, caught between the dilemma of showing suitable courage by facing his deadly opponent Achilles, or safeguarding his people by returning inside the walls of Troy (Haubold, 2000). The *Odyssey*, on the surface much less problematic (the baddies, the arrogant suitors of Odysseus' wife Penelope, get their come-uppance), still betrays social tension. The powerlessness of the 'people' (*demos*) of Ithaca to do anything to help the situation is presented vividly in *Odyssey* 2, and the divinely engineered 'happy ending' in *Odyssey* 22–4 (large numbers of predatory suitors are slaughtered and Odysseus is installed back in his kingdom) masks the somewhat patched-up conclusion of *Odyssey* 24 (which may be, in part, a later addition to the main poem). But these insights are not exclusive to modern scholars. 'Excellence' was, as we have seen, a major Greek object of aspiration. Nevertheless, the moral ambiguity inherent in Homer's presentation of an Agamemnon or an Odysseus was not lost on later Greeks, as fifth-century BCE tragedy vividly demonstrates: for example, Agamemnon, as either the arrogant destroyer or the wronged husband requiring revenge from his son Orestes (both aspects presented in Aeschylus' *Oresteia*); Odysseus, either treated unfavourably in Euripides' *Hecuba* or Sophocles' *Philoctetes* (this side of his character fixed in his Roman persona as the evil Ulysses in Virgil's *Aeneid*), or (less often) treated as noble and magnanimous, as in Sophocles' *Ajax*.

Conclusion: the Homeric poems in the twenty-first century

The advances in Homeric scholarship that continue to be made, with all the advantages of progress in literary and scientific techniques that scholars now enjoy, do not therefore necessarily lead to a rejection of the insights of the ancients. We are, for example, no longer so sure, as some scholars were in the middle of the twentieth century, that the idea of the individual genius of Homer, as understood by the Greeks and the Romans, can be discarded. A key question, hotly debated in current Homeric scholarship, is how oral composition might relate to individual artistic creation, or, to put it another way, should the poems be seen as a culmination of an oral tradition or essentially the work of an artist who, while still, perhaps, an oral poet, transcended the tradition? What part in this transition, if any, might have been played by the recently introduced written alphabet? What exactly was (and still is) the relationship between oral and literate composition (see Bakker and Kahane, 1997)? There are other ongoing questions: for example, how far was the transmission of the poems after the late eighth century BCE, about which, again, we know next to nothing, essentially the preservation of a largely fixed text (this has always been a problem – under what circumstances was it written down?) or, more radically, how much can the seventh- and sixth-century BCE transmission of the *Iliad* and the *Odyssey* have influenced not only details but the overall conception of each of the poems? We know that in certain respects the text of the poems remained fluid even into the fourth century BCE. The question arises: how fluid, and when was the main period of consolidation? Exactly what part may have been played by performances under the so-called editorial role of Pisistratus in the sixth century BCE (see above)? These questions are vital to consideration of how far Homer was not only an influence on, but perhaps even influenced by, the development of the early Greek city state (Seaford, 1994; Nagy, 1996). On this there is, as yet, no clear consensus.

The fascination of the Homeric poems is that they are so important for Greek culture, and we know so much, and yet so little, about them. The study of Homer remains open-ended. While we may now, from our twenty-first century vantage-point, find it easy to spot the fatal preconceptions of a Wolf or a Schliemann in earlier centuries, we must also constantly be aware of the limitations of our own perspectives, underpinned as they inevitably are by our own social and cultural concerns and those of our age.

Further reading

The *Iliad* and the *Odyssey* can be read in their entirety in a variety of stimulating translations, of which those used in this essay, by the scholar and poet Richmond Lattimore (*Iliad* 1951 and *Odyssey* 1965), are close in letter and spirit to the original. Among introductory survey books on each of the poems, recommended are Jasper Griffin (2004) on the *Odyssey* and Michael Silk (2004) on the *Iliad*, both in the Cambridge 'Landmarks of World Literature' series, along with another perspective from Barry Powell (2004). Compendious for up-to-date and scholarly discussion of all aspects of Homeric studies is *A New Companion to Homer* by Ian Morris and Barry Powell (1997). This is long and thorough, although at a price unlikely to be affordable by many! Richard Rutherford's recent (1996) survey of Homer in the Oxford 'Greece and Rome New Surveys in the Classics' series, gives an accessible short account of recent scholarship in the field of Homeric scholarship, with a useful bibliography. *The Cambridge Companion to Homer* (2004) by Robert Fowler comprises 22 stimulating studies of all aspects of Homer, in particular ancient and modern reception.

Passing to more specialist studies (but still well within the grasp of the general reader), Mark Edwards (1987) and Colin McLeod (1992) focus on the artistic qualities of the poet of the *Iliad*, the latter (originally designed as an introduction to an edition of Book 24 of the Greek text) particularly powerful on what he conceives as the spiritual force and pathos of the poem. Moving to the broader picture, Barbara Graziosi and Johannes Haubold (2004) consider the religious, cultural and cosmological scope of the Homeric poems, particularly in comparison and contrast with the other major Dark Age poet, Hesiod. Albert Lord's pioneering work on Homer as oral poetry (second edition 2001) was written by the man who did fieldwork in the Balkans in the 1930s as an assistant to Milman Parry. Ruth Finnegan's *Oral Poetry* (1977) will be of interest to those who wish to learn more about the wider picture of oral poetic traditions in modern times. Turning to history and archaeology, Ian Morris (1986) examines the value of the poems in constructing a social history of the late eighth century BCE, an exploration effectively complemented by Susan Sherratt (1992), whose study picks out what she discerns as the 'archaeological layers' in the poems from the middle Bronze Age to the eighth century BCE. For Homer's cultural influence, Susan Woodford (1993) traces the influence of Homer on the artistic tradition of Greece and Rome, and, with an even wider perspective, Diane Thompson (2004) considers Homeric reception in later European culture.

Bibliography

Ancient sources

Aeschylus, *Oresteia*, in Meineck, P. (trans.) (1998) Aeschylus: *Oresteia*, Indianapolis: Hackett.

Aristotle, *Poetics*, in Heath, M. (trans.) (1996) Aristotle: *Poetics*, Harmondsworth: Penguin.

Athenaeus, *Deipnosophists*, in Gulick, C.B. (trans.) (1930) Athenaeus: *Deipnosophists*, 7 vols, Cambridge, MA and London: Harvard University Press.

Euripides, *Hecuba*, in Morwood, J. (trans.) (2000) *The Trojan Women and Other Plays*, Oxford: Oxford University Press.

Euripides, *Helen*, in Davie, J. (trans.) (2002) *Heracles and Other Plays*, Harmondsworth, Penguin.

Hesiod, *Theogony*, in Wender, D. (trans.) (1973) *Hesiod and Theognis*, Harmondsworth: Penguin.

Hesiod, *Works and Days*, in Wender, D. (trans.) (1973) *Hesiod and Theognis*, Harmondsworth: Penguin.

Homer, *Iliad*, in Lattimore, R. (trans.) (1951) *The Iliad of Homer*, Chicago and London: University of Chicago Press.

Homer, *Odyssey*, in Lattimore, R. (trans.) (1965) *The Odyssey of Homer*, New York: Harper Perennial.

'Homeric Hymns', in Crudden, M. (trans.) (2001) *Homeric Hymns*, Oxford: Oxford University Press.

Philostratus, *Lives of the Sophists*, in Wright, W.C. (trans.) (1921) *Philostratus and Eunapius, The Lives of the Sophists*, Cambridge, MA: Harvard University Press.

Plato, *Apology*, in Tarrant, H. (trans.) (1993) *The Last Days of Socrates*, Harmondsworth: Penguin.

Sophocles, *Ajax*, in Cannon, R. (trans.) (1990) *Sophocles: Plays Two*, London: Methuen.

Sophocles, *Philoctetes*, in McLeish, K. (trans.) (1990) *Sophocles: Plays Two*, London: Methuen.

Virgil, *Aeneid*, in West, D. (trans.) (1991) Virgil: *Aeneid*, Harmondsworth: Penguin.

Modern scholarship

Bakker, E. and Kahane, A. (eds) (1997) *Written Voices, Spoken Epic: Tradition, Performance and the Epic Text*, Cambridge, MA and London: Harvard University Press.

Blegen, C.W. (1963) *Troy and the Trojans*, London: Thames & Hudson.

Clark, M. (2004) 'Formulas, metre and type scenes', in Fowler, 2004, pp.117–38.

Clay, J.S. (2003) *Hesoid's Cosmos*, Cambridge: Cambridge University Press.

Edwards, M.W. (1987) *Homer: Poet of the Iliad*, Baltimore and London: Johns Hopkins University Press.

Emlyn-Jones, C., Hardwick, L. and Purkis, J. (eds) (1992) *Homer: Readings and Images*, London: Duckworth and Milton Keynes: Open University Press.

Finnegan, R.H. (1977) *Oral Poetry: Its Nature, Significance and Social Context*, Cambridge: Cambridge University Press.

Fowler, R. (ed.) (2004) *The Cambridge Companion to Homer*, Cambridge: Cambridge University Press.

Graziosi, B. (2002) *Inventing Homer: The Early Recognition of the Epic*, Cambridge: Cambridge University Press.

Graziosi, B. and Haubold, J. (2004) *Homer: The Resonance of Epic*, London: Duckworth.

Griffin, J. (2004) *Homer, The Odyssey: A Student Guide*, Oxford: Oxford University Press (first published 1987).

Haubold, J. (2000) *Homer's People: Epic Poetry and Social Formation*, Cambridge: Cambridge University Press.

Korfmann, M. and Mannsperger, D. (1998) *Troia: ein historiker Überblick und Rudgang*, Stuttgart: K.Theiss.

Lord, A.B. (2001) *The Singer of Tales*, ed. S. Mitchell and G. Nagy, Cambridge, MA and London: Harvard University Press (first published 1960).

McLeod, C.W. (1992) 'Introduction to Iliad Book 24', in Emlyn-Jones *et al.*, 1992, pp.76–88.

Morris, I. (1986) 'The use and abuse of Homer', *Classical Antiquity*, vol.5, pp.81–138.

Morris, I. (2000) *Archaeology as Cultural History: Words and Things in Iron Age Greece*, Malden, MA and Oxford: Blackwell.

Morris, I. and Powell, B.B. (1997) *A New Companion to Homer*, Leiden: Brill.

Nagy, G. (1996) *Homeric Questions*, Austin: University of Texas Press.

Parry, M. (1971) *The Making of Homeric Verse: The Collected Papers of Milman Parry*, ed. A. Parry, New York and Oxford: Oxford University Press.

Powell, B.B. (2004) *Homer*, Malden, MA and Oxford: Blackwell.

Rutherford, R.B. (1996) *Homer*, Oxford: Oxford University Press.

Seaford, R. (1994) *Reciprocity and Ritual: Homer and Tragedy in the Developing City-State*, Oxford: Oxford University Press.

Sherratt, S. (1992) '"Reading the texts": archaeology and the Homeric question', in Emlyn-Jones *et al.*, 1992, pp.144–65.

Silk, M.S. (trans.) (2004) Homer: *The Iliad*, Cambridge: Cambridge University Press (first published 1987).

Thompson, D.P. (2004) *The Trojan War: Literature and Legends from the Bronze Age to the Present*, North Carolina and London: MacFarland.

Wolf, F.A. (1985) *Prolegomena ad Homerum*, trans. A. Grafton, G.W. Most and J.E.G. Zetzel, Princeton: Princeton University Press (original 1795).

Woodford, S. (1993) *The Trojan War in Ancient Art*, London: Duckworth.

Essay Three

Sing Muse: authorial voices in early Greek poetry

Naoko Yamagata

When we read a modern work of literature, we tend to take it for granted that we know the name of the author (albeit often a pseudonym), the title of the work given by the author, and something about the author's life and creation of the work. Even if the information is not forthcoming from the author, a determined biographer can research and obtain such details in due course. This biographical information often influences the way we read literary works – it can assist us in interpreting the works and enrich our reading experience, but it can also colour the way we judge their quality and hinder us from reading them for their own merit.

When we read authors from the ancient world, our reading experience is somewhat different. Take Homer for example. The history of Greek literature begins with Homer, who is the most celebrated of ancient Greek poets, but we know very little about the poet himself. He does not talk about his own person or name himself at all in his work, so it is not even certain whether the name given to the author of the *Iliad* and the *Odyssey* was indeed Homer, or for that matter whether or not those titles were given to the poems by Homer himself. We do not know where he was from, where he lived or even when he lived. Needless to say, we have little idea what he looked like, so all the so-called 'portraits' of Homer since antiquity are products of the imagination of later generations, and tell us more about the cultural climate and the attitude towards Homer of those who produced them, than give us an indication of Homer's true likeness (Figures 3.1–3.3).

This problem of not knowing who Homer really is, the so-called Homeric question, has exercised many a scholar's mind since antiquity, and is not likely ever to be resolved. The problem also applies to some extent to many other classical authors, both Greek and Roman. In this essay, I am going to examine the narrative 'voice' of three authors – Homer, Hesiod and Sappho – not so much as their autobiographical testimony but as their artistic creations, including when they are talking about their own persons in their works. After all, stories are often told from the points of view of characters in the story or an obviously fictitious narrator. It requires

EXPERIENCING THE CLASSICAL WORLD

Figure 3.1 Head of Homer, second century CE, marble, Vatican, Rome. Photo: Vatican Museums (neg N. XXXV.30.34)

Figure 3.2 Homer's portrait, from *Die Schedelsche Weltchronik*, Germany, 1493. Permission of Harenberg Kommunikation, Dortmund.

Figure 3.3 Jean-Auguste-Dominique Ingres, 1827, *The Apotheosis of Homer*, oil on canvas, 386 cm x 512 cm, Musée du Louvre, Paris. © Photo: RMN/© René-Gabriel Ojéda.

essentially the same procedure to listen to the poet as narrator in his or her work, whom we must regard as a persona (or identity) specially created for the purpose.

Such approaches to narrative texts have recently been enhanced by the branch of literary criticism called narratology. Narratology, among other things, has taught us to be aware of the existence of different narrators inside a story (for example, the author's voice and those of characters) as well as different 'focalisers' from whose perspectives given events or experiences in the story are perceived. This approach, first introduced to classics by Irene de Jong (2004, first published 1987), has provided classical scholars with a more refined tool for analysing narrative texts. Although there is not space to go into the technical details of narratological analyses in this essay, I would like to apply one of the key concepts of the narratological approach, that of differentiating between different perspectives within the narrative text, to some examples of early Greek poetry. More specifically, I would like to examine how the voices of different narrators with different perspectives interact with one another to create specific effects in the texts, whether they include the author's own voice or are those of the characters in the story. I would also like to touch on some of the issues arising from the difficulties in interpreting different voices from the past in the classical texts.

Homer's voices

Homer as narrator is renowned for his detached narrative voice, which tells his story without expressing his own emotions or opinions and seldom makes the reader aware of his presence. Very occasionally, however, we become conscious of the poet's voice when he directly addresses someone else. The most notable example of this is his address to the Muse or Muses at the start of his poems:

> Sing, goddess, the anger of Peleus' son Achilleus.
>
> (Homer, *Iliad* 1.1; in Lattimore, 1951, p.59)
>
> Tell me, Muse, of the man of many ways, who was driven
> far journeys, after he had sacked Troy's sacred citadel.
>
> (Homer, *Odyssey* 1.1–2; in Lattimore, 1965, p.27)

The question of exactly how we should interpret the divine inspiration is a complex issue. Some may wish to see in the lines the evidence for early Greek religious experience, if we are to believe that the author and his audience actually felt the presence of the Muse at the scene of performance. On the other hand, we can simply see the invocation to the Muse as the poet's literary device, which gives the overall framework and authority to his poetry. Whatever the reality behind the invocation, this mode of address creates a series of voices, in the sense that the poet is presenting himself as the Muse's mouthpiece, and therefore we are supposed to be hearing the Muse's voice through the poet's.

In the *Iliad*, Homer addresses the goddesses not only at the start of the poems, but also at other critical points of the plot. One of the most prominent examples is the address at the start of the so-called 'Catalogue of the Ships' where Homer lists the leaders of the Greeks and their ships:

> Tell me now, you Muses who have your homes in Olympos.
> For you, who are goddesses, are there, and you know all things,
> and we have heard only the rumour of it and know nothing.
> Who then of those were the chief men and the lords of the Danaans?
> I could not tell over the multitude of them nor name them,
> not if I had ten tongues and ten mouths, not if I had
> a voice never to be broken and a heart of bronze within me,
> not unless the Muses of Olympia, daughters
> of Zeus of the aegis, remembered all those who came beneath Ilion.
>
> (Homer, *Iliad* 2.484–92; in Lattimore, 1951, p.89)

This passage reveals something about the nature of the poet's divine inspiration. First, the Muses are called upon to bestow on him the accurate knowledge of the event that will enable him to sing a truthful song. The passage also shows his admission of the limitation of human memory and physical strength. The expressions 'ten tongues and ten mouths', 'a voice never to be broken' and 'a heart of bronze' seem to imply that physical strength and stamina are considered equally important in poetic creation as what we might call poetic skills. Artistically speaking, this interlude within the poem can be regarded as an effective literary device to create expectation and suspense at the transition from one episode to another. This also gives the impression that the poem is not simply dictated by the Muse to be repeated verbatim by the poet, but that the poet is creating it in conversation with the Muse or Muses, who will give him instructions as and when needed.

The poet also addresses a character within the story, again very occasionally. This device is what is commonly called 'apostrophe' and is used towards several characters in the *Iliad* and one in the *Odyssey*, as in the following examples:

> Then groaning heavily you answered, O Patroclus the rider.
>
> (Homer, *Iliad* 16.20; my translation)
>
> Then you said to him in answer, O swineherd Eumaeus.
>
> (Homer, *Odyssey* 14.55; my translation)

Different views have been proposed by scholars to explain the reasons for the use of this device (cf. Edwards, 1987, pp.37–41; Yamagata, 1989). Because the two characters most often addressed by the poet, Patroclus and Eumaeus, are gentle and sympathetic characters, ancient commentators speculated that the poet was expressing his sympathy for them. But that explanation does not seem to hold for other characters similarly addressed. The formal constraint imposed by the metre of epic verse (hexameter) may also have played a part. Maybe one effect was to create more immediacy in the singer's performance and to narrow the psychological gap between the past and the present.

The poet speaking his mind?

There is another type of passage in which the poet appears to speak for 'himself'. Very occasionally, he does throw in what seems like his own comment on the scene he is describing. For example, when characters act in ignorance of their fate, the poet sometimes interjects, 'fool [*nēpios*]!' (*Iliad* 2.38, 873, 12.113, 16.46, 686, 20.264, 466), which may be interpreted as an expression of his pity or contempt for the character (Edwards, 1991, p.5). Curiously, two of these cases (*Iliad* 16.46, 686) are addressed to Patroclus in the same context in which the poet's direct addresses to the hero occur, which adds some force to the theory that the poet is expressing his sympathy for the hero.

The poet also personally comments on Heracles' murder of his guest:

> These mares presently were to mean his doom and murder,
> at the time when he came to the son of Zeus, strong-hearted,
> the man called Herakles, guilty of monstrous actions,
> who killed Iphitos while he was a guest in his household;
> hard man, without shame for the watchful gods, nor the table
> he had set for Iphitos, his guest; and when he had killed him
> he kept the strong-footed horses for himself in his palace.
>
> (Homer, *Odyssey* 21.24–30; in Lattimore, 1965, pp.309–10)

In this passage, the poet's condemnation of Heracles' behaviour is clear to see. Although we should always remember that the poet as narrator is technically his own artistic creation, it is tempting to hear the author speaking his mind in a passage such as this.

The Muse speaking – the poet's divine perspective

As we have seen in Homer's invocation to the Muses at the start of the long list of Greek and Trojan leaders and their ships at *Iliad* Book 2, knowledge of events supposed to have been witnessed by human beings in the past but hard for human memory to recall can be ascribed to the Muse. More obviously, when the poet speaks of things in the realm of the gods, his voice can be regarded as that of the Muse. For example, when the poet introduces the opening episode of the *Odyssey* with Zeus lamenting human beings' false belief in the gods' role in human misfortunes (*Odyssey* 1.32–43), he is supposed to be drawing on the knowledge of the Muse about matters of the divine world. Clearly, the poet could not have been on Mount Olympus eavesdropping on the gods' conversation, and so it is necessary for him to call upon the deity of poetry to inspire and inform him and to authenticate his tales. It is a case of the narrator telling the tale not from his own perspective, but from that of the gods.

The poet narrating

About half of the *Iliad* and the *Odyssey* consist of the poet's narrative, the anonymous narrator's voice telling the tale (Griffin, 1986, p.37). However, the perspective through which he does so can be complex, as we have already seen in the case in which the poet draws on divine knowledge to describe scenes from the perspective of the gods. There are also passages in which the perspectives of the characters described in the narrative subtly interact with that of the poet as narrator. The following passage will provide an illustration. It comes immediately after the funeral games for Patroclus, which Achilles has hosted to honour his beloved friend:

> And the games broke up, and the people scattered to go away, each man
> to his fast-running ship, and the rest of them took thought of their dinner
> and of sweet sleep and its enjoyment; only Achilleus
> wept still as he remembered his beloved companion, nor did sleep
> who subdues all come over him, but he tossed from one side to the other
> in longing for Patroklos, for his manhood and his great strength
> and all the actions he had seen to the end with him, and the hardships
> he had suffered; the wars of men; hard crossing of the big waters.
> Remembering all these things he let fall the swelling tears, lying
> sometimes along his side, sometimes on his back, and now again
> prone on his face; then he would stand upright, and pace turning
> in distraction along the beach of the sea, nor did dawn rising
> escape him as she brightened across the sea and the beaches.
>
> (Homer, *Iliad* 24.1–13; in Lattimore, 1951, p.475)

In this scene, Achilles' actions are described from the point of view of the poet, but he also 'gets inside' Achilles' mind, as it were, when he describes Achilles' reminiscence of what he did with Patroclus and his longing for him. In other words, the poet is letting Achilles' perspective seep into his narrative, perceiving what Achilles is seeing and feeling in this context. In narratological terms, this is called 'embedded focalisation', that is, the perspective of Achilles as the focaliser is embedded in the poet's narrative (de Jong, 2004, p.111).

Essay Three Sing Muse: authorial voices in early Greek poetry

The characters speaking through the poet

The poet provides the mostly impersonal narrative (sometimes with his own perspective, sometimes with those of the characters) and the characters inside the story converse with each other in direct speech. In terms of narratology, the poet is the external narrator and the characters are the internal narrators. Some direct speech can continue for many lines. In the case of the *Odyssey* in particular, Odysseus tells his host Phaeacians of his adventures almost throughout Books 9 to 12, which add up to thousands of lines. It is worth considering the possible effects of making the hero of the story, rather than the poet himself, the main narrator in that part of the poem.

Let us take as an example the passage in which Odysseus finally reveals his identity to the Phaeacians:

> I am Odysseus son of Laertes, known before all men
> for the study of crafty designs, and my fame goes up to the heavens.
> I am at home in sunny Ithaka. There is a mountain
> there that stands tall, leaf-trembling Neritos, and there are islands
> settled around it, lying one very close to another.
> There is Doulichion and Same, wooded Zakynthos,
> but my island lies low and away, last of all on the water
> toward the dark, with the rest below facing east and sunshine,
> a rugged place, but a good nurse of men; for my part
> I cannot think of any place sweeter on earth to look at.
> For in truth Kalypso, shining among divinities, kept me
> with her in her hollow caverns, desiring me for her husband,
> and so likewise Aiaian Circe the guileful detained me
> beside her in her halls, desiring me for her husband,
> but never could she persuade the heart within me. So it is
> that nothing is more sweet in the end than country and parents
> ever, even when far away one lives in a fertile
> place, when it is in alien country, far from his parents.
> But come, I will tell you of my voyage home with its many
> troubles, which Zeus inflicted on me as I came from Troy land.
>
> (Homer, *Odyssey* 9.19–38; in Lattimore, 1965, pp.137–8)

Coming from the mouth of the man himself, who has been away from home for nearly 20 years, the passage has a particular poignancy. His description of his homeland is detailed as if his spirit is already wandering there, although of course there is a practical purpose to this – the Phaeacians are about to escort him home, so he needs to tell them his 'address' and how to get there. Nevertheless, the practical information naturally draws out the man's longing for home: he regards it as the sweetest of all places in the world. His confession that even the goddesses Calypso and Circe both wanted him for their husband can be seen as part of his self-advertisement (like his opening lines regarding his fame) to impress his hosts. However, what stands out more than that is where his heart is. To go home and see his family is dearer to him even than to gain immortality in a strange place far away. Home is what makes him human, what makes him who he is. Odysseus' speech shows us the truth about humanity, which is rendered more poignant in his own words than it would have been in the poet's narration.

The final line, 'But come, I will tell you of my voyage home', has a somewhat different tone. Here we almost hear the poet saying 'now let me tell you the tale of Odysseus' adventures', which his audience must have been impatiently waiting for. The lines fulfil virtually the same function as the poet's own introduction. However, in ancient Greece when the poem was orally performed, the device of the singer taking on Odysseus' persona as he sang the tale must have been more absorbing from the audience's point of view. They would have been listening to the storyteller as if to the hero himself – and at the same time Odysseus, in the story, would have appeared as an eloquent singer and story-teller (just like the singer Demodocus whom he has praised shortly before this passage: *Odyssey* 8.487–921). The voices of the narrator and the character subtly overlap to create a multiplicity of effect, especially in the long story-telling of Odysseus in the *Odyssey*.

There are, however, some occasions on which the perspective of the poet bursts through the framework of the speech of the 'character'. For example, in *Odyssey* 12.374–88, Odysseus displays in his speech an astonishing knowledge of the heavenly conversation that took place between Zeus and the Sun God Helios about Odysseus and his men. Helios was demanding punishment of Odysseus' companions who had killed the god's cattle, and Zeus acceded to his demand and promised to inflict punishment on the men by causing a storm. Odysseus' narration quotes the gods' direct speech and describes what went on in a manner normal for the poet's narration. But how did Odysseus know all this without the divine inspiration that is the preserve of the poet? Homer manages to circumvent this difficulty by letting Odysseus add an explanation at the end of the episode:

> All this I heard afterwards from fair-haired Kalypso,
> and she told me she herself had heard it from the guide, Hermes.
>
> (Homer, *Odyssey* 12.389–90; in Lattimore, 1965, p.195)

This sounds like an authorial voice thinly disguised as the character's speech. This example further enhances the identification of the poet's voice with that of the Muse – only the gods are supposed to know matters in the divine world, and if his characters are allowed to speak for the poet, then they have to give a plausible explanation for their knowledge. The poet must not forget when he is talking through a character's voice that on such occasions he cannot display the divine omniscience that he normally enjoys.

The characters speaking through others – what and how they quote

We hear another layer of voice when characters quote what others have said. In such cases, too, we need to pay attention not only to what the original speaker says and how the characters quote it, but also to the overall framework in which the poet placed such a speech. Take, for example, the words spoken by Odysseus just as he was departing for the war in Troy, recalled after nineteen years and quoted by Penelope:

> 'Dear wife, since I do not think the strong-greaved Achaians
> will all come safely home from Troy without hurt, seeing
> that people say the Trojans are men who can fight in battle,
> that they are throwers of the spear, and shooters of arrows,
> and riders with fast-footed horses, who with the greatest
> speed settle the great and hateful issue of common battle,
> I do not know if the god will spare me, or if I must be lost
> there in Troy; here let everything be in our charge.
> You must take thought for my father and mother here in our palace,
> as you do now, or even more, since I shall be absent.
> But when you see our son grown up and bearded, then you may
> marry whatever man you please, forsaking your household.'
> So he spoke then; and now all this is being accomplished.
>
> (Homer, *Odyssey* 18.259–70; in Lattimore, 1965, p.277)

Penelope is quoting these words in the presence of her suitors (and the disguised Odysseus himself whom she has yet to recognise). What effect does this have? The poet's exquisite touch is visible here. In a single stroke, he creates a psychological drama developing around the figure of Penelope. Her love for her missing husband is clear to see from her reminiscence; his love for her and his parents, and his trust in her, are evident in this quotation of the husband by the wife. At the same time the poet is bringing into relief the cleverness of Penelope – she manages to hint at her readiness to remarry, not by announcing it in her own words, but by quoting her husband, and presenting the proposal as *his* instruction, which she is prepared to follow, albeit reluctantly, for the love of Odysseus. The picture of Penelope here is that of ultimate fidelity: she would not take a second husband but for the specific instruction of her (presumed) dead husband.

In this passage, we hear Penelope's voice – and through hers Odysseus', but the author's voice is perfectly concealed and we only perceive the psychological drama unfolding in front of us. This is a typical mode in which Homer operates.

Hesiod – the farmer-poet from Boeotia

When we turn from Homer to Hesiod, we feel that we learn more about this author than Homer. From the language he uses, we can guess that Hesiod was roughly contemporary with Homer, but we appear to have more personal information about Hesiod through his works. There have been a dozen or so works attributed to Hesiod since antiquity, but today only two extant epic poems are regarded as his genuine works, namely the *Theogony* and the *Works and Days*. Through those two poems, we get to know his name, his occupation as a farmer-poet, his family's circumstances and even his motivation for becoming a poet.

The inspired poet

Hesiod, like Homer, addresses the Muses as his source of inspiration, and opens his *Works and Days* with his invocation to the goddesses. However, he makes his connection with them even clearer and more striking in his *Theogony*, by opening the poem with the 115-line long prelude dedicated to the goddesses who inspired him to sing of the family of the gods: 'From the Muses of Helicon let us begin our singing' (Hesiod, *Theogony* 1; in West, 1988, p.3). He then tells of his remarkable experience, which transformed him from a simple shepherd to an epic poet. He met the Muses in person while he was watching over his flock:

> And once they taught Hesiod fine singing, as he tended his lambs below holy Helicon. This is what the goddesses said to me first, the Olympian Muses, daughters of Zeus the aegis-bearer:
>
>> 'Shepherds that camp in the wild, disgraces, merest bellies: we know to tell many lies that sound like truth, but we know to sing reality, when we will.'
>
> So said mighty Zeus' daughters, the sure of utterance, and they gave me a branch of springing bay to pluck for a staff, a handsome one, and they breathed into me wonderous voice.
>
> (Hesiod, *Theogony* 22–32; in West, 1988, pp.3–4)

He goes on to explain that the subject matter of the poem, that is, the song of the family of the gods, was also given to him by the Muses themselves.

In this passage we are told that he regarded it as his calling to sing of the truth as instructed by the goddesses. But this declaration should also make us cautious about the 'reality' of the biographical details the poet might provide us with – are these based on his actual experience, or is he perhaps following some sort of literary formula to make his opening of the poem dramatic and authentic? Did he actually meet the goddesses on the mountain or was this perhaps a dream?

The question about the biographical details the poet provides is not a straightforward issue, not only in relation to miraculous experience such as this, but also regarding any author about any sort of experience. Is the author bound to provide absolutely accurate information about himself? This is a secondary question if our purpose is merely to appreciate the artistic effect that the poet creates by his setting of the scene and characters, one of whom happens to be himself, but we need to exercise caution if we try to treat an author's works as historical documents from which we extract information about the author, his background and the society in which he lived.

In the rest of the *Theogony*, Hesiod concentrates on telling the tale of the origins of the gods and their power struggles, from which Zeus emerges as the victor, and the poet does not talk about himself at all. In this respect, the Hesiod of this poem is as impersonal as Homer, acting out his role as the Muses' mouthpiece. However, in his *Works and Days*, which is considered to have been composed later than the *Theogony*, we get to hear much more about the poet's personal life and thoughts.

Hesiod speaking as 'himself'

As in Homer's poems, Hesiod's *Works and Days* begins with the poet's invocation of the Muses:

> Muses from Pieria, who glorify by songs, come to me, tell of Zeus your father in your singing.
>
> (Hesiod, *Works and Days* 1–2; in West, 1988, p.37)

This sounds as though this poem is about Zeus, and indicates that the poet is going to act as the Muses' mouthpiece as he does in the *Theogony*, of which the main theme was also Zeus as the ruler of the world. Hesiod praises the god's power and greatness, and then invokes him as the god of justice:

> O hearken as thou seest and hearest, and make judgment straight with righteousness, Lord; while I should like to tell Perses words of truth.
>
> (Hesiod, *Works and Days* 9–10; in West, 1988, p.37)

This is an astonishing opening for an epic poem in which we appear to be expected to hear three voices: that of the Muses as the source of poetic inspiration, that of Zeus who tells the poet what is right, and that of the poet with which he addresses his brother Perses. The use of 'I' is not confined to the poet's invocation of the Muses and Zeus, but used throughout the poem as the device through which the poet imparts his advice ostensibly to his brother, but in practice to his audience and readers. It is in his first person narrative, speaking as himself, that Hesiod tells us about himself and his background.

According to this poem, Hesiod's father used to live in Cyme in Asia Minor and was a sea trader, but emigrated to the Greek mainland to escape poverty. The place he settled in was the village of Ascra on the slope of Mount Helicon, which Hesiod describes as 'bad in winter, foul in summer, good at no time' (*Works and Days* 640). Hesiod and his brother are said to have grown up in this place, but after their father's death they fell out with each other in a dispute over the division of their father's estate. Each of them had already had their fair share, but after spending all of his share, Perses claimed some of Hesiod's share as his own, and took the case to the local 'kings' who acted as judges. Perses obtained a decision advantageous to himself by bribing the kings, whom Hesiod repeatedly criticises as 'bribe-swallowers' (*Works and Days* 39, 221, 264).

Against this background Hesiod sets out the theme of the poem, the 'works', which he recommends to his brother as the best means to gain wealth, and the 'days', lucky and unlucky, a good knowledge of which will help one avoid trouble in daily life. This then gives the poet a convenient framework to spin out in verse what could almost be described as a manual for agriculture and farming, as well as moral tales such as the myth of the five ages of men and the myth of Prometheus, both of which are designed to explain the origin of human labour and suffering. All this is told to educate his lazy brother, and incidentally his audience and readers, too.

The down-to-earth and personal contents of the poem are so convincing that we cannot help feeling we are actually hearing the voice of the poet himself telling a truthful life story. Perhaps it is. After all, would it be a fair and just thing to do to accuse the kings of unfair judgement against him in his poem if there was no such incident in real life? He even manages to squeeze in a reference to a proud moment in his life, when he won a singing contest at the funeral games for King Amphidamas in Chalcis on the island of Euboea and dedicated the trophy to the Muses (*Works and Days* 654–9), as well as describing his only experience of sailing as an overture to a manual for seafaring. The mention of the funeral games is, incidentally, the main evidence for giving Hesiod's date as late seventh century BCE, because Amphidamas is a historical figure who is reported to have died in a war for which we have an approximate date.

However, we must be constantly aware that this 'self-portrait' of the poet, true or false, remains his poetic creation aimed at certain literary effects. Nothing would have stopped him from composing a good story out of someone else's experience with changed names. Hesiod's poetry shows plenty of evidence of influence from ancient Near Eastern literature, including myths of the gods and the genre of wisdom literature. The latter commonly uses the framework of the narrator as the wise advisor, such as the father, and the addressee as the recipient of advice, such as his son. Hesiod may be using himself (or some other figure) as a convenient frame to fit his pictures. After all, has he not warned us through his Muses' words that they can tell 'many lies that sound like truth'? (*Theogony* 28). Some critics have detected slight inconsistency in Hesiod's autobiographical story, which may suggest that it is a fiction to suit his artistic purposes (Griffith, 1983).

Sappho – a female voice from ancient Greece

Finally, I would like to read a poem by Sappho, a lyric poet from the island of Lesbos who lived in the seventh to sixth centuries BCE. She composed choral wedding songs and solo love songs for and about other women. She also mentions a daughter and a brother in her poems, which survive in fragments. We do not know much about her life except that she lived in Mytilene in Lesbos and then spent some time in exile. Her poems were highly praised by ancients and she was even nicknamed 'the tenth Muse', but most of her poems have been lost and only some fragments remain, apart from one of her poems, which appears to have survived complete. This is thanks to an ancient author who quoted her poem as an example of a polished poetic style with skilful juxtaposition of words and euphony (Dionysius of Halicarnassus, *On Literary Composition* 23; in Mulroy, 1992, pp.92–3). We also need to be aware that reading the poem in such a context in itself colours our perception of the poem. It was no doubt intended to be sung, not to be read in a scholarly treatise:

> Rich-throned immortal Aphrodite,
>   scheming daughter of Zeus, I pray you,
> with pain and sickness, Queen, crush not my heart,
>
> but come, if ever in the past you
>   heard my voice from afar and hearkened,
> and left your father's halls and came, with gold
>
> chariot yoked; and pretty sparrows
>   brought you swiftly across the dark earth
> fluttering wings from heaven through the air.
>
> Soon they were here, and you, Blest Goddess,
>   smiling with your immortal features,
> asked why I'd called, what was the matter now,

> what was my heart insanely craving:
> 'Who is it this time I must cozen
> to love you, Sappho? Who's unfair to you?
>
> 'For though she flee, soon she'll be chasing;
> though she refuse gifts, she'll be giving;
> though she love not, she'll love despite herself.'
>
> Yes, come once more, from sore obsession
> free me; all that my heart desires
> fulfilled, fulfil – help me to victory!
>
> (Sappho, fragment 1; in West, 1994, p.36)

This poem, along with some of Sappho's other poems, has given the geographic adjective 'Lesbian' the connotation of female homosexuality. The poet appears to have had some close relationships with other women, judging by her poems, but most biographical details about her are conjecture based on her poems, and the nature of such relationships is only a matter of speculation. As always what we see here is the poet's self-portrait as she wants her listeners/readers to see it.

The entire poem is her address to the goddess Aphrodite. Unlike the epic poets, she does not address the Muses for inspiration or for reminding her of the story to tell. This is one twist – and also a female twist, for it is customary for women to call on Aphrodite for help on all sorts of occasions. But a further twist is that it has to be Aphrodite and no other goddess because the poet does not need the divine aid for the composition of the song, but for pursuing her love interest.

We can also see here another difference between the genres of epic and lyric poetry. This is not about a grand story of heroes and gods fighting with each other, but an intense expression of private feeling. On the other hand, epic elements are abundantly used, almost as if it is a mock-heroic poem. The poet's appeal to Aphrodite follows the pattern of Homeric prayers (e.g. *Iliad* 1.453–5, 16.236–8; cf. *Iliad* 14.234–5), in that she uses the fact of divine help in the past as a basis for believing in the availability of help in the future. In Homer, Aphrodite is carried in a horse-drawn chariot like any other gods, but here she uses a sparrow-drawn carriage, a delicate imagery perhaps to suit the goddess's and the poet's femininity better (*Iliad* 5.364–7; cf. Rissman, 1983, pp.9–10, 15).

The way the poet reports her past encounter with the goddess is rather like the epiphany of the Muses to Hesiod in the *Theogony*, but there is no sense of the wonder or surprise we might sense from Hesiod's passage. Here is a more Homeric, even heroic, proximity of the human to the goddess, almost like that enjoyed by Achilles to Thetis in the *Iliad* or Odysseus to Athena in the *Odyssey*. Sappho can pray to her patron goddess and expect her to come to her aid, to fight along with her, except that the victory in this context is to win another lover's heart, not to take the city of Troy.

The mock-heroic tone of the song, along with the love interest in women rather than men, could easily have led us to believe that this poem was composed by a man, except for the poet's signature, that is, her name in the poem itself, and other hints, such as the address to Aphrodite and the use of 'feminine' images such as the sparrow-drawn carriage. It gives us a pause to think what we would have made of the poem if we did not know that the poem was by a woman, for the poet has used elements of the 'male' epic genre, which blurs her feminine voice (cf. Wilson, 1996, p.23).

The difficulty in reading male and female styles in literature is particularly acute in the case of fragmentary works. Sappho worked at the same time as Alcaeus, a male lyric poet, in the same city in Lesbos. They composed their poems in similar styles, so much so that it is virtually impossible to tell to which poet some of the fragments belong, which are normally classified as 'Sappho or Alcaeus'. In addition, the need to be aware of the poet's use of more than one voice is no less acute in lyric poetry than in epic. Just as Homer can speak through his female characters such as Penelope, male lyric poets also composed songs for females to sing. Whether crossing the male-female boundary or not, we should always be aware that the authorial voice in literary works is a product of the author's art and to be listened to as such.

Voices down the ages

This brings us to another layer of complexity involved in listening to ancient voices. Sappho's is one of the few female voices from the ancient world that still survives today – and 'survive' is the right word to use, as many works by women poets, whose number was not thought to be numerous to start with, almost completely vanished before reaching us. For that matter, most male authors of both poetry and prose suffered the same fate as Sappho, in that the majority of their works have been scattered and lost, and in many cases only survive in the form of quotations by later authors or in papyrus fragments preserved in the dry climate of Egypt. This is another obstacle we encounter as we try to hear the voices from Greek and Roman antiquity. Even the epic poems of Homer and Hesiod, which are relatively well preserved in medieval manuscripts, also have variation in readings in different texts handed down though the ages. The branch of scholarship tackling this particular problem of text transmission is called philology, and all the edited texts and the translations based on them are its product. In other words, when reading edited texts we are listening to ancient voices through the interpretation of the philologists, and if we are reading them in translation, also through the interpretation of the translators. As readers of ancient texts we need to be constantly aware not only of the effects of varying voices that the authors intended but also of other effects introduced by the chances of transmission and the interpretations of the editors and translators.

Further reading

For a general introduction to Homer and on the Homeric question, see Essay Two, and its further reading, in this volume. The best introductions to narratology, especially its application to Classical Studies, are Irene de Jong's *Narrators and Focalizers: The Presentation of the Story in the Iliad* (2004) and the same author's *A Narratological Commentary on the Odyssey* (2001). On the relationship between the poet and the Muses, see Penelope Murray, 'Poetic inspiration in early Greece' (1999).

Concise introductions to Hesiod can be found in Dorothea Wender, *Hesiod and Theognis* (1973) and Martin West, *Hesiod: Theogony and Works and Days* (1988), and the works cited in their bibliographies, among which Hermann Fränkel's *Early Greek Poetry and Philosphy* (1975) may be particularly mentioned, along with his sections on Homer and Sappho. For more historical background of Hesiod's poems, see Andrew Burn, *The World of Hesiod* (1936).

For general introductions to Sappho and other lyric poets, David Mulroy, *Early Greek Lyric Poetry* (1992) and Martin West, *Greek Lyric Poetry* (1994) are particularly recommended. For stimulating recent readings of Sappho from gender studies' point of view, see Margaret Williamson, *Sappho's Immortal Daughters*, (1995) and Lyn Wilson, *Sappho's Sweetbitter Songs: Configurations of Female and Male in ancient Greek Lyric* (1996).

Bibliography

Ancient sources

Dionysius of Halicarnassus, *On Literary Composition*, in Mulroy, D. (trans.) (1992) *Early Greek Lyric Poetry*, Ann Arbor: University of Michigan Press.

Homer, *Iliad*, in Lattimore, R. (trans.) (1951) *The Iliad of Homer*, Chicago and London: University of Chicago Press.

Homer, *Odyssey*, in Lattimore, R. (trans.) (1965) *The Odyssey of Homer*, New York: Harper Perennial.

Hesiod, *Theogony*, in West, M.L. (trans.) (1988) Hesiod: *Theogony and Works and Days*, Oxford: Oxford University Press.

Hesiod, *Works and Days*, in West, M.L. (trans.) (1988) Hesiod: *Theogony and Works and Days*, Oxford: Oxford University Press.

Sappho, in West, M.L. (trans.) (1994) *Greek Lyric Poetry*, Oxford: Oxford University Press.

Modern scholarship

Burn, A.R. (1936) *The World of Hesiod*, London: K. Paul, Trench, Trubner.

de Jong, I.J.F. (2001) *A Narratological Commentary on the Odyssey*, Cambridge: Cambridge University Press.

de Jong, I.J.F. (2004) *Narrators and Focalizers: The Presentation of the Story in the Iliad*, 2nd edn, London: Bristol Classical Press (1st edn published 1987).

Edwards, M.W. (1987) *Homer: Poet of the Iliad*, Baltimore and London: Johns Hopkins University Press.

Edwards, M.W. (1991) *The Iliad: A Commentary*, vol.V, books 17–20, Cambridge: Cambridge University Press.

Fränkel, H. (1975) *Early Greek Poetry and Philosophy*, Oxford: Basil Blackwell.

Griffin, J. (1986) 'Homeric words and speakers', *Journal of Hellenic Studies*, vol.106, pp.36–57.

Griffith, M. (1983) 'Personality in Hesiod', *Classical Antiquity*, vol.2, pp.37–65.

Murray, P. (1999) 'Poetic inspiration in early Greece', in I.J.F. de Jong, *Homer: Critical Assessments*, London and New York: Routledge, vol.IV, chapter 73, pp.21–41.

Rissman, L. (1983) *Love as War: Homeric Allusion in the Poetry of Sappho*, Königstein/Ts.: Verlag Anton Hain.

Wender, D. (trans.) (1973) *Hesiod and Theognis*, Harmondsworth: Penguin.

Williamson, M. (1995) *Sappho's Immortal Daughters*, Cambridge, MA and London: Harvard University Press.

Wilson, L.H. (1996) *Sappho's Sweetbitter Songs: Configurations of Female and Male in Ancient Greek Lyric*, London and New York: Routledge.

Yamagata, N. (1989) 'The apostrophe in Homer as part of the oral technique', *Bulletin of the Institute of Classical Studies*, vol.36, pp.91–103.

Essay Four

Self and society in Classical Athens

James Robson

CONTESTANT Hello. I'm Pam, I'm 32 and I'm a market researcher from Lowestoft.

(British quiz show)

STUDENT Who's been knocking at this door?

STREPSIADES Strepsiades, son of Pheidon, of Cicynna.

(Aristophanes, *Clouds* 133–4; in Sommerstein, 1998, p.23)

How do people identify themselves to others? What does this tell us about the distinctions that are important in a society? How do group identities emerge and how do they influence the way in which individuals conceptualise the world they live in? In this essay, I address these questions in relation to Classical Greece and fifth-century BCE Athens in particular. Starting with how individuals define themselves, I shall look at some of the social categories that were important to Classical Athenians and begin to build up a picture of the complex nexus of groupings in existence in their society. I shall then go on to look at two broader group identities of particular importance in the fifth century BCE. First, I shall explore what our sources can tell us about the way in which Greeks characterised themselves as different from eastern 'barbarians', and second, how Athenians represented themselves and their city's values. Of course, the only way in which we have access to the thought world of fifth-century BCE Greece is through evidence – written, pictorial, architectural – that the ancients themselves have left behind, and so a central part of our study will, of necessity, concern reading and contextualising sources. In this way, we shall also explore the different contributions that various sources can make to building up a picture of individual and collective identities.

Self-identity

A simple way to explore identity is to consider how people introduce themselves and others. We have no equivalents of the contestant's introduction from a quiz show preserved for us from the ancient world, but we do have moments in comic drama where slaves are addressed:

Come here, come here, Xanthias!

(Aristophanes, *Clouds* 1485; in Sommerstein, 1998, p.153)

Midas, Phryx, come here and help! Masyntias too!

(Aristophanes, *Wasps* 433; in Sommerstein, 1996, p.47)

or when a citizen farmer introduces himself to a god:

HERMES By holy earth, you shall most certainly die if you don't tell me what your name is.

TRYGAEUS I'm Trygaeus of Athmonum, a skilled vine-grower.

(Aristophanes, *Peace* 188–90; in Sommerstein, 1990, p.21)

At the beginning of Plato's philosophical dialogues, we also find new characters being introduced:

When I reached the little gate that leads to the spring of Panops, I chanced there upon Hippothales, son of Hieronymus, and Ctesipus of Paeania.
(Plato, *Lysis* 203A; in Lamb, 1967, p.7)

After that I recognized ... Hippias of Elis, sitting on a seat of honour in the opposite portico.
(Plato, *Protagoras* 315B–C; in Guthrie, 1956, p.46)

Polemarchus, the son of Cephalus, caught sight of us from a distance as we were hastening homeward and ordered his slave run and bid us to wait for him.
(Plato, *Republic* 327B; in Lamb, 1953a, pp.3–5)

In Plato's *Euthyphro*, Socrates is asked who it is that has brought a charge against him:

SOCRATES I don't know the man very well myself, Euthyphro, for he seems to be a young and unknown man. His name, however, is Meletus, I believe. And he is of the deme of Pitthus, if you remember any Pitthian Meletus, with long hair and only a little beard, but with a hooked nose.

(Plato, *Euthyphro* 2B; in Lamb, 1953b, p.7)

A further source of information is tombstones. The following inscriptions from Attica all date from the Classical era:

Leocrates of Otryne (IG II^2 7016)

Hagnostrate daughter of Theodotos (IG II^2 10569)

[Char]mides son of Philon from Agryle (IG II^2 5297)

Philinna daughter of Praxion (IG II^2 12926)

Philodemus son of Philodemos of Euonymon (IG II² 6196)

Pausimache (IG II² 12435)

Dexitheos son of Dionysius (IG II² 11054)

The simple act of naming an individual had the potential for being highly significant in fifth-century BCE Athenian society, since it could reveal huge amounts about an individual's status. To start with the lowest rung of society, a slave would often possess a generic name that revealed his or her ethnic origins – Phryx, for instance, 'Phrygian' (a region of Asia Minor) – or which pertained to some other characteristic – Xanthias, 'golden-haired' or Masyntias, 'greedy'. That said, in practice Athenians seem often to have avoided using a slave's name, preferring 'slave' or 'one of my slaves' in the way the servants of the British upper classes might once have been referred to as 'the housekeeper' or 'cook'.

Moving up the social scale (leaving women to one side for the moment) we come to foreigners and metics (*metoikoi*), people of non-Athenian birth who lived and worked in Athens. The number of 'resident aliens', as they are often called, was large (perhaps half the size of the

Figure 4.1 Attic tombstone of Philokleia, Vandoeuvres, G. Ortiz Collection. From C.W. Clairmont (1993) *Classical Attic Tombstones*, Akanthus.

Figure 4.2 Attic tombstone of Xenocrateia, daughter of Eucleides of Oie, Staatliche Antikensammlungen und Glyptothek, Munich. Photo: Renate Kühling, Inv.487.

citizen population in the late fourth century BCE) and they formed a highly diverse group. In one of the quotations above we find a visitor to Athens – Hippias of Elis – referred to by his name and city of origin, and another – Polemarchus – referred to by a formula often used for citizens: 'son of ...'; in this case, 'son of Cephalus'.

Finally, at the top of the social scale, we come to citizens, such as the fictional Trygaeus, the real-life Meletus and the names from tombstones in the list above. To judge from these examples, a standard formula of introduction between Athenian citizens was to provide a name, and either a patronym ('son of ...'), the name of the man's *deme*, or both. To understand the significance of the latter term requires some knowledge of the social organisation of Athens in the fifth century BCE. The Athenian city state (*polis*) – Attica – was divided into ten tribes (*phylai*) named after heroes, each of which was further divided into three 'thirds' (*trittyes*) (Figure 4.3). *Demes* were a smaller unit still and acted as a form of local government with tax raising and spending powers and a role in the organisation of the city's religious and military life. Each of the 139 *demes* – perhaps best translated 'districts' or 'communes' – was allotted to a *trittys* in such a way that each *trittys* contained at least one *deme* from an urban area, one from a rural area and one from a coastal area. Thus, to know a citizen's *deme* was to know his *trittys*, tribe (*phyle*) and with whom he voted, fought and worshipped on a local level – and all this information could be conveyed in a name.

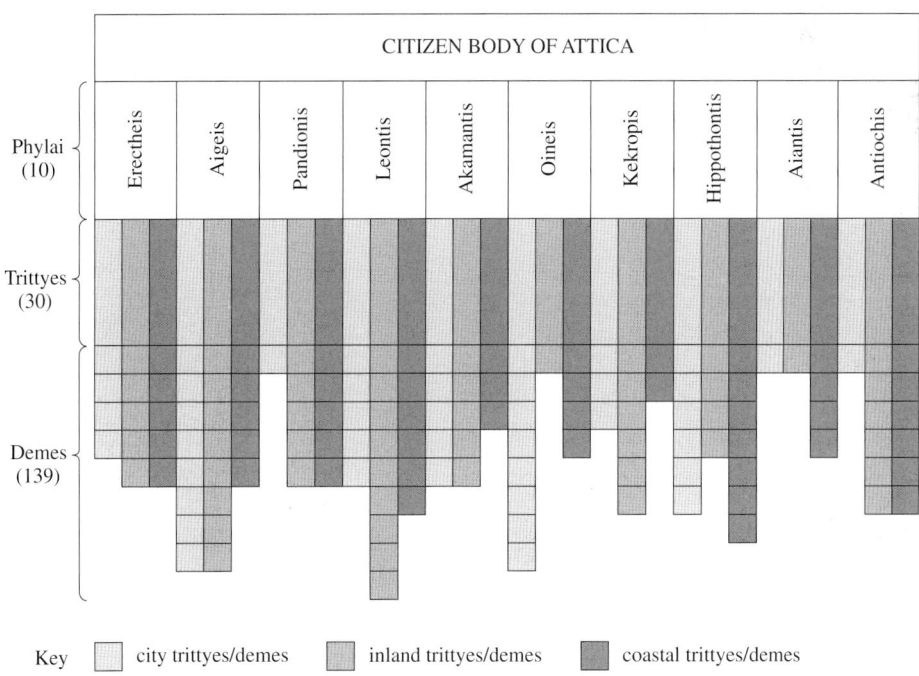

Figure 4.3 Political organisation of Attica in the Classical era.

In addition to a *deme*, each citizen belonged to a *phratry* or 'brotherhood', an institution about which we know relatively little. Like membership of a *deme*, *phratry* membership was inherited by the male line, and these brotherhoods seem to have concerned themselves chiefly with matters of legitimacy and descent. A prospective member had to convince the *phratry* that he was the legitimate freeborn son of an Athenian father (and, after 452/1 BCE, of an Athenian mother too). From the evidence of legal speeches dating from the fourth century BCE, it would appear that without *phratry* membership a man did not become a citizen. Whether this applied in the fifth century BCE as well is unclear: there is some suggestion that *deme* membership was sufficient to secure citizen rights.

We can, perhaps, push the importance of naming further if we consider the use of patronyms. On one level the use of a patronym may be thought equivalent to our surnames and indeed there is a parallel here with modern Icelandic culture where patronyms are used in place of surnames: Magnusson ('son of Magnus'), Gudmundsdottir ('Gudmund's daughter'), and so on. However, we may also detect in the use of patronyms an interest in genealogy and descent and in a city the size of Athens we should not discount the possibility of a father's name being familiar to a sizeable proportion of other citizens. What is more, the potential for identifying someone's family from their name plus patronym was compounded by the fact that the first- and second-born son were regularly named after the paternal and maternal grandfather respectively, with other sons named after uncles (it is interesting to consider what a small pool of names each family must have had and the way in which cousins must have shared names). The use of patronyms also underscores the importance of the household (*oikos*) in the social life of the city of which a man's father – if still alive – was the head (*kyrios*).

The way in which an individual was named provided important information to an Athenian and allows us, too, an insight into factors that were of importance to fifth-century BCE Athenian society. Even names themselves could suggest a person's class. Compound names and the element *hipp*- (suggesting the ownership of horses) were often associated with higher classes: rustic Strepsiades' aspirational, urban wife in Aristophanes' *Clouds* suggests naming their son Xanthippus, Chaerippus or Callippides, for instance (*Clouds* 63–4). It is equally important to note, though, information that is less often provided when a person is named. For example, our tendency to give an individual's age is seldom reflected in Classical Athenian sources and even information as to a person's occupation is relatively uncommon.

One group we have failed to discuss so far is women. Women's voices are rarely preserved for us from ancient Greece: not only are there few female authors but women's words are not often transmitted verbatim (the poets Sappho and Corinna are rare exceptions, both of whom predate the Classical era and neither of whom were Athenian). In addition, there is the tendency for freeborn Athenian women not to be named in literary sources (unless they are fictional). Thus, the speaker in the fourth-century BCE legal speech by Lysias, *On the Murder of Eratosthenes*, fails to name his wife, for instance, although her alleged adultery with the victim is key to the case. Foreign women and prostitutes were not subject to the same taboo, however, and female slaves seem to have been named and referred to in a similar way to their male counterparts. If we might suppose that the tombstones cited above belonged to freeborn women, then such women could, however, be named in death. Note that Hagnostrate's and Philinna's names are accompanied by those of their fathers. We can only speculate as to why Pausimache's name is not accompanied by a patronym.

The picture of Athens that emerges from this brief examination of naming is of a highly stratified society where citizens were commonly differentiated from foreigners, slaves and women and where local and family ties played an important role. But what other allegiances, aside from those largely determined by birth, would a citizen of Classical Athens have had?

We already have one hint from the way in which the *trittyes* were arranged that geography may have been a factor in determining a citizen's loyalties and preoccupations. The fact that each *trittys* comprised urban, rural and coastal *demes* indicates an engineered co-operation between parts of Attica whose diverse economies and ways of life might otherwise have set them at odds. This suspicion can be backed up with the evidence of a source such as Aristophanes' comedies, where we routinely find ageing rustics who are disgruntled with aspects of modern urban life. Indeed, not only do we have here confirmation of the existence of an urban/rural divide but also the hint of a generation gap.

In fact, the structure of tribes and *trittyes* outlined above was introduced by the politician Cleisthenes in the late sixth century BCE, in the early days of Athenian democracy. One important consequence of this political shake-up was to reduce the power bases of certain aristocratic families. This points to another important divide in Athenian society: wealth. There were four property classes in Athens, membership of which affected a citizen's eligibility to hold certain public offices. Those belonging to the lowest property class, the *thetes*, were characterised by their inability to afford armour and so in times of war served in Athens' fleet. Their role became crucial for Athens in the fifth century BCE, since the strength of its navy was the source of much of its influence. Wealthy Athenians, on the other hand, generally saw their power eroded in the course of the fifth century BCE as the democracy grew stronger, yet were still asked to meet various public expenses including the equipping of war ships. What is more, wealthy families would often have ties of marriage with aristocratic families in other city states and so would be painfully aware of the relative lack of influence enjoyed by the upper classes in Athens compared with elsewhere in Greece. Under the right conditions, the tensions between rich and poor in the city could certainly explode: in the late fifth century BCE, for example, there was more than one occasion on which wealthy Athenians seized power of the city in a *coup d'état* (411 and 404 BCE).

Here we have a selection of the more prominent distinctions and tensions that existed between the citizens of Attica, as well as an indication of some of the factors and mechanisms that served to hold Athens together. It is interesting to consider how these elements interacted and how they affected the attitudes and actions of real individuals. Which of these groups were naturally conservative or xenophobic? How could an individual's various loyalties clash? What is more, as we go on now to look at the topic of group identity, it will also be important to bear in mind just how diverse the individuals who made up the population of Athens in the fifth century BCE really were.

Social identity

We have already begun to consider the way in which Athenians' identities are dependent on how they are positioned relative to others in fifth-century BCE society, for example in terms of birth (citizen/foreigner), sex (male/female) and wealth (rich/poor). Of course, an individual's sense of identity will also be shaped by prevailing attitudes towards the groups to which he or she belongs and so I now want to consider the collective identity of large social groups. The two identities on which I shall focus take us beyond the level of groups *within* the city, however: they are those of the Greeks as a whole – 'Hellenism' – and of the city of Athens – 'Athenianism'.

Being Greek and being Athenian were both potent concepts in the fifth century BCE and I want to examine a range of sources in an attempt to establish what these concepts signified for Classical Greeks. In so doing, we shall also see the challenges that different sources present when we try to 'read' them for information about identity and shall consider the role of historical events in shaping notions of group definition.

Hellenism

The event in Greek history that traditionally marks the beginning of the Classical era is the end of the Persian Wars: that is, the successful repulsion of the threat posed to the Greek mainland first by Darius, then by Xerxes.

These events were significant for all Greeks and not least for the Athenians who had played such an important part in the campaigns in general and the battles of Marathon (490 BCE) and Salamis (480 BCE) in particular. Athens underwent terrible hardship with the sack of the city and destruction of its temples in 480 BCE. With the eventual defeat of the Persian invaders, however, the fledgling democracy could claim to have survived a notable test and to have established itself as a major military power.

Figure 4.4 Relief from Persepolis, early fifth century BCE. Darius is seated on his throne as Xerxes stands behind him. Courtesy of the Oriental Institute of the University of Chicago.

An interesting cultural consequence of the Persian Wars is the emergence in Greek art and literature of the figure of the barbarian. After the wars we find increasingly in our sources depictions of Persians and other eastern peoples as luxury-loving, effeminate and lacking self-control – and such 'barbarian' figures are often made to stand in contrast to Greeks who are presented as the opposite: frugal, courageous and well-ordered. In her book examining the portrayal of non-Greeks, *Inventing the Barbarian* (1989), Edith Hall considers a range of sources from Homer onwards and demonstrates the rapidity with which this derogatory image of the barbarian initially emerges. Prior to the fifth century BCE, she argues, Greeks were certainly aware of key differences between themselves on the one hand and Persians on the other – differences in language and customs, say – but what is absent until after the Persian Wars is the kind of depiction of 'barbarians' we see for the first time in Aeschylus' *Persians* (472 BCE).

The *Persians* is a fascinating play. It bucks tragedy's tendency to be set in the distant, mythical past and instead concerns itself largely with the battle of Salamis fought less than ten years before its production. The news of the Persian defeat is relayed to the Persian Queen, Atossa, and a Chorus of elders at the Persian court. The setting and theme allow constant references to oriental luxury and excess, and the Persian defeat at the hands of the Greeks is presented in a moral light, a just reward for arrogance and impiety. In battle, too, the Persian throng is depicted as a formidable force, but one that is less courageous, wily and disciplined than the plucky, outnumbered Greeks. In the following extract, for instance, a Persian messenger relays a key moment of the battle, where the superior organisation of the Greeks paves the way for the bloody rout of the Persian navy:

> Then charge followed charge
> On every side. At first by its huge impetus
> Our fleet withstood them. But soon, in that narrow space,
> Our ships were jammed in hundreds; none could help another.
> They rammed each other with their prows of bronze; and some
> Were stripped of every oar. Meanwhile the enemy
> Came round us in a ring and charged. Our vessels heeled
> Over; the sea was hidden, carpeted with wrecks
> And dead men; all the shores and reefs were full of dead.
>
> Then every ship we had broke rank and rowed for life.
>
> (Aeschylus, *Persians* 409–23; in Vellacott, 1961, p.134)

The image of the eastern barbarian such as we find in the *Persians* seems to have emerged over a short period of time, most likely in the 490s and 480s BCE as a direct consequence of the conflict with Persia. It is interesting to note, though, how the stereotype both endured and (as more recent work has shown) *evolved* in the course of the fifth century BCE. We gain a particularly fascinating glimpse of how the figure of the barbarian developed from Euripides' *Orestes*, a play probably produced in 408 BCE, through the figure of the Phrygian bodyguard who is characterised as effete and cowardly. In the play, Orestes and Pylades plot to kill Helen who has herself developed Persian tastes during her time in Troy. The two discuss how they will handle Helen's assassination:

> ORESTES How shall we manage? She has a barbarian bodyguard.
>
> PYLADES What bodyguard? I'm not afraid of Phrygians.
>
> ORESTES True – chaps who polish her mirrors and set out her scents.
>
> PYLADES Has she brought all her Trojan frills and trinkets here?
>
> ORESTES Hellas falls far below her standard for a home.
>
> (Euripides, *Orestes* 1110–14; based on Vellacott, 1972, p.339)

When we finally meet the Phrygian following the attempt on Helen's life, he is running for his life in a cowardly fashion. He addresses the women of the Chorus in high-flown Greek, sung in extraordinary rhythms:

> PHRYGIAN   Out of death I have escaped
> the Argive sword in Persian slippers
> over the boudoir's
> cedared timbers and the Doric triglyphs –
> gone, gone, O land, O land! –
> in my barbarian flight.
> Woe is me!
> Which way may I escape, ladies?
>
> (Euripides, *Orestes* 1369–75; based on West, 1980, p.153)

The Phrygian then goes on to describe how he and the other bodyguards were worsted by Orestes and Pylades:

> So we joined sword-points: then indeed the Phrygians
> showed up outstandingly
> how far in martial prowess we were born
> inferior to Greek arms,
> one fled, another dead, another wounded,
> another begging to protect his life.
>
> (Euripides, *Orestes* 1483–8; in West, 1980, p.161)

Unlike the Persians in Aeschylus' play, the Phrygian in the *Orestes* seems, to a large extent, to be a figure of fun. On one view we could choose to see the Phrygian as simply a development of the figures we find in the *Persians*, but it will be important to bear other factors in mind too. Aeschylus' play is peopled exclusively by Persians and for the tragedy of the play to unfold effectively the audience no doubt needs to feel respect and not just contempt for their plight. In addition, Aeschylus' portrayal of the Persians as a formidable adversary not only reflects what was no doubt a historical reality but also serves to highlight the magnitude of the Greeks' victory. The character of the Phrygian, on the other hand, is peripheral to the plot of the *Orestes* and this allows Euripides a freer hand in the way he is portrayed. Of course, the fact that Euripides has chosen to include this character in his telling of the myth despite the fact that he is, to all intents and purposes, a dispensable part of the plot is itself just as interesting as Aeschylus's decision to dramatise the Persians' defeat 64 years earlier.

Like most racial stereotypes, the images of the Persian barbarian that prevailed in the fifth century BCE most likely had some basis in fact but owed much to invention. No doubt some Persians really *did* wear Persian slippers and because of the comparative wealth of their empire and their un-Greek tastes and customs Persians may quite reasonably have struck Greeks as luxury loving. Above all, though, the figure of the barbarian was a popular and convenient cultural stereotype, which (at different times in different ways) served an important sociological purpose in demonising a race whose power and proximity gave Classical Greeks particular cause for concern – and, it might be added, proved a singular source of fascination.

The phenomenon of the barbarian figure demonstrates a much-discussed tendency in Greek thought, namely to conceive of categories in terms of binary opposites: male/female; Greek/barbarian; free/slave, etc. Thus, there are key respects in which a male is the opposite of a female, a Greek the opposite of a barbarian, and so on. An interesting point to consider, though, is that unlike male and female the dividing line between Greek and barbarian is not so clear. The inhabitants of mainland Greece and the Greek islands were not the only Hellenes. Greek city states had established colonies as far afield as Sicily, North Africa and Asia Minor and, what is more, certain mainland inhabitants, such as the Macedonians, were regarded by others as not wholly 'Greek' at all. Attempts to classify as Greek all those who, say, speak a common language or share a common set of values are equally fraught with problems. Local customs and dialects could vary enormously and studies of the interaction between Greeks and non-Greeks such as Jonathan Hall's *Hellenicity* (2002) tend to stress the cultural continuum between Greek and non-Greek peoples. Hall even highlights the prevalence of bilingualism in certain communities, thus challenging the idea that language can be considered a defining characteristic of 'Greekness'. It is also worth stressing that there were numerous ways in which mainland Greeks, too, may have had direct contact with 'barbarians' (through trade and travel, for instance) – nor were eastern art and customs without their imitators in Hellas.

What we have identified here is an interesting tension between the sharp Greek/barbarian divide apparent from many of our sources and the spectrums that in fact existed in the fifth century BCE in terms of language, race, customs and religion. We should note two points here, however. First, in modern discourse too we often find categories used that many of us would find hard accurately to define – 'European' or 'working class', for instance – but which are none the less potent for that. Second, we should note that on the spectrum of 'Greekness' an Athenian or Spartan citizen is hardly likely to have placed himself in the middle – rather, he would undoubtedly have thought of himself and his city as paradigms of what it was to be Greek. Aside from anything else, if we recall the Greek obsession with genealogical descent as enshrined in various citizenship laws, the very fact of being a legal citizen of a city state was proof to an Athenian, say, of his ethnic purity. And what were his city's language, customs and religious practices if not Greek?

In sum, Greek language, Greek customs and Greek religion were potent concepts in the fifth century BCE, and the conflict with Persia had played an important role in establishing their prominence in Greek thought. In the following extract, we can see these ideas of a common Greek identity being appealed to in a speech that appears in Herodotus' account of the Persian Wars. The historical date of the speech is 479 BCE and Spartan envoys have come to Athens, concerned that the Athenians will be persuaded to make an alliance with Persia. The Athenians, however, reassure the Spartans of their resolve:

> There is not so much gold in the world nor land so fair that we would take it for pay to join the common enemy and bring Greece into subjection. There are many compelling reasons against our doing so, even if we wished: the first and greatest is the burning of the temples and images of our gods – now ashes and rubble. It is our bounden duty to avenge this desecration with all our might – not to clasp the hand that wrought it. Again, there is 'Greekness' (*to Hellēnikon*) – the community of blood and language, temples and ritual; our common customs; if Athens were to betray all this, it would not be well done.
>
> (Herodotus, *Histories* 8.144; based on Marincola, 2003, p.553)

Of course, the speech that Herodotus records, writing as he was in the middle of the fifth century BCE, is unlikely to be a verbatim transcript of what was actually said. This need not trouble us, though, since of more importance is that he could present this speech as a credible historical record: regardless of its accuracy, it nevertheless allows us insight into the thought-world of the fifth century BCE. The mention of the 'Greekness' (*to Hellēnikon*) and the shared concepts of ethnicity, language and religion are thus all highly significant.

We have seen how the concept of 'Greekness' was influenced by the Persian Wars, a conflict which had served to define the enemy barbarian as a villain but which also had its heroes: the Greeks themselves. No doubt the individual city states grew in confidence through their victory but, just as importantly, the unity that the Greeks had displayed in meeting the Persian threat became a cultural symbol for successive generations. Never before – or afterwards – did the Greek city states collaborate on such a scale. The number of Greek cities that had in fact combined their forces against the Persians was small – 31 out of the 181 *poleis* were involved – but many a Greek would afterwards look back to this golden period as evidence of what a panhellenic – 'all-Greek' – force could achieve. The historian Herodotus, a native of Halicarnassus in Asia Minor – a Greek city under Persian rule (and, interestingly, with an ethnically mixed population) – was one admirer of the panhellenic achievement but there were certainly others, most notably the Athenian orator Isocrates, who in the fourth-century BCE was to appeal for the Greeks to unite against Persia once again under the leadership of Athens and Sparta.

Athenianism

Another major effect of the Persian Wars was to crystallise a new power structure between the Greek city states. The two prime movers in the conflict had been Athens and Sparta and it is these city states that subsequently emerged as the two major powers in the Greek world. Between the end of the Persian Wars and the beginning of the Peloponnesian War in 431 BCE – a time known as 'The Fifty Years' (*pentakontaetia*) – Athens enjoyed a period of particular prosperity and self-confidence.

One of the factors that accounts for Athens' prosperity at this time is the Delian League, an anti-Persian alliance of mostly maritime city states set up by Athens soon after the Persian Wars. The League soon turned into what amounted to an Athenian empire (in the sources it is described as an *archê*, which can mean both 'leadership' and 'rule') and some of the tribute paid by the member states – nominally to contribute to the continuing struggle against Persia – was directed into a huge public building programme in Athens in the 440s and 430s BCE. The most remarkable product of this programme was without doubt the Parthenon, an enormous temple to Athena on the Athenian Acropolis, which was built in contravention of an oath taken by the member states of the Delian League to leave their sacked temples in ruins as a permanent reminder of the Persian threat.

It is interesting to consider the Parthenon and the other Acropolis buildings from the point of view of 'identity' and to ask what they can tell us about the way in which Athenians perceived themselves in the middle of the fifth century BCE. The question is complex and requires careful consideration, both of the buildings and sculptures themselves and of the contemporary cultural and historical context. Nevertheless, even a brief analysis can suggest interesting points for further thought.

The Parthenon was built between 447 and 432 BCE and its construction involved some of the most skilled craftsmen in the Greek-speaking world. The quality of the workmanship and the sheer size of the temple (at the time the biggest in Greece) are important points to note – these at once suggest a building conceived of as being a national symbol for Athens. Its position is noteworthy too: the temple was in the centre of Athens but also visible from afar to the numerous traders and other visitors who came to Athens each year.

Essay Four Self and society in Classical Athens

"a celebration of civilisation"
Russ

Figure 4.5 Acropolis from afar: view from the west. The Propylaea, the gate marking the entrance to the Acropolis, can be seen on the left-hand side, near the site of the Temple of Athena Nike. © The Open University. Photo: James Robson.

The Parthenon and its sculptures can certainly be viewed as celebrating Athens' spiritual life, military prowess and cultural pre-eminence. The pediments at the east end of the temple depict the birth of Athena, while the west pediment sculptures show the contest between Athena and Poseidon to decide who would become the patron god of the city (a competition that Athena won, of course). The continuous frieze running along all four sides of the temple is thought by most scholars to have depicted the yearly Panathenaic ('all-Athenian') procession in honour of Athena, the final destination of which was the was the home of the ancient olive-wood statue of the goddess: originally the Old Temple of Athena Polias, later the Erechtheion, both of which temples lay to the north of the Parthenon. The metopes too – the 92 carved square panels that line all four sides of the temple – pick up themes we explored earlier in our discussion of Greeks and barbarians. They depict various battles between the powers of civilisation and groups that are somehow *un*civilised – the gods battle against the giants, the Greeks battle against the Amazons – in all of which mythical struggles the forces of order and civilisation prevail.

One interesting feature of the Acropolis sculptures is the way in which imagery is echoed in different locations. For example, the giant gold and ivory statue of Athena Parthenos ('the virgin') that stood inside the Parthenon held a shield sculpted with scenes of the battles between both gods and giants and Greeks and Amazons, and she also wore sandals whose decoration included the battle between Lapiths and centaurs (all motifs found on the temple's metopes). The Parthenos statue could itself be said to

a celebration of

Partheno

99

Figure 4.6 South metope from the Parthenon (Lapith and centaur), *c.*440 BCE. Elgin Collection, British Museum, London. © Copyright The Trustees of the British Museum.

complement the older statue of Athena Promachos ('she who fights *for*'), which had been dedicated on the Acropolis nearly 20 years earlier and looked towards Salamis, where the Athenians had led the Greeks in the decisive sea battle of 480 BCE. After the completion of the Athena Parthenos, this earlier Promachos statue was revisited by sculptors and decoration was added that included scenes of fighting Lapiths and centaurs – one effect of which was surely to create a sense of unity between the various pieces of statuary and sculpture.

A further example of reflected imagery may be found in the richly decorated temple of Athena Nike ('victory'), which was built some time in the 420s BCE and lay perched just outside the Acropolis gate (the Propyleia; see Figure 4.5). Once more there is imagery of battling Amazons and giants (on the west and east pediments, respectively). Perhaps most remarkable, though, is the temple's frieze, which contains an assembly of gods over the temple entrance and various battles on the other sides. The subject matter of the north and west friezes is disputed (are the battles mythological, allegorical or historical?) but the south frieze almost certainly depicts the battle of Marathon. Is this a singular case of 'real' historical figures becoming the subject matter of temple sculpture, or are we to take it that Marathon had already entered the world of myth?

Even in this brief discussion of the Acropolis we can see the way in which its buildings and sculptures can be thought of as promoting 'Athenianism', that is, a sense of Athens's military and cultural superiority.

Figure 4.7 Section of south frieze from temple of Athena Nike, British Museum, London. © Copyright The Trustees of the British Museum.

But superiority over whom? To a large degree, over the Persians whom the Athenians played a decisive role in defeating in war. However, the celebration of Athena, the foundation of the city and the specific role played by Athens in the Persian Wars also suggests an Athens that is setting itself apart from other Greek states. Indeed, this 'reading' of the Acropolis buildings fits well with what we know about the way in which Athens was positioning itself at this time, namely establishing itself at the head of its empire and becoming embroiled in conflicts with other powerful cities, most notably Sparta.

Naturally, the Athenian self-confidence as represented by buildings such as the Parthenon is also discernible in other sources that date from this era. Tragedy makes a particularly interesting case study when it comes to questions of identity, owing to the complex relationship it has with the 'real' world of contemporary Athens. In order to glean information from tragedies, we have to negotiate issues such as the relationship of the mythical settings of the plays to the historical present, the context of the plays' performance and the diverse composition and expectations of the audiences. Although it may not always be easy to interpret, tragedy offers us a considerable range of information when it comes to issues of Athenian identity. To take a simple example, as has often been noted tragedies are only very rarely set in Athens or Attica – the tragic action (which regularly involves transgressive activity) usually takes place elsewhere. When plays *are* set in Attica, Athens is either seen to derive some lasting benefit from the events of the play (the support of the previously harsh Furies in Aeschylus' *Eumenides*; the blessings bestowed by Oedipus' death in Sophocles' *Oedipus at Colonus*) or is portrayed as a place of refuge and protection for displaced suppliants (Euripides' *Suppliant Women* and *Children of Heracles*).

Another seemingly straightforward instance of 'Athenianism' in tragedy is explicit praise of the city. In the following extract from Euripides' *Medea*, for example, produced in 431 BCE, the Chorus describes Athens as a place beloved of the gods, resistant to conquest, and as a cradle of 'excellence' (the Greek *aretê* can indicate moral as well as technical superiority). Note the local colouring here with the reference to the river Cephisus:

> CHORUS The men of Athens have been fortunate of old,
> Children of the blessed gods:
> Their land is holy, never plundered,
> They feed on their famed wit
> And sprightly step through bright, clear air,
> Where, they say, the nine Muses of sacred Pieria
> Created golden Harmony.
>
> By the streams of lovely Cephisus
> They say that Aphrodite, drawing water, breathed
> Down the valley gentle sweet-breathed airs;
> Always wearing on her hair
> A fragrant crown of roses,
> She sends young Loves to sit with Wit,
> Helping create their diverse arts.
>
> (Euripides, *Medea* 824–45; in Harrison, 2000, p.59)

Athens is also praised by the Chorus of Euripides' *Suppliant Women* (422 BCE), who appeal to Athens, 'the city of Pallas', to save them:

> Come, city of Pallas, come to a mother's aid;
> Save from dishonour the laws of mankind.
> You reverence Justice;
> Injustice you despise;
> To those in distress you bring deliverance.
>
> (Euripides, *Suppliant Women* 377–80; in Vellacott, 1972, p.205)

In tragedy, then, we perhaps gain glimpses of the qualities for which Athenians are wont to praise themselves in the fifth century BCE. The Chorus of *Medea* highlights Athens' good fortune, invincibility and excellence, for instance, whereas the Chorus of *Suppliant Women* evokes the city's reputation for justice and as a place of refuge. What is interesting to note here, though, is that just as we saw with the stereotype of barbarians the qualities ascribed to Athens are somewhat vague, and entail sweeping generalisations about the city and its inhabitants. What is more, the mythical setting of the plays adds a further layer of ambiguity – are these qualities that apply to the mythical Athens, present-day Athens or both?

To take this discussion further, I should like to consider other ways in which Athens and its qualities are discussed in tragedy. Let us focus briefly on a feature of Athenian society we often find highlighted in tragedy, namely the city's democratic constitution and the freedom (especially freedom of speech, *parrhesia*) enjoyed by its citizens. The following extract from Euripides' *Suppliant Women* is of particular interest in this regard. Here we find Athens' mythical king, Theseus, involved in a heated exchange with a Theban Herald, who has just arrived in Athens. The Herald asks 'Who is the sovereign here?', to which Theseus replies:

> THESEUS First, stranger, you began your speech on a false note,
> Enquiring for a king absolute. This state is not
> Subject to one man's will, but is a free city.
> The king here is the people, who by yearly office
> Govern in turn. We give no special power to wealth;
> The poor man's voice commands equal authority.

(Euripides, *Suppliant Women* 403–8; in Vellacott, 1972, p.206)

The first point to note is the anachronism involved in Theseus, a king from Athens' distant mythical past, extolling the virtues of a democracy only established in 508 BCE – a reminder, if one were needed, of the complexities involved in reading tragedies. Further, though, we should note that unlike the praise given to Athens by the Choruses of *Medea* and *Suppliant Women*, Theseus' praise of the democracy does *not* go unchallenged. On the contrary, the Theban Herald has harsh words to say in reply:

> HERALD There you concede a point which gives me half the game.
> The city that I come from lives under command
> Of one man, not a rabble. None there has the power
> By loud-mouthed talk to twist the city this way and that
> For private profit – today popular, loved by all,
> Tomorrow, blaming the innocent man for the harm he's done,
> Getting away with every crime, till finally
> The law-courts let him off scot-free! The common man!
> Incapable of plain reasoning, how can he guide
> A city in sound policy?

(Euripides, *Suppliant Women* 409–18; in Vellacott, 1972, p.207)

Here we have a key feature of Athenian life debated in the most public of contexts – a theatrical performance. What is more, this debate is not atypical: on the contrary, it would be truer to say that the discussion of moral values and political issues is central to fifth-century BCE tragedy. But where does this take our discussion of identity? At first glance, the presence of this debate about democracy may seem problematic if the question we wish to ask is 'What did the Athenians think about their system of government?', since no single view emerges. However, what its presence *does* allow us to infer is that the nature and success of democracy as a form of government was a potential topic of interest in Athens in 422 BCE, the date of the play's production. Thus, while we cannot with any certainty judge the playwright's own viewpoint on this or any other issue discussed in his plays, we might reasonably conclude that topics we find under discussion in tragedy either reflect live, contemporary debates (about which different members of the audience no doubt held differing opinions) or, at the very least, ideas that the playwright thought would resonate with his audience.

This tendency of tragic playwrights to frame debates has interesting repercussions for our topic of identity, since in tragedy we also find stereotypes of Greeks and barbarians challenged and thus issues of identity implicitly discussed. It is Euripides in particular who brings such issues to the fore. In his plays we find cases of noble barbarians who are treated badly by scheming Greeks (*Iphigenia in Tauris*, *Helen*), for instance, and his *Trojan Women* takes as its focus the passive victims of the Trojan War – the Trojan women of the title – who suffer greatly at the hands of the Greek victors. The reaction of Andromache, wife of the dead Hector, when she hears of the Greeks' plans to kill her son displays Euripides' subversion of Greek/barbarian stereotypes particularly neatly when she exclaims, 'Hellenes! Inventors of barbaric cruelties!' (*Trojan Women* 764).

It is another Euripdean play bearing the name of this same woman, *Andromache*, in which a particularly complex and revealing conflict occurs. Neoptolemus, son of Achilles, takes Andromache from Troy as his concubine and has by her a son, Molossus. Neoptolemus also takes a Greek wife, Hermione, daughter of Menelaus, who fails to bear him children. Hermione's barrenness becomes a source of conflict between the two women – a barbarian on the one hand, a Spartan on the other. In the war of words between them, Hermione characterises Andromache as an immoral barbarian. She cruelly accuses Andromache of actively seeking the marriage with Neoptolemus into which she was forced and tells her that she should know her place:

> ... And learn where you live now – there is no Hector here,
> Nor Priam decked in gold; this is a Greek city.

> And you have the effrontery, you immoral wretch,
> To sleep with the man whose father killed your husband, bear
> Children with the blood of his murderer in their veins!
> You orientals are all alike – incest between
> Father and daughter, brother and sister, mother and son;
> And murder too – the closest of family ties outraged,
> And no law to forbid such a crime! You can't
> Import your foreign morals here. It's a disgrace
> In Hellas for one man to be the master of two women;
> Unless a man wants trouble at home, he must enjoy
> The pleasures of marriage with one wife, and be content.
>
> (Euripides, *Andromache* 168–80; in Vellacott, 1972, p.151)

The imagery of oriental luxury and immorality is familiar, but what is striking about Euripides' choice of Andromache is that he has opted to portray a barbarian who is traditionally characterised as sympathetic in Greek literature – a tradition that he is at pains to uphold. By choosing to depict Andromache, Euripides can be said once more to be framing a debate about the nature of barbarians and challenging his audience's assumptions – just as in *Trojan Women* Greeks are shown to be capable of great cruelty towards their barbarian captives. The particular interest in this play, though, is that it is not Greeks in general who are cast as unforgiving, but Spartans in particular. Hermione and her father Menelaus both show great cruelty towards Andromache, for instance, and when she is later seized and threatened with death, Andromache accuses Spartans of being cruel, greedy, power-hungry liars:

> ANDROMACHE Spartans! The whole world hates you above all other men!
> Lies are your policy, treachery your accomplishment,
> Your craft is crime and cruelty; your hearts warped and sly,
> Your minds diseased, you lord it over the Hellenic world;
> Justice lies dead! What wickedness is not in you?
> You add murder to murder, you make gold your god;
> The whole world knows your speech is one thing, your intent
> Another. My curse on you!
>
> (Euripides, *Andromache* 445–53; in Vellacott, 1972, pp.159–60)

A simple reading of this conflict might be that the 'message' of Euripides' play is that Spartans are even worse than barbarians – and indeed a member of the audience in 426 BCE, at the height of Athens' conflict with Sparta, might reasonably have left the theatre having understood the play in that way. While it is interesting to speculate as to Euripides' intended 'message' as an author or the reactions of audience members (and these would no doubt have differed widely from spectator to spectator), we are on safer ground if we simply state that Euripides has chosen a theme – the nature of Spartans – likely to resonate with his audience. This theme stands in stark contrast to that of Aeschylus' *Persians*, and the differences between the two plays lead us to speculate about changes in Athenian self-definition in the intervening 50 years. Throughout the fifth century BCE, Athenians were no doubt conscious of the differences between themselves and Persian 'barbarians', on the one hand, and between themselves and other Greeks (Thebans, Spartans), on the other. If our sources are representative, though (and we must always bear in mind the limitations of our evidence, especially for the beginning of the century), in the wake of the Persian Wars, the 'other' in opposition to which Athenians were wont to define themselves most prominently were Persian barbarians. Later in the century, however, the situation becomes more complex. Barbarians continue to be portrayed in art and literature and – in Euripidean tragedy at least – the image of the barbarian is held up to scrutiny. However, a matter of increasing interest to Athenians is the relationship between Athens and other Greek city states – and none more so than Sparta. (It is interesting to note that later, in the fourth century BCE, when the Peloponnesian War is over and Greeks once more see Persia as a very real threat, further shifts in attitudes are perceptible, not least the emergence of new panhellenic ideals.)

Conclusions

Of course, the cultural shifts no doubt happened in a far more complex and intricate way than I have outlined here, but nevertheless through our study we can begin to see how our sources might be read for information about identity and to discover the type of information that such an investigation can reveal. What does become apparent even from a short survey such as this is the complex interaction of historical and sociological factors and how this determines the ways in which group identities crystallise and change. Equally apparent is the care with which we need to treat each source if we are not to arrive at an oversimplistic or inappropriate understanding of our evidence.

At this point it may be worth making a distinction that has not formerly been made explicit, namely that there is an important difference between defining the enemy as the 'other' and defining the 'other' as an enemy. To take a simple example, just because men and women perceive themselves as fundamentally different from each other (as was no doubt the case in Classical Athens), it does not follow that either sex *necessarily* looks upon the other with hostility. In terms of the oppositions we have been looking at here, it is interesting to note that at certain points during the Peloponnesian War (431–404 BCE) – especially towards the end – Persia was seen by both Athens and Sparta as a potential ally whose intervention in the war might prove decisive in their favour. In this case, the barbarian 'other' was looked upon as a potential friend. Perhaps more interesting still, though, is to contemplate the extent to which the opposite may be true – that is, does an enemy just *sometimes* or *routinely* come to be perceived as 'other'? Certainly this is the fate that befell both the Persians and later the Spartans in fifth-century BCE Athens, but what of other examples from the Greek world – or, indeed, from other eras and cultures? Is it inevitable that we come to characterise our adversaries as being different from us?

When talking of group identity (as I have done throughout the latter half of this essay), we should also be careful to bear the obvious in mind, namely that a large group such as 'the Athenians' comprises a number of smaller groups and a myriad of individuals. The voices we have preserved in our literary sources are generally those of the articulate élite and it is difficult or impossible to trace the relationship of most groups and individuals to the city at large. The tantalising glimpses we do get of the complex nature of individuals' loyalties indicate that we should certainly be wary of regarding Athenians as a homogenous whole. One notable tension, for example, was that many aristocrats had pro-Spartan leanings, a fact that must have caused particular disquiet in the lead-up to and during the Peloponnesian War. What is more, the Spartans even exploited this tension in 430 BCE when, in their invasion of Attica, they left Pericles' farmland untouched – doubtless a deliberate ploy to undermine the citizens' confidence in one of their most prominent politicians. When considering matters of identity, we must be careful to look at the detail as well as the broader picture – that is, to consider the self as well as the society.

Further reading

The theme of Greek identity is the central theme of Paul Cartledge's *The Greeks: A Portrait of Self and Others* (1993). An influential book on the Greek image of barbarians is Edith Hall's *Inventing the Barbarian* (1989), for which Aeschylus' *Persians* and Herodotus' *Histories* are key sources. Other plays worth reading on this theme include Euripides' *Medea* and *Orestes* (for the character of the Phrygian slave). *The Shadow of Sparta*, edited by Anton Powell and Stephen Hodkinson (1994) is strong on Athenian images of Sparta and the essay it contains by William Poole, 'Euripides and Sparta' discusses in more depth issues raised towards the end of this essay.
The Shadow of Sparta is usefully read in conjunction with Thucydides' *History of the Peloponnesian War* (see especially the Funeral Speech at Book 2.35–46) and Euripides' *Andromache*. Plays by Aristophanes, such as *Acharnians* and *Lysistrata*, provide an interesting perspective on issues of identity from the viewpoint of late fifth-century BCE comedy.

Other strands in this essay can be pursued in Mary Beard's *The Parthenon* (2002); Edith Hall's 'The sociology of Athenian tragedy' (1997); Jonathan Hall's *Ethnic Identity in Greek Antiquity* (1997); Jeffrey Hurwitt's *The Athenian Acropolis: History, Mythology, and Archaeology from the Neolithic Era to the Present* (1999) and *The Acropolis in the Age of Pericles* (2004); and David Whitehead's *The Demes of Attica, 508/7–ca. 250 B.C.: A Political and Social Study* (1986).

Bibliography

Ancient sources

Aeschylus, *Eumenides*, in Meineck, P. (trans.) (1998) Aeschylus: *Oresteia*, Indianapolis: Hackett.

Aeschylus, *Persians*, in Vellacott, P. (trans.) (1961) Aeschylus: *Prometheus Bound, The Suppliants, Seven Against Thebes, The Persians*, Harmondsworth: Penguin.

Aristophanes, *Acharnians*, in Sommerstein, A.H. (trans.) (2002) Aristophanes: *Lysistrata and Other Plays*, London: Penguin (first published 1973).

Aristophanes, *Clouds*, in Sommerstein, A.H. (trans.) (1998) Aristophanes: *Clouds*, Warminster: Aris & Phillips (first published 1982).

Aristophanes, *Lysistrata*, in Sommerstein, A.H. (trans.) (2002) Aristophanes: *Lysistrata and Other Plays*, London: Penguin (first published 1973).

Aristophanes, *Peace*, in Sommerstein, A.H. (trans.) (1990) Aristophanes: *Peace*, Warminster: Aris & Phillips (first published 1985).

Aristophanes, *Wasps*, in Sommerstein, A.H. (trans.) (1996) Aristophanes: *Wasps*, Warminster: Aris & Phillips (first published 1983).

Euripides, *Andromache*, in Vellacott, P. (trans.) (1972) Euripides: *Orestes, Children of Heracles, Andromache, Suppliant Women*, etc., Harmondsworth: Penguin.

Euripides, *Children of Heracles*, in Vellacott, P. (trans.) (1972) Euripides: *Orestes, Children of Heracles, Andromache, Suppliant Women*, etc., Harmondsworth: Penguin.

Euripides, *Helen*, in Morwood, J. (trans.) (1997) Euripides: *Medea, Hippolytus, Electra, Helen*, Oxford: Oxford University Press.

Euripides, *Iphigenia in Tauris*, in Morwood, J. (trans.) (1998) Euripides: *Iphigenia among the Taurians, Bacchae, Iphigenia at Aulis, Rhesus*, Oxford: Oxford University Press.

Euripides, *Medea*, in Harrison, J. (trans.) (2000) Euripides: *Medea*, with an introduction to the Greek theatre by P.E. Easterling, Cambridge: Cambridge University Press.

Euripides, *Orestes*, in Vellacott, P. (trans.) (1972) Euripides: *Orestes, Children of Heracles, Andromache, Suppliant Women*, etc., Harmondsworth: Penguin.

Euripides, *Orestes*, in West, M.L. (trans.) (1980) Euripides: *Orestes*, Warminster: Aris & Phillips (first published 1972).

Euripides, *Suppliant Women*, in Vellacott, P. (trans.) (1972) Euripides: *Orestes, Children of Heracles, Andromache, Suppliant Women*, etc., Harmondsworth: Penguin.

Euripides, *Trojan Women*, in Morwood, J. (trans.) (1999) Euripides: *The Trojan Women and Other Plays*, Oxford: Oxford University Press.

Herodotus, *Histories*, in Marincola, J. (trans.) (2003) Herodotus: *The Histories*, Harmondsworth: Penguin.

Lysias, *On the Murder of Eratosthenes*, in Todd, S.C. (trans.) (2002) Lysias: *On the Murder of Eratosthenes*, Austin: University of Texas Press.

Plato, *Euthyphro*, in Lamb, W.R.M. (trans.) (1953b) *Plato in Twelve Volumes*, vol.1, Cambridge, MA: Harvard University Press and London: William Heinemann.

Plato, *Lysis*, in Lamb, W.R.M. (trans.) (1967) *Plato in Twelve Volumes*, vol.3, Cambridge, MA: Harvard University Press and London: William Heinemann.

Plato, *Protagoras*, in Guthrie, W.K.C. (trans.) (1956) Plato: *Protagoras and Meno*, Harmondsworth: Penguin.

Plato, *Republic*, in Lamb, W.R.M. (trans.) (1953a) *The Republic in Two Volumes*, vol.1, Cambridge, MA: Harvard University Press and London: William Heinemann.

Sophocles, *Oedipus at Colonus*, in Meineck, P. and Woodruff, P. (trans.) (2003) Sophocles: *Theban Plays*, Indianapolis: Hackett.

Thucydides, *History of the Peloponnesian War*, in Warner, R. (trans.) (1972) Thucydides: *The History of the Peloponnesian War*, London: Penguin.

Modern scholarship

Beard, M. (2002) *The Parthenon*, London: Profile.

Cartledge, P. (1993) *The Greeks: A Portrait of Self and Others*, Oxford and London: Oxford University Press.

Hall, E. (1989) *Inventing the Barbarian*, Oxford: Oxford University Press.

Hall, E. (1997) 'The sociology of Athenian tragedy', in P.E. Easterling (ed.) *The Cambridge Companion to Greek Tragedy*, Cambridge: Cambridge University Press, pp.93–126.

Hall, J.M. (1997) *Ethnic Identity in Greek Antiquity*, Cambridge: Cambridge University Press.

Hall, J.M. (2002) *Hellenicity: Between Ethnicity and Culture*, Chicago and London: University of Chicago Press.

Hurwitt, J.M. (1999) *The Athenian Acropolis: History, Mythology, and Archaeology from the Neolithic Era to the Present*, Cambridge: Cambridge University Press.

Hurwitt, J.M. (2004) *The Acropolis in the Age of Pericles*, Cambridge and New York: Cambridge University Press.

Poole, W. (1994) 'Euripides and Sparta', in Powell and Hodkinson, 1994, pp.1–33.

Powell, A. and Hodkinson, S. (eds) (1994) *The Shadow of Sparta*, London and New York: Routledge.

Said, E. (1979) *Orientalism: A Brief Definition*, New York: Vintage.

Saïd, S. (1984) 'Grecs ou Barbares dans le théâtre d'Euripide: la fin des différences', *Ktema*, vol.9, pp.27–53.

Whitehead, D. (1986) *The Demes of Attica, 508/7–ca. 250 B.C.: A Political and Social Study*, Princeton: Princeton University Press, 1986.

Essay Five

Performance, competition and democracy in Athenian culture

Lorna Hardwick

Is there a significant cultural relationship between sport, the arts and politics? Is theatre an illusion or does it represent the realities of life? Is the power of performance transient or does it have a lasting effect on participants and spectators? Is an emphasis on victory in competition compatible with a democratic society that claims to value participation by all? These kinds of question are sometimes asked in our own times but they also represent key questions asked in recent scholarship concerning the practices and ideology of fifth-century BCE Athens. The aim of this essay is to consider how performance aspects of Greek society were defined, represented and criticised in the ancient sources and to discuss the extent to which modern scholars have been justified in describing Athenian culture as a performance culture (Goldhill and Osborne, 1999; Boedeker and Raaflaub, 1998, chapters 1 and 15).

Performed activities in ancient Greek culture: ancient and modern approaches

The *Oxford English Dictionary* definition of 'performance' identifies two distinct aspects of meaning. The first emphasises successful action – 'carry into effect, execute, [a] notable feat'. The other aspect is concerned with what is done – a public function, a play, a piece of music. These two aspects are closely linked in the ancient contexts. The *Oxford Classical Dictionary* (third edition, 1996) does not have a separate entry under performance. The entry on 'tragedy' includes a section by P.E. Easterling on form and performance and comments that competing in honour of the gods was an important characteristic of Greek culture. The entry under *agones* ('competitions'/'contests') identifies a variety of competitive panhellenic festivals, including the Olympic Games, that combined athletics, music, poetry and equestrian events, and includes information on the rewards of victory (wreaths of various kinds, money, gold crowns and amphorae (large jars for oil or wine)). The consequences of failure (shame, depression and even mental illness) were also great.

The conceptual analogy between social and cultural practices on the one hand and theatricality and performance on the other is drawn from modern anthropology, especially the work of Victor Turner and Clifford Geertz. Turner explored the relationship between politics and conflict as a kind of 'social drama'. Geertz examined ways in which deep social structures were reflected in various kinds of 'play' in which the individual and the socio-cultural came together (Turner, 1957; 1974; 1982; Geertz, 1993 (first published 1973); discussed in Ober and Strauss, 1990, pp.245–6). The conjunction has been summarised by Simon Goldhill: 'A politician's speech, a footballer's game, a musician's concert, a lover's antics, can be linked directly enough in a contemporary English discourse through the category of "performance"' (Goldhill and Osborne, 1999, p.1). The term 'performance' in modern English often reflects unexamined assumptions about the activities of individuals, audiences and social patterns of description, approval and disapproval. Attention and applause, explicit or implicit, is what is desired. The activities have their own rules and customs. Goldhill moves the focus of the analysis to ancient Athens and suggests that in Athens the connections between activities were rather more specific: 'When the Athenian citizen speaks in the Assembly, exercises in the gymnasium, sings at the symposium, or courts a boy, each activity has its own regime of display and regulation; each activity forms an integral part of the exercise of citizenship' (*ibid.*). Goldhill is one of many modern scholars who see the concept of performance as a useful tool for understanding the (largely public) culture of the Athenian democracy.

How success was achieved and recognised: victory and fame in Homer

Of course, there are problems in imposing modern categories on ancient evidence and practices, and one of the purposes of this essay is to consider how far generalisation on the basis of such categorisation is justified. Furthermore, a culture that valued performance was not something that suddenly emerged in the Athens of the fifth century BCE. Performance was deeply embedded in the Hellenic cultural frame of reference and we have substantial evidence of this at least from the Homeric poems onwards. In the chapter 'Performance' in *The Cambridge Illustrated History of Ancient Greece* (Cartledge, 1998), Edith Hall starts from the viewpoint that 'of all the cultural legacies left by the ancient Greeks, the three which have had the most obvious impact on modern western life are athletics, democracy and drama' (Hall, 1998, p.223). Hall goes on to argue that all of these involved public and competitive exhibitions and contexts in which 'success conferred

Essay Five Performance, competition and democracy in Athenian culture

the highest prestige and failure brought personal disappointment and public ignominy' (p.223). Prestige might be attached primarily to the individual and his family and descent (note, not 'her' family, although there were contests for women in some of the panhellenic festivals), or to the successful person in conjunction with his city.

The variations in priority in these associations are significant. Throughout the history of Hellenic culture it is possible to chart adjustments and larger shifts in descriptions of the types of performance, the particular traditions of competition (including rules, conventions and terms of praise or criticism) and the way in which success is represented in social and political contexts. For example, in Book 8 of the *Odyssey*, Odysseus, who has been shipwrecked in the land of the Phaiacians during his attempt to return home from Troy, grieves as the bard Demodocus sings of

> the famous actions
> of men on that venture, whose fame goes up to the wide heaven,
> the quarrel between Odysseus and Peleus' son, Achilleus,
> how these once contended, at the gods' generous festival,
> with words of violence, so that the lord of men, Agamemnon,
> was happy in his heart that the best of the Achaians were quarreling.
>
> (Homer, *Odyssey* 8.73–8; in Lattimore, 1965, p.123)

The passage emphasises the importance of fame for Hellenic values. It attests the importance of verbal contest, as a substitute for violence, in the contest for political supremacy. It also points to the importance in an oral and aural culture of being present and hearing the words (as well as viewing the accompanying visual phenomena).

The Phaiacians then organise athletic contests (running, wrestling, boxing, jumping and discus) and Odysseus is invited to participate. When he refuses because he is so careworn, a hostile young man accuses him of being

> a man who, careful of his cargo and grasping for profits,
> goes carefully on his way. You do not resemble an athlete.
>
> (Homer, *Odyssey* 8.163–4; in Lattimore, 1965, p.125)

The episode from which these extracts are drawn is significant in many ways. First, the musical performance of Demodocus is combined with discussions of speech-making as well as the practice of athletics (Hall, 1998, p.224). These are all characteristics of a wealthy and cultivated society. Second, the athletic games are put on, not to distract Odysseus from his misery but to impress him:

so that our stranger can tell his friends, after
he reaches his home, by how much we surpass all others
in boxing, wrestling, leaping and speed of our feet for running.

(Homer, *Odyssey* 8.101–3; in Lattimore, 1965, pp.123–4)

Third, as Hall points out in her discussion (1998, p.225), Euryalus' criticism of Odysseus for being a trader and not an athlete suggests tensions in socio-economic developments and their associated values. Sea-faring in the archaic eastern Mediterranean was opening up trade and creating a new social stratum of wealth and aspiration, which was potentially at odds with the aristocratic culture that praised athletic achievement in skills suited to individual combat in war. Fourth, when he rebukes Euryalus for his arrogant stress on personal beauty, Odysseus wins the day partly because of his superior powers of speech – his rhetoric – and partly because he can also out-throw the others with the discus. In the society depicted in the poems, both physical and rhetorical skills can be expected in members of the élite (variations on these characteristics continued throughout antiquity, see Figure 5.1). Victory is all. The disguised Athena praises Odysseus' throw:

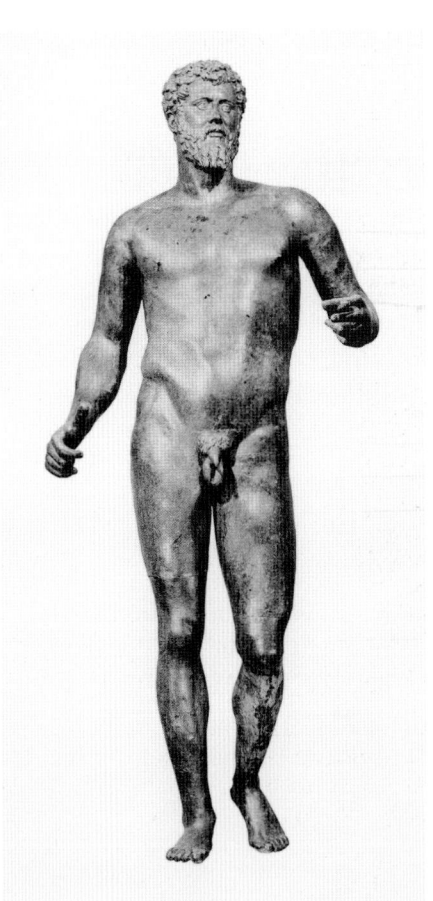

Figure 5.1 Bronze statue of the Roman emperor Septimus Severus, from Kythrea, CE 193–211, bronze, height 2.08 m, Cyprus Museum, Nicosia. The design combines several traditional forms of representation. The emperor is depicted nude with the body of an athlete, the severe face of a philosopher and the gestures of an orator. The piece indicates the persistence through antiquity of the dual status of physical power and rhetorical skill among the élite.

Essay Five Performance, competition and democracy in Athenian culture

> Even a blind man, friend, would be able to distinguish your mark
> by feeling for it, since it is not mingled with the common
> lot, but far before. Have no fear over this contest,
> No one of the Phaiakians will come up to this mark or pass it.

(Homer, *Odyssey* 8.195–8; in Lattimore, 1965, p.126)

Victory and patronage

In Greek culture the celebration of victory was associated with the patronage of various aristocratic art forms. One example is the bronze sculpture of the Delphi Charioteer (Figure 5.2). This was dedicated in the

Figure 5.2   Bronze statue of the Charioteer, Delphi Museum, Greece, dedicated in the sanctuary of Apollo at Delphi as a thank-offering for the victory of Polyzelus in the chariot race, 470s BCE. (© Ministry of Culture, Archaeological Receipts Fund)

sanctuary of Apollo at Delphi, a centre of display for the whole Hellenic world. The original sculpture was probably part of a group, including horses and chariot, and was dedicated by Polyzelus, tyrant of Gela in Sicily, as a thank-offering for the victory of his charioteer and horses in a chariot race at the Pythian Games at Delphi in the 470s BCE. The statue, like the victory, proclaimed Polyzelus' wealth and magnificence, in this case to all the visitors to the sanctuary. The particular prestige attached to victory in the chariot race drew on its status in epic poetry, for example in the funeral games given for Achilles' close friend the charioteer Patroclus in *Iliad* 23, and also had mythological associations with the foundation myth attached to the Olympic Games.

Lyric poetry was also used in celebration. The derivation of the word 'lyric' indicates poetry sung to a lyre (and by extension other stringed and wind instruments). A major exponent of the Victory Ode was the Boeotian poet Pindar (*c.*518–438 BCE). Many of Pindar's *Odes* reflect commissions placed by the cities and families of victors at the Olympic, Pythian, Isthmian and Nemean Games. The victory songs were designed to be sung shortly after the event or on the victor's return home. The Chorus of singers was usually made up of friends of the victor. The festivals were open only to Greeks and it is notable that, among the Greeks, Athenians were not conspicuous by their success. In fact, there are only two references to Athenian successes in the period covered by Pindar's poetry, both of them in rather short Odes. *Nemean Two* is in honour of Timodemus of Acharnae, winner of the pancratium, probably in 485 BCE. It refers to the glory brought to Athens by Timodemus' achievements as well as to previous victors from Acharnae (Figure 5.3). Pindar also wrote a victory ode, *Pythian Seven*, to celebrate the victory of the Athenian Megacles in the chariot race of 486 BCE and to pay tribute to his family, the Alcmaeonidae, one of the most distinguished in Athens.

The political connotations underlying the promotion of personal glory are important. Pindar's *Odes* could be commissioned as tools for political competition with a persuasive as well as a commemorative function, and underneath the apparent linking of the individual and the city, whether or not it was democratic, could lie deep-seated rivalries (Kurke, 1991). The persuasive function of Pindar's poetry depended on the association of victory with fame, rather than on the details of the event itself. This kind of victory was presented as achieved by heroic physical prowess allied to social status, rather than by the verbal dexterity that had come to be associated with Odysseus, which in *Nemean Eight* Pindar attacks ('hateful trickery', 'wheedling words', 'does violence to glory,' 'sets up a flimsy fame for the unknown'; in Bowra, 1969, pp.215–18; quotes at p.216).

Essay Five Performance, competition and democracy in Athenian culture

Figure 5.3   Athletic scenes from three Attic Black-figure Panathenaic amphorae, showing a foot race, boxing and old men and athletes with victor's head ribbons, c.500, 500–480, c.500 BCE, heights 37.5, 40, 37.5 cm, British Museum, London, BM 137, BM 140, BM 138. © Copyright The Trustees of the British Museum.

From the panhellenic to the Athenian context: some problems in how victory was valued in the democracy

The chariot race was the most aristocratic of the spectacular competitions, probably because of the wealth required to breed or purchase and to train the winning horses and its connection with exploits in war. Nevertheless, its status persisted well into the time of the developed democracy. In his account of the opposing speeches made by Nicias and Alcibiades in the debate in the Athenian Assembly in 415 BCE, about whether to mount a naval expedition to Sicily in connection with the war against Sparta, the Athenian historian Thucydides (c.460–400 BCE) represents Alcibiades' response to the suggestion by Nicias that he is too young and unstable to be considered a wise source of political advice and leadership:

> Athenians, I have a better right to command than others – I must begin with this as Nicias has attacked me – and at the same time I believe myself to be worthy of it. The things for which I am abused, bring fame to my ancestors and to myself, and to the country profit besides. The Hellenes, after expecting to see our city ruined by the

> war, concluded it to be even greater than it really is, by reason of the magnificence with which I represented it at the Olympic games, when I sent into the lists seven chariots, a number never before entered by any private person, and won the first prize and was second and fourth, and took care to have everything else in a style worthy of my victory. Custom regards such displays as honourable, and they cannot be made without leaving behind them an impression of power. Again, any splendour that I may have exhibited at home in providing choruses or otherwise, is naturally envied by my fellow citizens, but in the eyes of foreigners has an air of strength as in the other instance. And this is no useless folly, when a man at his own private cost benefits not only himself but his city.
>
> (Thucydides, *History of the Peloponnesian War* 6.16; in Crawley, 1997, p.321)

Although we have to be cautious about taking this as a verbatim report (see Thucydides 1.22 for the historian's rather opaque discussion on reporting what he thought the occasion demanded or what ought to have been said rather than what actually was said), the passage is very instructive as a pointer to stresses and strains in the cohesiveness of Athenian society and values. Alcibiades wants to be leader of the Athenians and in charge of the invasion of Sicily, so he appeals to what he has done to glorify the reputation of the city. However, he is clearly on the defensive, especially since his Olympic successes were gained through wealth, not by his own skills as a charioteer – he just bought or hired the best driver. He also refers to his financing of performances in the theatre (through paying for and arranging the training of the Chorus just as Pericles had done many years previously for Aeschylus' *Persians*). In the democracy personal wealth and glory might therefore be counter-productive, unless these could be clearly allied to promotion of the status and reputation of the *polis* itself. These also had to be justified by oratory in the Assembly. Ironically, although Alcibiades' oratory carried the vote for the Sicilian expedition, he was disgraced and exiled before he could exercise full command, and the reluctant Nicias was made general. Nicias lost the debate and he went on to lose the war in Sicily and his own life.

Thucydides' presentation of the debate reveals what the historian himself considered to be the underlying issues. Moreover, at the very beginning of his *History*, Thucydides incorporates direct authorial comment to display a comparably sceptical attitude to the relationship between public display and actual power:

> For I suppose if Lacedaemon [Sparta] were to become desolate, and the temples and the foundations of the public buildings were left, that as time went on there would be a strong disposition with posterity to refuse to accept her fame as a true exponent of her power ... as the

city is neither built in a compact form nor adorned with magnificent temples and public edifices, but composed of villages after the old fashion of Hellas, there would be an impression of inadequacy. Whereas, if Athens were to suffer the same misfortune, I suppose that any inference from the appearance presented to the eye would make her power to have been twice as great as it is.

(Thucydides 1.10; in Crawley, 1997, pp.7–8)

The passage provides a critical context for the claim attributed to Pericles in the Funeral Speech (Thucydides 2.34–46) that 'everywhere, whether for evil or for good, [we] have left imperishable monuments behind us' (2.41; in Crawley, 1997, p.97). It is significant, however, that Pericles' rhetoric distances Athenian communal civic pride in its deeds (its performances) from the traditional poetic tributes to the reputation of the Homeric heroes and Olympic victors as individuals: 'far from needing a Homer for our panegyrist, or other of his craft whose verses might charm for the moment only for the impression which they gave to melt at the touch of fact, we have forced every sea and land to be the highway of our daring' (*ibid.*).

From physical to verbal competition: oratory in Athens

The passage above, together with others in Thucydides and other fifth-century BCE sources, draws attention to contrasts in how the power of words was characterised and valued. In Homer, skilful use of words by the poet or by individuals within the poems was inspired by the Muses and speaking in public was an activity reserved for the élite. For example, Thersites' attempt in *Iliad* 2 (211–77) to sway the Greeks against their commanders was brutally repressed by Odysseus even though Thersites' view was very similar to that expressed by Achilles in *Iliad* 1 (148–71). The status of the speaker was what mattered. However, in the fifth century BCE skilful use of words was regarded as something that could be taught. Furthermore, the citizens in the Athenian Assembly and in juries had the right and duty to make their judgements and cast their votes on the basis of the speeches made. So, in the fifth-century BCE democracy, oratory increasingly became refined not only as an art of performance but as a political and civic instrument.

There were three main types of oratory (inter-related in some respects):

(i) *Epideictic* or *display* oratory was practised by some fifth-century BCE sophists. These sophists were 'experts', mostly non-Athenians, who moved round the leading Greek *poleis* producing speeches and debates for wealthy patrons and educating young men in public speaking.

Epideixis involved a public virtuoso performance that attracted students and provided models for the training of ambitious (and rich) young men. The word *epideixis* was also used to indicate physical display of wealth, status and power and military prowess (see Herodotus 1.11).

(ii) *Forensic* oratory was the branch used in litigation to develop the style and arguments that would convince a jury. By the late fifth and fourth centuries BCE it evolved into a highly specialised art, examples of which have been preserved in the speeches of Lysias, Demosthenes and Aeschines, whose contests in the courts also had a strong political dimension.

(iii) The dominant type of *political* oratory in the fifth century BCE related directly to the Assembly, in which rival contenders for influence and power in leadership and decision making competed to win over the citizens. Thus, the situation in Athens, in which there was a combination of public democratic institutions with citizen participation on a wide scale and intense rivalry for political prominence and positions of leadership, intensified the development of rhetoric for public occasions.

Competition and the audience

There are two particularly important features of oratory in relation to performance. The first is that there is an audience. Oratory creates and mediates power rather than exercising it physically (as would the performance of military acts). Depending on the nature of the audience, oratory extends the performance to include various kinds of participation by others (as attenders, admirers, applauders, judges, critics). Secondly, oratory is intimately connected with competition. This may take a variety of forms, ranging from competition between sophists to win high fees for educating young men, to competition between litigants and, in the Assembly, competition for votes. The term *agon* is generally used to indicate this kind of direct confrontation. It is also used to cover the physical struggles in contact sports such as wrestling and boxing, while in the *Persians* Aeschylus used the word to indicate total conflict between Greeks and Persians (405).

In the democracy of the fifth century BCE, oratory could hold in balance tensions between the individual desire for prominence and the desire of the spectators for participation in power rituals. The hint by Pericles in the Funeral Speech that the Athenians did not need skilful words to express their power is one of several examples in Thucydides of anti-rhetorical rhetoric. In recent scholarship the term 'anti-spin rhetoric' has been used to describe this feature (see Hesk, 2000, chapter 4, which has a

Essay Five Performance, competition and democracy in Athenian culture

section on 'spin' and 'anti-spin' in rhetoric). Another occurs in the Mytilene debate when Cleon (cast by Thucydides as the arch-demagogue or crowd-pleaser) appeals to the 'ordinary' Athenian in the Assembly not to be persuaded into voting for a change in the previous day's decision to punish the revolt against Athens in Mytilene by killing all the males and enslaving the women and children (Thucydides 3.36–50). Cleon's populist appeal has two aspects. First, he appeals to the citizens' anti-intellectualism – 'bad laws which are never changed are better for a city than good ones that have no authority; that unlearned loyalty is more serviceable than quick-witted insubordination; and that ordinary men usually manage public affairs better than their more gifted fellows' (Thucydides 3.37; in Crawley, 1997, p.151). He goes on to say that the best judges are precisely those people who know that they lack the ability to 'pick holes in the speech of a good speaker' (*ibid.*) and who are not people taking part in a contest (a verb relating to the *agon* is used at this point and is rendered by the Victorian translator Richard Crawley as an allusion to the rivalry of athletes). This appeal to the 'ordinary man' is paralleled in Aristophanes' play *Clouds*, which satirises both the intricacies of sophistic education and the resistance to change of the traditionalists (see lines 545–9 for a parallel to Cleon's claim). Cleon flatters the citizens by saying that politicians should try to be more like them rather than trying to display their cleverness and intelligence.

The second significant aspect of Cleon's approach is that his attack on intellectuals and clever speaking is expressed by using terms like 'competition' and 'spectacle' in association with 'slaves'. He continues:

> In such contests the state gives the rewards to others, and takes the dangers for herself. The persons to blame are you who are so foolish as to institute these contests; who go to see an oration as you would go to see a sight [spectacle] ... the easy victims of new-fangled arguments, unwilling to follow received conclusions; slaves to every new paradox, despisers of the commonplace.
>
> (Thucydides 3.38; in Crawley, 1997, p.151)

He taunts the citizens by saying that they are themselves frustrated orators wanting to compete but able only to expand clever points rather than grasping the implications: 'very slaves to the pleasures of the ear, and more like the audience of a rhetorician than the council of a city' (Thucydides 3.38; in Crawley, 1997, p.152). This last sentence emphasises the oral focus of Athenian public culture and contains the only direct reference in Thucydides to the sophists, the teachers of rhetoric. This is thought by some to reflect the fact that in 427 BCE, the year of the Mytilene debate, the sophist Gorgias had arrived in Athens as part of a delegation from Leontini in Sicily, and was dazzling and puzzling the Athenians with the intricacies of his oratory and his stress on the persuasive power of speech (see also Aristophanes, *Clouds* 331–4). In the event, Cleon narrowly lost the vote. His attack on the 'spin' and the 'spectacle' aspects of oratory is not only one of the great ironies in Thucydides but is also important additional evidence both that oratory was regarded as a competitive performance art and that its role in the democracy could be problematic.

In his *History of the Peloponnesian War*, Thucydides normally presents public debate as an *agon* and pairs opposing speeches at moments of critical decision – Cleon and Diodotus in the Mytilene debate, Nicias and Alcibiades in the debate concerning the Sicilian expedition. The way in which he uses opposing speeches delivered in front of critical audiences at moments of political climax has caused commentators to stress the affinities with the theatre, in which the form and style of debate between leading figures parallels the *agon* found in rhetorical debate. In Thucydides, the *strategos* ('general') Pericles (*c.*495–429 BCE) is given the status of delivering solo speeches on public occasions. One of these is the Funeral Speech, which marks the communal funeral of those killed in the first year of the war and does not take place in the Assembly. Significantly, Pericles' Assembly speeches are also not presented in terms of conflict with other named individuals, and his Last Speech, in which Thucydides represents Pericles' defence against criticism, is set out as a solo speech (Thucydides 2.65). In this way, Thucydides presents Pericles, whom he much admires, as in some sense standing above the personal confrontations and 'point-scoring' of the demagogues whom he, Thucydides, despises. Demagogues were populist politicians who competed for the approval of the *demos* or ordinary citizens and so it might be said that, in achieving election to office and maintaining his leadership despite many setbacks, Pericles was the most successful demagogue of them all.

Performance culture in the Athenian democracy

The Athenian theatre is, along with the Assembly and the jury courts, the institution most heavily cited in support of arguments that Athenian culture was a performance culture and that this was a defining feature of the democracy. Like the law courts and the Assembly, the dramatic festivals were an institution that provided civic ceremonials or 'events' at which a large body of citizens congregated. Standard estimates are that at the performances of tragedy and comedy at the Great Dionysia between 14,000 and 17,000 spectators could be accommodated (compared with about 6,000 for the Assembly and up to 6,000, although usually considerably fewer, for the Courts; see Sommerstein, 2002, chapter 1; Goldhill in Rowe and Schofield, 2000, p.62). In addition, representatives of other *poleis* attended the theatre, as did other foreign visitors. The

Essay Five Performance, competition and democracy in Athenian culture

ambassadors had special seats. Therefore the theatre, like the games, provided an important aspect of inter-*polis* display. The ceremonies that preceded the plays provided an enactment of civic ideals. For example, the ten *strategoi* (elected military and political leaders) poured the libation for the opening sacrifice. Then the heralds announced the names of those who had provided benefits for the Athenian *polis*. By the middle of the fifth century BCE there was a procession and display of silver paid in tribute by the allies (aka subject *poleis*) of the Athenian *arche*, or empire. This was followed by a parade of those orphans of the war-dead who, having been educated at public expense, were now themselves entering military service and who took an oath recognising their civic obligation. These ceremonies and displays have been routinely cited by scholars as evidence that theatre was institutionally and ideologically embedded in the democracy and that the dramatic festivals fostered an ethos of participation (see Goldhill, 1990, 2000, p.38; Goldhill and Osborne, 1999, p.63; Cartledge, 1997, p.5). The performances themselves were competitive. A panel of judges drawn from the citizen groups selected the winning dramatist and records were kept (*didaskaliai*). From the mid-fifth century BCE, there was also a prize for the best actor.

Nevertheless, there is continuing debate about the extent to which the Athenian drama festivals in themselves constitute a distinctive product of the democracy and about the slightly different point of whether they are overwhelmingly democratic in character. The view of Goldhill and others is that 'the [drama] festival itself, in organization and structure, despite earlier origins and later development, is in the fifth century fully an institution of the democratic polis, and that the plays constantly reflect their genesis in a fifth-century Athenian political environment' (Goldhill, 2000, p.35). The argument that drama was a democratic phenomenon rests to a large extent on the association between the performance culture represented by all the activities at the festival and the definition of Athenian civic identity. For example, Paul Cartledge has described the play festivals of Dionysus as 'a device for defining Athenian civic identity, which meant exploring and confirming but also questioning what it was to be a citizen of a democracy' (1997, p.6). Those who take a contrary view argue that to see the Athenian drama festivals only in the context of the Athenian democracy is to narrow unacceptably the implications of the plays, as well as to promote an Atheno-centric interpretation of their subject matter.

It has been argued that although the festivals obviously took a particular institutional form in democratic Athens, the institutional setting was actually a version of what was found more widely in the Greek world and that even the Athenian version was not distinctively democratic (Rhodes, 2003). For example, the themes in particular plays that have often been held to be democratic may more accurately be described as themes common to the Greek *poleis* in general, rather than democratic *poleis* in particular. Certainly, it is true to say that the tragedians reworked myths and legends that were common to all the Greeks. Very few of the plays refer directly to Athens, let alone have an Athenian setting, and in any case the settings of surviving tragedy, unlike comedy, are not contemporary (with few exceptions, of which the *Persians* is one). Of course, the lack of direct reference to the contemporary situation in Athens by no means rules out relevance, nor did it preclude the spectators from interpreting the meaning of the plays in terms of their own experiences and socio-political concerns. The characters may come from myth and the settings from outside Athens but the rhetoric and the debates are in the vocabulary and frames of reference of fifth-century BCE Athens. Furthermore, the subsequent history of performance of Greek plays demonstrates very clearly their potential for serving as an artistic and political site for addressing metaphorically or directly the contemporary problems of the societies in which they are staged (Hardwick, 2000, chapter 4; Rehm, 2003; Garland, 2004).

In favour of the distinctive democratic character of Athenian tragedy it has been argued that both tragedy (indirectly) and comedy (directly) question democratic values and that to permit them to do so was part of the ethos of the democracy. Against this the point can be made that most regimes adapted festivals to political purposes and that the so-called 'democratic' features were not new inventions but were democratic versions of customs and institutions found in other cities, whether democratic or not. Furthermore, some aspects were not distinctively democratic at all – for example, the recruitment of the (non-professional) Chorus members by the *choregoi* (rich men who funded the training of the Chorus as a public service or liturgy), the special seats for distinguished members of the audience and charges for admission. It might also be argued that the *choregia* as an institution indicates the need for any political structure, whether or not it is democratic, to find ways of mediating between the claims of the community and prominent individuals (Thorpe, 2004). So far as the plays themselves are concerned, there is little direct reference to democracy in the figures, situations or language of the extant plays. The notable exceptions usually cited are the dramatisation of the ideas and origins of the democracy in Aeschylus' *Suppliants* and *Eumenides* (the final play in the *Oresteia* trilogy), the justification of democracy in Euripides' *Suppliant Women* and the treatment of contemporary political issues in Old Comedy.

In my view, this debate has become overly polarised. It is, after all, possible to hold that the Athenian dramatic festivals were grounded in Hellenic *polis* performance culture and also to show that this was adapted by the Athenians to meet the needs of the forms and context of democracy. Spectators probably accepted the festivals in the context of the political and cultural environment that they knew. Equally, it is possible to show that the plays both reflected and contributed to the culture of debate in democratic Athens without having to reduce their political application solely to that of the immediate context. Furthermore, one of the crucial difficulties about conducting this kind of scholarly debate is that, apart from the lists of winners, there is a lack of evidence about how the judges operated and about the reactions of the spectators and the citizen community as a whole. Such evidence as there is refers mainly to the spectators in the fourth century BCE, although there is some indication that in the fifth century riotous behaviour was tolerated and even expected (Wallace, 1997, pp.97ff.). However, this type of evidence does not prove that audiences viewed the plays as stimuli for introspection concerning their own sense of civic identity or that it is possible to generalise about audiences as a whole.

Contests and debates in drama

It is, however, clear from the study of the text and contexts of staging Athenian theatre that drama, like oratory, provided a public field on which overlaps and oppositions could be articulated, examined and renegotiated, and that the 'performances' (in the festivals as a whole as well as in the plays themselves) embodied power relations – between Athenians and other Greeks and within Athens itself. Josiah Ober has pointed out with reference to Old Comedy (which, unlike tragedy, was peppered with contemporary political allusions including scurrilous attacks on individuals) that audiences were themselves part of the theatrical context:

> As in the Assembly, the demos in the theater was both spectator and judge of virtuoso verbal performances ... Thus, classical Athenian dramas meant something to the original audience of citizens that is necessarily quite different from what they have meant to all subsequent audiences and readers – from Hellenistic revivals to the present ... That context, informed as it was by democratic knowledge, has an important bearing on the issue of how comedy worked as a form of political criticism.
>
> (Ober, 1998, p.123)

Impact on the audience was shaped by the forms of theatrical performance as well as its contexts. Verbal and physical aspects of contest came together in performance. Central to this were the *agon*, or conflict between opposing ideas or characters, the *stichomythia*, or line-by-line exchanges between characters, and the Chorus, which often combined the functions of giving a voice to the politically marginalised (women, slaves, foreigners, the victims of war) with a capacity for moral and religious comment as well as allowing interaction with the main characters. In Old Comedy, the *agon* sometimes began with mutual abuse and took a variety of forms. These might involve debate between the main character and the Chorus or between two opposing arguments or points of view (the clash between the Better and Worse Arguments in Aristophanes' *Clouds* may have been initially staged as a duel between fighting cocks; Slater, 2002, p.113). In Aristophanes' *Frogs*, the competition between the tragic poets Euripides and Aeschylus for the throne of tragedy (and recall from Hades) takes the form of an *agon* (Figure 5.4). In Aristophanes' *Wasps*, the structure of the play was shaped by successive contests involving the main character. In his *Lysistrata*, two semi-Choruses meet and mock and threaten one another in a series of songs and speeches. The old men portray themselves as traditional defenders of Athens; the old women assert their rights to a political role on the basis of their traditional contributions to civic life – the provision of males and the maintaining of religious rituals (638–47; discussed in MacDowell, 1995, pp.239–40).

So far as the forms of tragedy are concerned, the *agon* generally used paired speeches to represent an encounter or conflict between the leading figures. These set up opposing arguments and also explored the problems inherent in them. For example, in Sophocles' *Antigone*, Antigone's conflict with Creon about whether burial should be denied to her brother Polyneices after his death in civil war was not a simple competition between the old values of religious observation of burial rituals and the new pressures of maintenance of civic order (Figure 5.5). Creon held power and exercised it, yet in the successive *agones* with Tiresias and Haemon his power was shown to be inadequate and misdirected, in that it rested on might and not on persuasion or negotiation. The *agon* between Creon and Tiresias is a struggle about which of these can best identify and represent the interests of the *polis*.

In drama, the formal elements and language may encode competition (and the festivals themselves involved competition between dramatists), yet the outcome of the performance is more a transformation of awareness than straight 'victory' for one figure or one perspective. A balanced assessment of the relationship between the competitive theatre performances and the democracy might indicate that the theatre was grounded in panhellenic traditions of competition at festivals dedicated to the gods but developed in a particular way in the context of the Athenian democracy, especially in respect of the relationship between the democratic conventions of free speech and the dramatic forms used to communicate the clash of ideas.

Essay Five Performance, competition and democracy in Athenian culture

Figure 5.4 *The Frogs*, front cover of playbill for the Lincoln Center Theater, New York, 2004. *The Frogs* was a musical that had been freely adapted from Aristophanes by Burt Shevlove for a 1974 production in a swimming pool at Yale University, and then even more freely adapted by Nathan Lane for the 2004 production (without swimming pool). In the 2004 production, music and lyrics were by Stephen Sondheim and direction and choreography by Susan Stroman. This production used the Aristophanic context of debates about drama and democratic values to lampoon and critique President George W. Bush's policy towards Iraq. (Courtesy of Lincoln Center Theatre, New York City, 10023)

EXPERIENCING THE CLASSICAL WORLD

Figure 5.5 After the Beldam painter, *Woman at Tomb*, Attic white-ground *lekythos* ('small oil bottle'), provenance unknown, *c*.480–75 BCE, height of vase 38.7 cm, British Museum, London, BM.D65; ARV 752.2. *Lekythoi* are a major source of evidence about the role of women in religious rituals relating to family tombs.
© Copyright The Trustees of the British Museum.

Overview and future directions for the debate

A review of the approach of Hall, discussed at the beginning of this essay, provides a useful reminder of the extent to which selection of themes and genres from antiquity is governed by what has been influential since, and therefore necessarily draws in interpretations and concepts that are different from those of the Greeks. Hall selected athletics, democracy and drama as key influences. In their Greek forms all required performance and all included competition. Analysis of the specifically Athenian versions shows that fifth-century BCE forms, contexts and criticisms all involved negotiation between Greek and Athenian and between traditional and newer expressions and values, between contenders for power and between different political ideologies.

Examination of the ancient evidence shows that the fifth-century BCE Athenians wanted their world to be constituted as a balance between conflicting interests, and that in the Assembly and the dramatic festivals they constructed a relationship between performance, competition and democracy that would enact that balance. Performance, competition and democracy were constituents of Athenian culture, yet their shifting relationships are as revealing of actual or potential stresses or even gaping faultlines as of cohesion and unity. The task of the student of cultural history is to probe underneath this construction and to identify the contending and potentially destructive elements that had to be held in balance. Even though these forms of civic negotiation in fifth-century BCE Athens were for the most part successful in avoiding internal civic fracture and preventing the dreaded *stasis* (civil strife), at least until the oligarchic revolutions at the end of the century, analysis of their inter-relationship prevents easy generalisations about social, political or cultural unity. The sources discussed in this essay show that Athenian democracy was not simply a form of government but a socio-cultural structure. There was a general framework of cultural politics that held the democracy together, but this only partly disguised or resolved real issues of social, political and economic inequality and conflict (Ober and Strauss, 1990, pp.237–42). Current research on 'the politics of cultures within cultures' is very much concerned with the relationship between 'thin' and 'thick' aspects of cultures, that is, between particular practices, the groups associated with them and the larger social and political framework that contained or failed to contain them (Dougherty and Kurke, 2003). This suggests a new phase of debate about what in fifth-century BCE culture is Greek, what is Athenian and what is democratic, and how and why they were 'performed' together.

Further reading

In addition to the items cited in this essay, there is further relevant material in P.E. Easterling (1997) *The Cambridge Companion to Greek Tragedy*. This includes essays by Simon Goldhill ('The audience of Athenian tragedy', pp.54–68 and 'The language of tragedy: rhetoric and communication', pp.127–50); Edith Hall ('The sociology of Athenian tragedy', pp.93–126) and P.E. Easterling ('A show for Dionysus', pp.36–53 and 'Form and performance', pp.151–77). In D. Boedeker and K. Raaflaub (1998)

Democracy, Empire and the Arts in Fifth-Century Athens there is a useful Introduction (pp.1–13) and a concluding chapter by the joint editors ('Reflections and conclusion: democracy, empire and the arts in fifth-century Athens', pp.319–44). However, the most valuable further reading would be to test some of the ideas explored in this essay against a close reading of the ancient sources, especially (i) Thucydides' discussions of the Athenian democracy in action and (ii) the tragedies and comedies of the fifth century BCE. Sophocles' *Antigone* is particularly important. Many recent stagings of Greek plays (in translation or in adaptation) have used the ancient themes and contexts to open up critique of modern politics and culture and these provoke a re-examination of the language and ideas of the ancient texts and of the socio-political contexts in which they were presented.

Bibliography

Ancient sources

Aeschylus, *Eumenides*, in Meineck, P. (trans.) (1998) Aeschylus: *Oresteia*, Indianapolis: Hackett.

Aeschylus, *Persians*, in Hall, E. (trans.) (1996) Aeschylus: *Persians*, Warminster: Aris & Phillipps.

Aeschylus, *Suppliants*, in Ewans, M. (ed. and trans.) (1996) *Suppliants and Other Dramas: Persians, Seven Against Thebes, Suppliants, Fragments, with Prometheus Bound*, London: J.M. Dent.

Aristophanes, *Clouds*, in Sommerstein, A.H. (trans.) (1998) Aristophanes: *Clouds*, Warminster: Aris & Phillips (first published 1982).

Aristophanes, *Frogs*, in Sommerstein, A.H. (trans.) (1996) Aristophanes: *Frogs*, Warminster: Aris & Phillipps.

Aristophanes, *Lysistrata*, in Sommerstein, A.H. (trans.) (1996) Aristophanes: *Lysistrata*, Warminster: Aris & Phillipps.

Aristophanes, *Wasps*, in Sommerstein, A.H. (trans.) (1983) Aristophanes: *Wasps*, Warminster: Aris & Phillipps.

Euripides, *Suppliant Women*, in Davie, J. (trans.) *Electra and Other Plays*, London: Penguin.

Herodotus, *Histories*, in Marincola, J. (trans.) (2003) Herodotus: *The Histories*, Harmondsworth: Penguin.

Homer, *Iliad*, in Lattimore, R. (trans.) (1951) *The Iliad of Homer*, Chicago and London: University of Chicago Press.

Homer, *Odyssey*, in Lattimore, R. (trans.) (1965) *The Odyssey of Homer*, New York: Harper Perennial.

Pindar, *Odes*, in Bowra, C.M. (trans.) (1969) *The Odes of Pindar*, Harmondsworth: Penguin.

Sophocles, *Antigone*, in Franklin, D. and Harrison, J. (trans.) (2003) Sophocles: *Antigone*, Cambridge: Cambridge University Press. (This also contains an introduction to the Greek theatre by P.E. Easterling.)

Thucydides, *History of the Peloponnesian War*, in Crawley, R. (trans.) (1997) Thucydides: *The History of the Peloponnesian War*, Ware: Wordsworth Press (first published 1876, revised R.C. Feetham, 1903).

Modern scholarship

Boedeker, D. and Raaflaub, K. (eds) (1998) *Democracy, Empire and the Arts in Fifth-Century Athens*, Cambridge, MA and London: Harvard University Press.

Cartledge, P. (ed.) (1998) *The Cambridge Illustrated History of Ancient Greece*, Cambridge: Cambridge University Press.

Cartledge, P. (1997) 'Deep plays: theatre as process in Greek civic life', in Easterling, 1997, pp.3–35.

Dougherty, C. and Kurke, L. (eds) (2003) *The Cultures within Ancient Greek Culture*, Cambridge: Cambridge University Press.

Easterling. P.E. (ed.) (1997) *The Cambridge Companion to Greek Tragedy*, Cambridge: Cambridge University Press. (This volume also includes lists of the main scholarly editions of the Greek texts of the tragedies, together with modern commentaries and translations.)

Garland, G. (2004) *Surviving Greek Tragedy*, London: Duckworth.

Geertz, C. (1993) *The Interpretation of Cultures: Selected Essays*, London: Faber (first published New York: Basic Books, 1973).

Goldhill, S. (1990) 'The great dionysia and civic ideology', in Winkler and Zeitlin, 1990, pp.97–129.

Goldhill, S. (2000) 'Civic ideology and the problem of difference: the politics of Aeschylean tragedy once again', *Journal of Hellenic Studies*, vol.120, pp.34–56.

Goldhill, S. and Osborne, R. (eds) (1999) *Performance, Culture and Athenian Democracy*, Cambridge: Cambridge University Press.

Hall, E. (1998) 'Performance', in Cartledge, 1998, pp.219–49.

Hardwick, L. (2000) *Translating Words, Translating Cultures*, London: Duckworth.

Hesk, J. (2000) *Deception and Democracy in Classical Athens*, Cambridge: Cambridge University Press.

Kurke, K. (1991) *The Traffic in Praise: Pindar and the Poetics of the Social Economy*, Ithaca and London: Cornell University Press.

MacDowell, D.M. (1995) *Aristophanes and Athens*, Oxford: Oxford University Press.

Ober, J. (1989) *Mass and Elite in Democratic Athens: Rhetoric, Ideology and the Power of the People*, Princeton: Princeton University Press.

Ober, J. (1998) *Political Dissent in Democratic Athens*, Princeton and Oxford: Princeton University Press.

Ober, J. and Strauss, B. (1990) 'Drama, political rhetoric and the discourse of Athenian democracy', in Winkler and Zeitlin, 1990, pp.237–70.

Rehm, R. (2003) *Radical Theatre*, London: Duckworth.

Rhodes, P.J. (2003) 'Nothing to do with democracy', *Journal of Hellenic Studies*, vol.123, pp.104–19.

Rowe, C. and Schofield, M. (eds) (2000) *The Cambridge History of Greek and Roman Political Thought*, Cambridge: Cambridge University Press.

Slater, N.W. (2002) *Spectator Politics: Metatheatre and Performance in Aristophanes*, Philadelphia: University of Pennsylvania Press.

Sommerstein, A.H. (2002) *Greek Drama and Dramatists*, London and New York: Routledge.

Thorpe, M. (November 2004) Private communication.

Turner, V. (1957) *Schism and Continuity in an African Society*, Manchester: Manchester University Press (for the Institute for African Studies, University of Zambia).

Turner, V. (1974) *Drama, Fields and Metaphors: Symbolic Action in Human Society*, Ithaca and London: Cornell University Press.

Turner, V. (1982) *From Ritual to Theatre: The Human Seriousness of Play*, New York: Performing Arts Journal Publications.

Wallace, R.W. (1997) 'Poet, public and theatocracy: audience performance in Classical Athens', in L. Edmunds and R.W. Wallace (eds) *Poet, Public and Performance in Ancient Greece*, Baltimore and London: Johns Hopkins University Press, pp.97–111.

Winkler, J.J. and Zeitlin, Z. (eds) (1990) *Nothing to do with Dionysus? Athenian Drama in its Social Context*, Princeton: Princeton University Press.

Essay Six

Roman reputations: famous figures and false impressions in the late republic

Paula James

Famous figures

Rome in the first century BCE is a time we tend to access through the famous figures who loomed large on its political landscape. Julius Caesar lives on in modern consciousness as a strong symbol of conquest, Roman style. There are many books written about Caesar as both a historical phenomenon and a charismatic legend. Twenty-first century works include distinct and accessible studies by Michael Parenti (2003), Robert Garland (2004) and Tom Holland (2004). Books about Caesar's career and rise to power invariably involve an examination of the troubled politics of the last years of the republican government. Gaius Julius Caesar (to give him his first name, family name and finally the personalised and identifying name of Caesar) went on to become sole ruler, albeit briefly, at the centre and capital of a vast empire. 'Caesar', as Garland (2004, pp.96–8) points out, turned out to be a tenacious title for emperors and kings long after the passing of the Roman empire: 'Kaiser' and 'Tzar', for instance, are derivations.

Perhaps for this reason, Caesar's high profile in the history of the Roman empire has in popular perceptions placed him on the brink, or at the beginning, of rule by emperors. Suetonius, writing over 100 years after Caesar's assassination in 44 BCE, called his history *The Twelve Caesars* and took Julius Caesar as his starting point. Indeed, once Julius' young heir Octavian (the emperor Augustus) had gained the monopoly of military strength, offices and power, the establishment of a Caesarian (called the Julio-Claudian) imperial dynasty marked a turning point in Roman history. Julius Caesar rose to prominence at a time when Rome was ruled by the senate, the policy-making assembly formed of the wealthy and influential members of society. A contemporary recorder of the conflict between the senate and powerful generals like Pompey and Caesar was Cicero, an orator and statesman (Figure 6.1). His surviving speeches and personal correspondence give us fascinating insights into what it was like to be a main player in Roman republican politics.

Cicero was a member of the Roman senate, but, unlike Caesar, Cicero was not born into the ruling élite. He managed nevertheless to be elected consul. This was a top position – there were two consular officers elected annually – and it was monopolised by the *nobiles* (literally, 'known'), men from old-established families who effectively functioned as an oligarchy enjoying the first choice of most magistracies. Cicero's career had some famous highs and lows: he was hailed as saviour of the Roman state at one point and later temporarily exiled for the very actions that had allegedly protected the republic from a violent overthrow. Like Caesar, whose assassination he approved and celebrated as the death of a tyrant, Cicero came to a sticky end.

Another significant republican male is the Italian poet Catullus, although he is a less obvious candidate for celebrity treatment than Caesar

Figure 6.1 Bust of Marcus Tullius Cicero, first century BCE, marble, Apsley House, London. (V&A Images/ Victoria and Albert Museum)

or Cicero. During his relatively brief life, he did not aspire to high office and is probably less familiar to general readers of the twenty-first century. For students of the Latin language and the literary culture of ancient Rome, Catullus is most famous for the poetry he wrote as a gentleman of leisure. Catullus' poems are generally studied for their passionate and personal tone (he traces an unhappy love affair in some detail). The following extract will give you a flavour of his style:

> My Lesbia, let us live and love
> And not care tuppence for old men
> Who sermonise and disapprove,
> Suns when they sink can rise again
> But we, when our brief light has shone,
> Must sleep the long night on and on.
>
> (Catullus, Poem 5; in Michie, 1998, p.9)

However, Catullus was also a man of the moment in the volatile times of Caesar and Cicero (we shall return to Catullus for an unfavourable view of Caesar). He had powerful connections and aspired to make his mark at Rome, even if this was primarily as a poet rather than in politics. Catullus moved in the upper-class spectrum of society and he was certainly an interested commentator or spectator on the sidelines of the power struggles that so preoccupied Cicero and Caesar. Catullus' life interacted with Caesar's and Cicero's and his poetic voice forms part of a contemporary commentary upon the stresses and strains of republican society. Catullus spent a great deal of time in the capital and at the centre of things. The struggle for power and high office in a physically crowded and socially claustrophobic society would inevitably have confronted and affected those who had the money and leisure to move in the right circles and observe the wheeling and dealing among the politically proactive.

Scene setting

The Roman empire and especially its emperors have provided rich material for film and television. Historical surveys in a modern technological age are able to create a vivid visualisation of the densely populated and bustling city that was Rome; estimates of the total population have settled on the conservative number of 450,000 but it may have peaked even higher at times. The producers of imaginative dramatisations dealing with colourful characters like Julius Caesar and the more notorious of the emperors who followed him do not necessarily aspire to strict factual accuracy. In practice, both the documentary and the dramatisation approach should be treated with care. The straight history programme may confidently portray events and personalities, but sometimes gives anecdotal evidence from ancient sources a weighty and factual sound by means of an authoritative voice-over commentary. However, the Greek and Roman historians quoted are rarely put into either a chronological or a cultural context. Suetonius (author of *The Twelve Caesars* and a popular choice as a witness) is a good illustration, as he was writing some time after the events he describes. He researched into available written records and was aware of the pitfalls and contradictions of orally transmitted accounts, but he selected and presented his material against his own particular socio-political background.

Even those ancient commentators closer to or contemporary with the period under scrutiny were bound to have their own agendas. Historical works were expected to be high quality and absorbing literary narrative, so historians relished writing up dramatic reconstructions of important historical moments – their readership, like a modern television audience, probably appreciated vivid visualisation and interpretation of events rolled into one as a neat and plausible package. None of these considerations discredits the ancient evidence; it is our privilege to hear what the Classical authors have to say but also our responsibility to tease out their particular partisanship and the rules of the genre. 'Voices from the past' is a recurring theme in this collection of essays and you will be becoming accustomed to cautionary remarks about how we hear and receive them.

Republican values

For anyone new to a study of republican Rome, a central point to establish is that its system of rule by the few had survived for many hundreds of years. For Caesar, Cicero and Catullus the right to profit from the provinces of the empire was an inalienable one. Rome had acquired substantial territory, first after conquering Italy, then in the Mediterranean and by the last century BCE on a global scale across Europe, Asia and Africa – in other words an empire was established well before emperors rose from the ranks of the élite to possess it. The republican form of government was treasured by Cicero because he had been able to break into its aristocratic circle and had a stake in its wealth, status and power (Figure 6.2). The extent of Cicero's devotion to the republic and his place in it is well illustrated by the correspondence he had with a friend and fellow senator, Sulpicius. These letters were exchanged in a period of personal tragedy for Cicero, the death of his daughter Tullia who died after giving birth. Sulpicius starts with sympathetic sentiments that highlight his humanity and understanding of his friend's bereavement:

> When the report reached me of the death of your daughter Tullia, I was indeed duly and deeply and grievously sorry, and I felt that the blow had struck us both. Had I been in Rome, I should have been with you and shown you my grief in person. And yet that is a

melancholy and bitter sort of comfort. Those who should offer it, relations and friends, are themselves no less afflicted. They cannot make the attempt without many tears, and rather seem themselves to stand in need of comfort *from* others than to be capable of doing their friendly office *for* others. None the less, I have resolved to set briefly before you the reflections that come to my mind in this hour, not that I suppose you are unaware of them, but perhaps your grief makes them harder for you to perceive.

What reason is there why your domestic sorrow should affect you so sorely? Think how fortune has dealt with us up to now. All that man should hold no less dear than children – country, dignity, standing, distinctions – has been snatched away from us. Could this one further mishap add appreciably to your grief? How should not any heart practised in such experience have grown less sensitive and count all else as of relatively little consequence?

(Cicero, *Selected Letters*, n.102; in Shackleton Bailey, 1982, pp.183–4)

Figure 6.2   Veiled head of old republican, *c*.75–50 BCE, marble, Museo Gregoriano Profano, Vatican City.
(Photo: Alinari Archives – Anderson Archive, Florence)

Putting one's personal sorrow in perspective, in this case a particularly Roman political perspective, has a Stoical ring to it. Stoicism was one of the Greek philosophical schools that Romans active in public life found adaptable to their psychological needs, especially when they embarked upon stressful career paths. Cicero's reply suggests that Tullia had been his solace as he mourned the death of his career and the republic itself. He mentions other prestigious Romans who had lost children but points out that they could take solace in their state duties:

> But they lived in periods when the honourable standing they enjoyed in public life assuaged their mourning. *I* had already lost those distinctions which you yourself mention and which I had gained by dint of great exertions. The one comfort left to me was that which has now been snatched away. Neither my friends' concerns nor the administration of the state detained my thoughts. I had no wish to appear in the courts, I could not endure the sight of the Senate-House. I considered, as was the fact, that I had lost all the fruits of my work and success. However, I reflected that I shared this situation with yourself and certain others; I conquered my feelings and forced myself to bear it all patiently. But while I did so, I had a haven of refuge and repose, one in whose conversation and sweet ways I put aside all cares and sorrows.
>
> Now this grievous blow has again inflamed the wounds I thought healed. When in the past I withdrew in sadness from public affairs, my home received and soothed me; but I cannot now take refuge from domestic grief in public life, to find relief in what it offers. And so I stay away from home and Forum alike, for neither public nor private life can any longer comfort the distress which each occasions me.
>
> (Cicero, *Selected Letters*, n.103; in Shackleton Bailey, 1982, pp.186–7)

The letters of Cicero introduce a modern reader to an alien environment, but the sentiments can be 'universal'. We could add to this that, despite our abiding image of controlled and pragmatic personalities, many literate and leading Romans were not embarrassed about baring their souls and could do so with surprising frequency and candour. Sulpicius and Cicero reveal their traumatised state about the republic. At this time, the greatest threat to senatorial hegemony was Caesar, by then dictator of Rome. He was following in a line of powerful army generals (Figure 6.3) who had used the personal loyalty of their troops, gained over prolonged periods of campaigning, to build up an independent power base.

The Sulpicius letter and Cicero's response demonstrate the depth of depression both men felt at the state of the republic in the spring of 45 BCE and how difficult it was to sustain equanimity as Caesar rose from strength to strength in spite of their efforts to put obstacles in his way. One

Essay Six Roman reputations

Figure 6.3   Statue of Roman general from Tivoli, first half of first century BCE, from the period of the Mithridatic Wars, marble, Museo Nazionale, Rome. (Photo: Alinari Archives – Anderson Archive, Florence)

interesting question to ask from the outset is at what point we move from empathising with the trials and troubles of these articulate men and start to contextualise them historically and culturally in order to get to grips with their actions and attitudes. Reaching beyond the individual human condition into the social reality in which it is embedded is one of the most exciting processes of a historical study of the past. Both these letters could be used as sources for the grieving processes over children, whether infant or adult, who predeceased their parents (see Essay Eight). As personal letters between Cicero and Sulpicius, they were not written with an eye on publication; nevertheless, they provide more than one kind of evidence for a student of the Roman empire.

Placing our figures

In economic terms, Caesar, Cicero and Catullus were classed as *equites* ('cavalry class'; Goodman, 1997, pp.172–4). The term relates to the expectation that an individual *eques* was wealthy enough to equip a horse for military service. *Equites* were citizens of independent means and the wealthiest were enrolled in the top groups of the *comitia centuriata*. This body was an assembly where citizens were subdivided according to property qualifications into blocks, each of which cast a vote on important matters of policy and legislation. As there were far more blocks containing the numerically much smaller numbers of the well off, their collective interests could prevail over those of the poorer citizens at the other end of the economic scale, who were lumped together effectively en masse into fewer blocks. Of course, the wealthy did not necessarily form a united front when it came to deciding on matters of state.

I indicated in my introduction that Caesar belonged to a prestigious order of society; he was one of the patrician Julii family, which traced its ancestry back to the beginnings of Roman settlement and expansion. However, political privileges had been extended beyond a few families, as the spoils of empire helped make fortunes for men of commerce and their financial interests placed them firmly within the republican plutocracy.

Cicero was one of the non-aristocratic *equites* to break into the top political echelons. He stands out because his impressive entry into the top tier of government was accelerated by his skills as an orator in the law courts. He became part of the establishment partly by sheer self-exposure in key legal cases of his day. You have already read about his fervent love for republican rule and he was deeply committed to the continuation of a very stratified society. Cicero roundly condemned allowing the common people or 'mob' to make policy, especially when, as he saw it, they were being manipulated by renegade members of the senatorial stratum. Cicero's attitude towards the majority of the Roman citizenry pinpoints the limited and paternalistic notion of democracy that operated in ancient society. The ruling group could claim to be champions of the people and their liberty when it suited them. The Roman concept of *libertas* covered freedom from domination (being a citizen not a slave, having the protection of the laws), but also encompassed the privileges and wealth that came with conquest and empire. Obviously, privileges and wealth were not equally divided. Cicero believed in maintaining the proper hierarchies in the distribution of the empire's spoils at both ends of the social scale. He was not alone in his concerns about too much influence, status and money falling into the hands of an individual at the top end.

Years abroad gave opportunities to ex-magistrates on active service to create a network of rich backers in the provinces (the magistrates were assigned areas of responsibility as governors and commanders on completion of their offices at Rome). Pompey, Caesar's one-time ally and eventually defeated opponent, was a past master at such personal empire building. He had sufficient clout as a young man to bypass the usual stages of a political career and stand successfully at an unprecedentedly early age for one of the two consulships in Rome, the office that put its holder at the centre of running the empire for two years. The careers of men like Pompey and Caesar attracted insulting lampoons, in which their sexual appetites were portrayed as symptomatic of their acquisitiveness in general.

In the following poem Catullus alludes to the reputation for greed, corruption and sexual excess associated with Caesar and his protégé, Mamurra, who was Caesar's officer of engineers (*praefectus fabrum*) in Spain and Gaul:

> Nicely suited to the role of shameless debauchees
> The lust puppies, Mamurra and Caesar
> No surprises here – they match each other in corruption
> One in the forum and the other in Formiae.
> Mud sticks and this won't wash away.
> Equal in sickness, the diseased twins.
> Both little literary men in their cramped bed,
> They compete for the title of sex addict
> And are locked in comradely rivalry
> Over barely marriageable girls.
> Nicely suited indeed!
>
> (Catullus, Poem 57; my translation)

Suetonius comments that:

> Valerius Catullus had also libelled Caesar in his verses about Mamurra, yet Caesar, while admitting that these were a permanent blot on his name, accepted Catullus' apology and invited him to dinner that same afternoon, and never interrupted his friendship with Catullus' father.
>
> (Suetonius, *Julius Caesar* 73; quoted in Godwin, 1999, p.178)

It is worth noting that Catullus' family had business connections and influence in the rich Italian city of Verona.

Catullus penned quite a few frank and spiteful 'sketches' of well-known public figures. He was perfectly capable of producing disturbing images, including the graphically and aggressively sexual, when firing off his insults at both soft and hard targets. Peter Wiseman (1985, pp.4–8) draws attention to the Rome of Catullus, with its public torture and public executions, so that the modern reader can gain some sort of insight into the metaphors of violence that intersperse the poet's work. Without this context the strong expressions used might encourage us to overestimate the strength of Catullus' feelings. Catullus' tone of outrage and explicit accusations were an accepted part of ancient invective.

Satire of this sort is supposed to be entertaining, even in the most telling political exposures, but it is also possible that Catullus' negative portrayal of the powerful generals could be effective and damaging. Caesar was forced to spend prolonged periods away from the capital city, so he would be sensitive to any knocks that his image was taking in his absence. In her research on Catullus' role in Roman politics, Kate Hammond (Classical Association Conference, 2004) has reopened debates on the poet's life and influence in the empire's capital. To reinforce my earlier point, the interpretation of the events, social processes and individual careers in the Roman republic is a controversial and exciting area and not so readily reduced to a straightforward narrative as documentaries and introductory books might suggest.

As Caesar's military career advanced and he was able to call the political shots, his reputation for sexual voracity could be positively celebrated as part of his image as a campaigning soldier who fought and played hard! According to Suetonius (*The Twelve Caesars* 49.4.51), Caesar's legionary veterans chanted obscene songs about his sexual prowess when he celebrated his triumph over the Gauls in the usual huge procession of prisoners and booty through the streets of Rome. Although disrespectful ribaldry functioned as a reminder to celebrity generals that they were still fallible humans, the licence to laugh in affection at one's commander was also part of the relaxed atmosphere of such events. Caesar's personal shortcomings had positive cachet, but for his social peers his wanting and getting too much of everything was seen as a dangerous vulgarity, especially if arrogant acquisitiveness seriously disturbed the balance of wealth and power in the propertied classes.

Caesar was certainly not the first of the senatorial order to break ruling-class ranks by, as Cicero would have perceived it, pandering to the popular interests. Fifty years before, Tiberius and Gaius Gracchus had been prime movers in legislation that would benefit the lower orders. It is a complicated social and economic issue, but their reforms to land distribution were not wholly (and some scholars would argue, not at all) motivated by liberal and altruistic concerns. These very terms conjure up modern notions of progressive politics. However, Parenti has some valid observations on what he calls 'the rule of contextual immersion' (2003, pp.205–8). He suggests that in avoiding 'presentism' and seeing ancient society simply on its own terms (if indeed that were possible), the past will be filtered uncritically through the ideology of the predominant ancient (and literate!) class.

The tactics of the Gracchi brothers – they used their positions as tribunes (officers) of the people to advance their political programme – caused some consternation among the ruling élite, but these tactics had certainly 'caught on' by the time of Caesar. He also proposed legislation on the cancellation of debts and a more equitable distribution of the land. The senate at the time had ensured that the Gracchi both met violent ends in clashes on the streets between rival factions. Caesar was in a much more powerful position with a professional army behind him. He marched on Rome and took the title of 'dictator', which settled the matter of who would make policy in Rome (Figure 6.4). As a commander with veteran soldiers to reward, Caesar's strategy on reforms was a self-interested one, although that does not mean he had no vision of an internally better-run and relatively strifeless empire.

Figure 6.4   Silver denarius of Julius Caesar, struck by C. Cossutius Maridianus, legend reads 'DICT. IN PERPETUO', 44 BCE, Staatliche Museen zu Berlin – Preußischer Kulturbesitz, Münzkabinett. (Photo: 2004 © Bildarchive Preußischer Kulturbesitz, Berlin)

Double standards and dramatic licence

One prestigious historian of the Roman empire, Ernst Badian, concluded about senatorial rule in the late republic: 'No administration in history has ever devoted itself so wholeheartedly to fleecing its subjects for the private benefit of the ruling class as Rome of the last age of the Republic' (1968, p.87). Catullus describes in his poetry his disappointment at making so little money out of his trip abroad when he was on the governor's staff in the province of Bithynia (in his service abroad Catullus was following a traditional public career by playing a minor role in provincial government).

Catullus also documents in painful detail an affair in Rome, which took him into the heart of an aristocratic nexus that produced some of the racier 'copy' of the time. Catullus' mistress had a brother, Clodius, who relinquished his aristocratic name (Claudius) and used his position as a tribune of the people's assembly to expand his influence in Rome. He was useful to Pompey and Caesar, as the tribuneship could be used as legislative lever for the advancement of their interests (as had been done by the Gracchi). Clodius, like several key figures in political life at the time, moved about Rome with armed men at his side. He certainly seems to have been a 'wild card' in the heady mix of 'senatorial' versus 'popular' conflict. He played fast and loose with his alliances and his time as an independent force was eventually spent. In 52 BCE, he was murdered by Milo, an equally unreliable and violent associate of Pompey and Cicero.

One of Clodius' sisters, and possibly the same Clodia later authors identified as Catullus' mistress (who was mentioned in his poems), features in Cicero's most entertaining trial speeches in defence of Marcus Caelius Rufus. In what was at the time and still is regarded as a brilliant piece of advocacy, Cicero successfully defended Caelius against a series of charges including civil disturbance, damage to property, borrowing money to bribe slaves to commit murder and being involved in a direct murder himself. There were invariably a number of political angles to both the prosecution and defence of Caelius. By this time, Cicero was operating in a highly charged network of powerful players, many from aristocratic circles and all quite ruthless in their tactics. Most men who held high office walked the streets of Rome with armed bodyguards and trials were far from immune from bully-boy tactics. (This reached a climax when Cicero was later prevented from defending Milo in court by the intimidating presence of Pompey's men.)

Even if the conduct of a trial was regular, the political ramifications must have given a dramatic edge to legal proceedings and the atmosphere of menace and tension would have been paramount. We cannot easily recreate this experience or always get a sense as performance of the legal speeches Cicero published subsequently. As a key prosecution witness in the Caelius case, Clodia Metelli (i.e. Clodia, wife of Metellus) added theatrical colour to the proceedings:

> Yet since the elimination of this woman from the case will also mean the elimination of every single charge with which Caelius is faced, we who act as his counsel are left with no alternative; if someone attacks Clodius we are obliged to show they are wrong. Indeed, my refutation would be framed in considerably more forcible terms if I did not feel inhibited by the fact that the woman's husband – sorry, I mean brother, I always make that slip – is my personal enemy. Since that is the situation, however, my language shall be as moderate as I can make it, and I will go no farther than my conscience and the nature of the action render unavoidable. And indeed I never imagined I should have to engage in quarrels with women, much less with a woman who

has always been regarded as having no enemies since she so readily offers intimacy in all directions.

(Cicero, *In Defence of Marcus Caelius Rufus* 13; in Grant, 1972, p.32)

The deliberate slip about Clodius as husband was particularly pointed, as gossip had it that Clodius was incestuously involved with his sisters. The long-held assumption that Clodia (according to a much later Latin author Apuleius this was the real name of Catullus' mistress Lesbia) was Catullus' Clodia has been disputed by scholars like Wiseman, who have made a study of the configurations of the Claudii's aristocratic family. It is still an attractive idea that this particular sister of Clodius was the wayward and manipulative mistress of Catullus' poems. Cicero's discrediting of her as a witness and his wholesale destruction of her character builds a picture of Clodia that ties in nicely with the image we have of the woman who tormented Catullus with an on/off affair, that of the society woman working her way through a succession of lovers and ensnaring young men of good character.

In his commentary on the speeches of Cicero, Paul MacKendrick (1995, p.264) suggests that Cicero's wittily rhetorical performance at the trial has taken advantage of comic techniques. Caelius' trial took place in the midst of the Megalensian Games, when comic plays were performed as part of the entertainment. MacKendrick identifies several well-known comic play types in Cicero's characterisation of Clodia (cunning prostitute) and Caelius (gullible playboy), with their assorted supporting cast of curmudgeonly old men, slapstick slaves and so on. Incidentally, Catullus' affair with Clodia portrayed in fits and starts throughout his poems is rather like a drama unfolding before the eyes. Indeed, Classical scholars have questioned Catullus' sincerity and suggested that the whole sorry affair with Lesbia is more poetic fiction and fantasy than a genuine *cri de coeur* across the centuries. The closeness or remoteness of the actual author to the person the literary work presents as 'I' is a big critical issue in the interpretation of texts whenever and wherever they were written.

What kind of testimony?

Whatever the truth of Catullus' relationship with Lesbia/Clodia, the important point to reiterate is that the voices of the time come with a context – cultural, social and political – and cannot be uncritically quoted. What contemporary writing does give us are fascinating insights into the Roman way of doing things. Cicero's treatment of Clodia, wife of Metellus, exposes the viciousness of the cut and thrust in the law courts, just as Catullus' poetic insults show us a polemical world where slander, libel and defamation came with the territory. Cicero was no saint, and he has left so much of himself in his writing that it is easy to judge and condemn him for hypocrisy and dissembling when it was expedient. His vanity knew no bounds, but neither did his sense of insecurity, his feelings of fear and fallibility in his personal and political relationships. Cicero's personal correspondence reveals at least as much angst as Catullus' love poetry.

Caesar provides an interesting contrast, choosing to write up the progress of his military campaigns not in first-person narrative but referring to himself as 'Caesar' or simply 'he'. His works on the wars in Gaul and the Civil War need careful handling as a historical record, but his perspective on power, the Roman right to rule and upon his own place in the grand scheme of things speak out from his text. Caesar's works have great narrative fluency and plausibility and can read like a polished history of the wars he describes. However, there is a school of thought that believes Caesar's *The Conquest of Gaul* was circulated as war despatches from the front, with all the immediacy and excitement of a contemporary war correspondent.

As for Cicero in the law courts, it is worth trying to imagine the original reception of the text. Wiseman (1998) has strengthened the argument that Caesar's work on Gaul was disseminated, read and perhaps heard while the conquest of Gaul was taking place. He analyses specific episodes that have clear inconsistencies if Caesar was writing his war memoirs at the end of the wars in Gaul with the benefit of hindsight (for instance, Caesar mentions a tribe he clearly thought he had obliterated in battle and yet the tribe reappears later in the description of the conflict!). Wiseman observes that Caesar mentions the Roman people 41 times in the first book and suggests that he had them in mind as an audience for his campaigns as soon as he could feasibly relay his reports to Rome. Here is a flavour of one episode, in which Caesar reprimands Ariovistus, leader of the Suebi tribe in Germany and once saluted friend of the Roman senate, who had fallen out of favour when he seized large parts of the Aedui and Sequani tribes' territory in Gaul. The Roman people figure in this passage as the injured party, with Caesar as their champion:

> At this Caesar sent a second embassy to remind Ariovistus of the important privilege conferred upon him by himself and the Roman government, when during Caesar's consulship he received from the Senate the titles of 'King' and 'Friend'. Since his way of showing gratitude was to refuse an invitation to a conference for the discussion of matters affecting their common interest, the envoys were instructed to deliver him an ultimatum: first, he was not to bring any more large bodies of men across the Rhine into Gaul; secondly, he was to restore the Aeduan hostages he held, and to authorize the Sequani to restore those whom they held; finally, he was not to oppress the Aedui or to

make war on them or their allies. On these conditions Caesar and the Roman government would maintain cordial and friendly relations with him. If these demands were refused, then, in accordance with a decree of the Senate passed in the consulship of Marcus Messala and Marcus Piso, directing all governors of the Province of Gaul to do everything consistent with the public interest to protect the Aedui and other Roman allies, Caesar would not fail to punish his ill-treatment of them.

(Julius Caesar, *The Conquest of Gaul*; in Handford, 1982, p.46)

Wiseman produces a persuasive argument that Caesar was writing up the events of his campaign on a regular basis to promote and publicise his achievements and keep himself in the public eye. He would still have to rely on friends and allies at Rome to spread the word and make sure the readings of his reports were truly public. Recitation of all kinds of works was evidently quite customary in the ancient Greek world, and under the Roman emperors colourful speeches on a whole range of topics attracted very large audiences, as a theatrical performance would. The wider oral dissemination of Caesar's *The Conquest of Gaul* answers the objection that low levels of literacy and the high price of papyrus books militated against mass consumption. Wiseman quotes Cicero on 'the pleasure that people of humble station with no expectation of a public career, or even artisans, take in history' (1998, pp.4–5). Caesar posed as a man of the people and Wiseman believes that the people would have been spellbound by the narrative swiftness of Caesar's narrative. History was supposed to be entertaining and read aloud. These delayed dispatches from the front are what kept Caesar's victories in the public eye.

False impressions or problematising the past

There was so much written by contemporaries about this time that we might feel quite confident in producing a plausible narrative about the last years of republican government and the processes that ushered in the reign of the emperors. It should be stimulating to discover that such a confidence would be misplaced! The short extracts you have been reading from very different kinds of literature (poetic, epistolary and 'historical') emanate from educated and literary men with distinct personal agendas. They frequently raise either explicitly or implicitly the issues of power, empire, freedom and political representation in republican Rome.

Modern scholarship has also entered the picture at points in this essay. For many years, scholars have written about the stresses and strains the republican system suffered once Rome expanded out of its parochial parameters, acquiring land and wealth, and needing a permanent recruited army to keep conquered territory under control. This makes for a neat picture of cause and effect, but it no longer satisfies the historians as the whole story. There are a number of fascinating and open-ended debates about just how Rome and its empire was being run once powerful generals could dictate terms to the senate and the senate resigned itself to phases of autocratic rule.

We can learn a great deal from the methods of the historians and of the literary and cultural commentators as they tease out the political and social scenarios of the past as accurately as they can. Of course, in a lively intellectual milieu conclusions are no sooner drawn than they are challenged. We may have to resign ourselves to living with a degree of uncertainty about life and strife in the late republic or moving sometimes one step forward two steps back in our understanding of its political machinery.

The jury is still out, too, on the issue of people participation in the capital and whether the people's assemblies really involved the mass of the citizens in electing their magistrates. Henrik Mouritsen (2001) suggests that all kinds of practicalities would have prevented the city dwellers from participating very much in formal democratic processes, let alone those from the environs of Rome who would have needed to make a special trip into the city for the rural tribe assembly days. In any case, Mouritsen, drawing upon archaeological studies of the spaces and places reserved for voting and the counting of votes, concludes that only a small percentage of Roman citizens could have been manoeuvred around the 'pens' constructed for these purposes. The political institutions continued to work on the premise of a face-to-face society, but the number of citizens had grown exponentially (2001, p.32).

This raises the question of which citizens were exercising their political rights. As most Romans had to eke out a living and continued to be ruled by economic imperatives, even when a state handout of grain (the corn dole) had become a regular feature, they simply did not have the leisure time to be politically active. On the other hand, it is worth asking where the prosperous Romans who fell short of *eques* status by a few sesterces expressed their political aspirations and exercised their influence if not in the 'plebeian' assemblies. In other words the 'mob' manipulated by the powerful politicians might itself have been made up mostly of wealthy men!

Of course, the élite would meet the masses in more relaxed circumstances. Boundaries could certainly be blurred when the Romans were at play, a cultural and political phenomenon Nicholas Horsfall explores in his book on *The Culture of the Roman Plebs* (2003). Essay Nine below discusses the gladiatorial games and beast shows (even more lavish and large under the emperors) as, historically, arenas for mutual manipulation and control at all levels of the social spectrum. Pompey and Caesar were both willing to spend a fortune on these entertaining and 'sporting' displays, which were simultaneously a statement about the spoils and benefits of empire and the kudos of the military men who extended and defended its boundaries. The occasional shows would doubtless make the commanders popular, but it is questionable whether in the republican era these displays would or could translate automatically into votes in the next round of elections.

Analysing the relationship between the élite and the rest of the free population in Rome has never been straightforward. Painstaking research has been done on the bribery and intimidation that undoubtedly went on with open voting systems. This includes the influential persuasion that candidates could exercise upon their freedmen – these freed slaves automatically became citizens upon manumission (formal freeing from slavery), but their independence was hedged around by the obligations they had to former masters (Figure 6.5). How elaborate and effective this 'patron–client' system was and who, apart from freed slaves, might join the ranks of those beholden, morally or economically, to the richer citizens has been the subject of many separate studies. Mary Beard and Michael Crawford (1999, pp.88–92) raise this and other challenges in a postscript to their book *Rome in the Late Republic*, an update aptly entitled 'New directions'.

Figure 6.5 Silver denarius of Marcus Junius (reverse), showing Cap of Freedom (*pileus*) between two daggers, legend reads 'EID MAR', 43–42 BCE, British Museum, London, RR East BMC69. © Copyright The Trustees of the British Museum.

It seems that when we read about colourful episodes of 'people power' as related by the literate and educated we are not exactly meeting the masses and developing a sense of their everyday lives in Rome. Nevertheless, archaeological investigation continues to uncover evidence about the material conditions and the activities and aspirations of the lower and less literate classes in Rome and throughout the empire. The words and visual evidence we encounter on their tombstones, in graffiti or the transactions that survive in legal documents regulating roles in trade and industry do not give us a detailed ideology or class perspective. However, Horsfall (2003), using a rich variety of evidence, provides fascinating insights into their political awareness expressed in song, sloganising and a whole wealth of leisure activities that blurred hierarchical cultural boundaries.

Further reading

I suggested at the beginning of this essay that there was much to read and absorb about republican Rome. There is certainly plenty to choose from just by concentrating on Caesar, Catullus and Cicero, who were selected here to evoke something of the atmosphere and dynamics of the 30 years before the rule of the emperors. I have alluded to three timely and topical 'takes' on Caesar during this essay. Robin Seager's biography of Pompey (reissued in 2002) and Michael Grant's *Julius Caesar* (1969) would make an interesting comparison with the volumes by Michael Parenti (2003), Robert Garland (2004) and Tom Holland (2004).

You will have gathered that a great deal of the literary output of Caesar, Cicero and Catullus appears in paperback translations and these books come with useful introductions that fill out the sketchy portraits of the preceding pages. For instance, Dominic Berry (2000) gives an interesting introduction to the historical context, the literary significance and the forensic style of several key defence speeches of Cicero that he has translated. Even more recently, Josephine Balmer (2004) has produced lively renderings of Catullus' poems, giving his more graphic expressions of love and hate something of their original flavour.

You may find interesting approaches to the late republic in historical novels that have Cicero and Catullus at the centre or at least in cameo roles. There are a number of lively and controversial historical surveys of the republican period that introduce the generals Pompey, Marius and Sulla, and the aristocratic 'champions of the people' Tiberius and Cornelius Gracchus, among other colourful characters of the period. For a survey of the Roman republic, *The Cambridge Companion to the Roman Republic*, with a useful appendix on republican institutions, covers such subjects as the role of women, the household, economy, law and religion.

Bibliography

Ancient sources

Cicero, *In Defence of Marcus Caelius Rufus*, in Grant, M. (trans.) (1972) Cicero: *Selected Political Speeches*, Harmondsworth: Penguin.

Cicero, *Selected Letters*, in Shackleton Bailey, D.R. (trans.) (1982) Cicero: *Selected Letters*, Harmondsworth: Penguin.

Julius Caesar, *The Conquest of Gaul*, in Handford, S.A. (trans.) (1982) Caesar: *The Conquest of Gaul*, Harmondsworth: Penguin.

Suetonius, *Julius Caesar*, in Graves, R. (trans.) (1957) Suetonius: *The Twelve Caesars*, Harmondsworth: Penguin.

Modern scholarship

Badian, E. (1968) *Roman Imperialism in the Late Republic*, Oxford: Blackwell.

Balmer, J. (2004) Catullus: *Poems of Love and Hate*, Gwynedd, North Wales: Bloodaxe Books.

Beard, M. and Crawford, M. (1999) *Rome in the Late Republic: Problems and Interpretations*, London: Duckworth.

Berry, D. (2000) Cicero: *Defence Speeches*, Oxford: Oxford University Press.

The Cambridge Companion to the Roman Republic (2004) ed. H. Flower, Cambridge: Cambridge University Press.

Garland, R. (2004) *Julius Caesar*, Bristol: Bristol Phoenix Press.

Godwin, J. (1999) *Catullus: The Shorter Poems*, Warminster: Aris & Phillips.

Goodman, M. (1997) *The Roman World: 44BC – AD180*, London and New York: Routledge.

Grant, M. (1969) *Julius Caesar*, London: Wiedenfeld & Nicolson.

Holland, T. (2004) *Rubicon: The Triumph and Tragedy of the Roman Republic*, London: Abacus (first published New York: Little, Brown, 2003.)

Horsfall, N. (2003) *The Culture of the Roman Plebs*, London: Duckworth.

MacKendrick, P. (1995) *The Speeches of Cicero: Context, Law, Rhetoric*, London: Duckworth.

Michie, J. (1998) *Poems of Catullus*, Ware, Herts: Wordsworth Classics of World Literature.

Mouritsen, H. (2001) *Plebs and Politics in the Late Roman Republic*, Cambridge: Cambridge University Press.

Parenti, M. (2003) *The Assassination of Julius Caesar: A People's History of Ancient Rome*, New York and London: New Press.

Seager, R. (2003) *Pompey the Great*, Malden, MA and London: Blackwell (first published 1972).

Wiseman, T.P. (1985) *Catullus and his World*, Cambridge: Cambridge University Press.

Wiseman, T.P. (1998) 'The publication of *De Bello Gallico*', in K. Welch and A. Powell (eds) *Julius Caesar as Artful Reporter: The War Commentaries as*

Political Instruments, London: Duckworth with the Classical Press of Wales, pp.1–9.

Essay Seven

Seneca: a philosophy of living

Carolyn Price

Philosophy, as it was practised by the Romans, had its origins in Greece in the philosophical schools that sprung up there in the fourth century BCE. The first Greek philosophers known to have visited Rome came, some two centuries later, as ambassadors, using their spare time to deliver lectures on philosophical subjects. They drew large crowds and seem to have provoked a suspicious response from some leading Romans: the republican statesman Marcus Porcius Cato the Elder (234–149 BCE) is said to have urged his fellow senators to settle one diplomatic dispute as quickly as possible, to prevent impressionable young Romans from attending too many lectures on philosophy (Plutarch, *Cato the Elder* 22).

By the later years of the republic, however, the philosophical schools were well established at Rome, and some leading citizens had Greek philosophers permanently installed in their homes (Plutarch, *Brutus* 2.2; *Cato the Younger* 16). Romans began to write philosophical treatises for themselves, drawing on Greek sources: the philosophical works of Lucretius (*c.*99–*c.*55 BCE) and of the orator Cicero (106–43 BCE) are significant additions to western philosophical literature. By the early years of the Principate, the historian Tacitus reports that the tenets of the major schools were common knowledge at Rome, so that speakers could no longer use them to dazzle their audiences (Tacitus, *Dialogue on Oratory* 19; in Hutton *et al.*, 1914, quoted in Griffin, 1989, p.5).

Each of the philosophical schools was identified with a particular founder and with a particular philosophical outlook or set of doctrines. The oldest of the four major schools was the Academy, which was established by Plato (*c.*429–347 BCE) at Athens at the beginning of the fourth century BCE. The Peripatetic School was founded by Plato's pupil Aristotle (384–322 BCE), who set up his school in the Lyceum, on the other side of the city. At the end of the fourth century BCE, Epicurus (341–271 BCE) established his school just outside the city gates. At around the same time, Zeno of Citium (334–262 BCE) created the Stoic School, which was named after its meeting place in the Stoa Poikile ('Painted Colonnade') in Athens' main market place.

Under the republic, these schools seem to have enjoyed equal popularity at Rome, but under the Principate, the Stoic School achieved a degree of ascendancy. It is not surprising that Stoicism should have proved attractive to the Romans: as Miriam Griffin points out, its austere ethical doctrines could be seen as a justification for traditional Roman values, and the resolute life and heroic suicide of Marcus Porcius Cato the Younger (95–46 BCE) provided the school with a gripping example of the ideal Roman Stoic (Griffin, 1989, pp.8–10). Indeed, under Nero and his Flavian successors, Stoicism became associated with senatorial resistance to imperial power: a Greek philosophical system set up in defence of Roman political tradition (see Tacitus, *Annals* 16.20–32).

The best-known Roman Stoic of this period, however, was Nero's own tutor and minister, Lucius Annaeus Seneca the Younger (*c.*4 BCE to CE 65) (Figure 7.1). Seneca had been born in Cordoba in Spain into a wealthy family of equestrian rank. His father, Seneca the Elder (*c.*55 BCE to CE *c.*40) was an expert on rhetoric, but Seneca and his elder brother Novatus, later known as Gallio, were the first members of the family to pursue a senatorial career. Gallio eventually became governor of Achaea. Seneca himself was exiled by the emperor Claudius, but later recalled due to the influence of Claudius' fourth wife Agrippina, who wanted him to act as tutor for her son – soon to become the emperor Nero. Tacitus reports that, along with the military officer Burrus, Seneca all but ruled the empire during the early years of Nero's reign. But after Burrus' death in CE 62, Seneca became isolated, and asked for permission to retire from public life. He spent his last three years living in retirement, enjoying his country villas and furthering his study of philosophy.

Seneca was prominent, not only as a politician but also as a writer, primarily on philosophical subjects. In the ancient world, philosophical writings took a variety of forms: Plato wrote dialogues; Epicurus expounded his doctrines in letters; Lucretius explained Epicureanism to his Roman audience in a poem. Seneca himself made use of a number of literary genres. He was the author of several tragedies, which reflected his philosophical convictions. He wrote a number of treatises, for example: *On Mercy* (addressed to the young Nero), *On Anger*, *On the Happy Life* and *On Tranquillity of Mind*. He also wrote three *Consolations* – one to his mother Helvia, consoling her on his exile; one to a woman named Marcia, on the death of her son; and one to the imperial freedman Polybius, on the death of his brother. Perhaps his most interesting philosophical work is a set of letters that were composed towards the end of his life. Although they are addressed to his friend Lucilius Junior, an adherent of the rival Epicurean School, they were probably always intended for publication. This choice of genre enables Seneca to write what is, in effect, a series of short essays, addressing a broad range of topics and presented in a friendly, personal tone. The form is ideally suited to the task of explaining Stoicism to a non-

Essay Seven Seneca: a philosophy of living

Figure 7.1 Herm of Lucius Annaeus Seneca the Younger (frontal view), Roman double herm, first half of third century CE, height 28 cm, Antikensammlung, Staatliche Museen zu Berlin, Germany. (Inv. Sk 391. Photo: Johannes Laurentius. © 2006 bpk)

specialist audience, and allows Seneca to draw on the circumstances of his own life at the time. We learn of his daily runs, accompanied by his young slave Pharius (*Letters to Lucilius* 83.4); of his struggle with bouts of asthma (*Letters* 54); and of his wife Paulina's concerns for his health (*Letters* 104.3).

The purpose of this essay is to investigate Seneca's philosophical views and, in particular, to consider what Seneca took his commitment to Stoicism to imply – theoretically, at least – with respect to his everyday conduct. This question must be distinguished from a rather different question: how far Seneca's philosophical beliefs did in fact influence his conduct – for example, in the political decisions that he made as Nero's minister or in his life at home. Many philosophers who have upheld certain ethical principles in their writings have been accused of back-sliding or hypocrisy, and Seneca was no exception. However, in the absence of detailed and reliable biographical evidence, these issues are impossible to judge. Here, my primary purpose is not to examine Seneca's life, but to investigate, through the claims that he makes in his writings, his understanding of how Stoicism ought to have influenced his conduct.

I shall concentrate, not on Seneca's career as a politician, about which he gives us very little information, but on issues that must have arisen for many Romans of his wealth and status. In particular, I shall consider what Seneca has to say about the proper attitude to wealth; about the relationship between slave-owner and slave; and about the ever-present threat of bereavement and death. I shall end by considering Seneca's attitude to suicide. In places, I shall contrast Seneca's views with those of members of other philosophical schools, particularly the Epicureans and Peripatetics, and with another Stoic, Epictetus (CE *c.*55–*c.*135). I shall begin by setting out, very briefly, the basic principles of Stoic ethics, and by explaining Seneca's place in the history of the school.

The Stoics on well-being, reason and choice

One issue on which the major philosophical schools were united was their conception of the kinds of question that ought to concern a philosopher. This conception was strikingly broad. Proper subjects for philosophical investigation were taken to include the fundamental constituents of the universe; the possibility of an afterlife; the limits of human knowledge; the nature of god; and the value and purpose of human life. Even more striking, perhaps, was the extent to which these questions were recognised to be interdependent. As a result, the doctrines of each school provide a coherent and complete account of the world and the individual's place within it. In this essay, I am going to concentrate primarily on Seneca's ethical views. However, it is important to bear in mind that Seneca's views on ethics were underpinned by his understanding of Stoic philosophy as a whole.

The ancient schools shared the assumption that the primary concern of ethics is to explain how each individual may achieve the best possible human life. In this respect, ancient philosophers differ from many modern ethical theorists, who hold that the goal of ethics is to determine how we should behave towards other people. On this more recent conception, it makes sense to ask how we should balance the demands of ethics (which concern our duties to others) with those of prudence (which concern our own interests). In contrast, ancient philosophers took ethics to be concerned, in the first instance, with the individual's own well-being. Each individual is assumed to be in pursuit of *eudaimonia* – a state of well-being or flourishing that incorporates everything of real value in a human life. However, this is not to say that ancient philosophers recommended selfishness: they tended to think that the best life for a human being will include unselfish relations with others.

What, then, is the best life for a human being? Of all the ancient schools, the Stoics offered the most radical and challenging answer to this question.

Essay Seven Seneca: a philosophy of living

Suppose that you meet someone – a middle-aged man, say. Let us call him Felix. Felix is handsome, charming and in excellent health. He has a moderate amount of money – enough to live a comfortable life. He has an excellent reputation and a wide circle of interesting and admirable friends. He has a loving relationship with his partner, and two charming and healthy children. Moreover, Felix is a very good person – he is kind, courageous, fair-minded, and respectful towards others. Above all, he is wise; in other words, his judgements and choices are governed by reason.

Felix, it seems, is leading an excellent life. But in what respects, exactly, is his life excellent? Do his good looks matter? Does his money, his health or his reputation matter? Do his friendships matter? The Stoics held that none of these things are of any real importance: Felix could lose any of these things without it in the least diminishing his *eudaimonia*. What matters is Felix's character – his courage, kindness, fair-mindedness and so on. In fact, since the Stoics thought that having a good character was simply a matter of making correct judgements and choices, they would have held that the only thing relevant to Felix's well-being is his wisdom.

To put the point bluntly: suppose that Felix is arrested by a tyrant, his wealth confiscated, his reputation destroyed, Felix himself imprisoned, tortured and eventually executed. None of this, the Stoics held, would detract from his *eudaimonia*. All that would matter is that Felix endures these things as reason dictates: that is, with courage and dignity. So long as Felix is living in accordance with reason, his life is as good as it can be.

On this point, the Stoics were opposed by the Peripatetics. Aristotle argued that the best life was, first and foremost, a life of virtuous activity, directed by reason. But he also argued that virtue and wisdom are not sufficient for *eudaimonia*: health, moderate wealth and friendship are also required. Indeed, he remarked that the suggestion that a virtuous person would be happy even while being tortured is nonsense (*Nicomachean Ethics* 1153b). Nevertheless, Aristotle also claimed that a virtuous person who was destitute, friendless or tortured, although not in a state of *eudaimonia*, would at least not be wretched: a virtuous person cannot sink as low as someone who lacks virtue (*Nicomachean Ethics* 1101a). Seneca attacks this position as inconsistent: if virtue is not enough to secure *eudaimonia*, why should it be enough to save someone from wretchedness (*Letters* 92.26)?

In contrast, the Epicureans questioned the Stoics' claim that wisdom is good in itself. According to Epicurus, health, wealth, good reputation, friendships and wisdom are all worth having, but they are worth having only because they lead to something else – that is, a pleasant life. However, when the Epicureans claimed that the pleasant life is best, they did not mean (as Roman writers sometimes implied) that the best life is one of riotous self-indulgence. They held that the supreme form of pleasure is a state of tranquillity, and that a pleasant life could be secured only by living quietly, away from the public eye, by enjoying a simple, healthy diet and by making warm, but not passionate, friendships with others (Epicurus, *Letter to Menoeceus* 127–32).

There is one issue on which the Epicureans and Stoics were in agreement against the Peripatetics. As we have seen, the Peripatetics accepted that people's *eudaimonia* depends in part on things that they cannot completely control, including their health, their finances and their relationships with others. On this view, a person's well-being can be impaired or even destroyed by chance. The Stoics, in contrast, held that everything that is required for a good life depends on the person alone, and cannot be removed by chance. The Epicureans took a similar view. They argued that the pleasant life is very easy to attain: a simple diet, for example, is available to all. More importantly, they claimed that, even in times of loneliness, illness or pain, a person can enjoy pleasure by choosing to concentrate on pleasant thoughts or memories. Both Stoics and Epicureans, then, sought to make *eudaimonia* immune to luck, by arguing that it depends, not on the individual's external circumstances, but on his or her mental attitude.

By making *eudaimonia* independent of factors that the person cannot control, the Stoics freed the wise person from the vagaries of chance. Equally, on the Stoic view, a wise person will also be free from control by other people. According to the Stoics, a wise person cannot be threatened or coerced by a tyrant, because there is nothing that a tyrant can do to diminish the wise person's *eudaimonia*. Both freedom from chance and freedom from coercion are important themes in Stoic ethical writings.

It might be thought that the Stoics are open to a fatal objection. If only wisdom is valuable, how can it be exercised? Why should a wise person choose one thing rather than another? For example, if health has no value, why should Felix choose to eat healthily rather than dine on chocolate éclairs? The Stoic response is that, although health has no value in itself, it is rational to choose a healthy diet, because in choosing to eat healthily we are acting in accordance with our human nature. But why is it rational to choose in accordance with human nature? In order to understand the connection between nature and reason in Stoic philosophy, it is necessary to consider the Stoics' conception of god.

The Stoics believed that the world was governed by one god, of which the traditional gods of Greek and Roman religion were symbols or representations. The Stoics did not think of god as existing outside the natural world, but as pervading it and constantly shaping it. Above all, the Stoics identified god with reason: they held that god shapes the world in accordance with a rational and benevolent plan. Like the rest of nature, our human nature has been formed by god. So to choose in accordance with human nature is to choose in accordance with god's providential plan – that is, in accordance with (divine) reason.

However, this is not to say that the things that we ought to choose are themselves valuable. What is valuable is our choice. If Felix acts on his decision to eat healthily, but becomes ill anyway, this does not matter. What matters is that he made the healthy choice. Seneca makes the point clear in an imagined dialogue with Lucilius:

> 'What, then,' comes the retort, 'if good health, rest and freedom from pain are not likely to hinder virtue, shall you not seek all these?' Of course I shall seek them, but not because they are goods, – I shall seek them because they are according to nature and because they will be acquired through the exercise of good judgment on my part. What, then, will be good in them? This alone, – that it is a good thing to choose them.
>
> (*Letters* 92.11)

As an ethical theory, Stoicism is extremely demanding. It implies that almost all commonsense judgements about what is valuable in life are both false and pernicious. Stoics must strive to rid themselves of the belief that solitude, poverty, ill health, bereavement and death are evils, to be feared and lamented. Equally, they must strive to rid themselves of the belief that friendship, wealth, health, worldly success and a long life are good things – fit objects of greed or pride. Early Stoics seem to have made some claims that shocked their contemporaries. Chrysippus (289–207 BCE), the third head of the school, was said to have argued that incest is not unnatural (Plutarch, *On Stoic Self-contradictions* 1044F–1045A). He is also reported to have argued in favour of cannibalism (Sextus Empiricus, *Outlines of Pyrrhonism*). Later Stoics, however, seem to have been less inclined to question conventional institutions. Seneca's writings, certainly, concern how Stoic principles can be applied by Romans of his class, living in accordance with established traditions and institutions.

Perhaps unsurprisingly, the Stoics thought that *eudaimonia* was almost impossible to achieve: most held that there had never yet been a wise person, although the Greek philosopher Socrates (469–399 BCE) was presented as having come close to the ideal. Among Roman Stoics, Cato the Younger was given a similar status. Here, the Stoics were closer to the Peripatetics, who regarded *eudaimonia* as difficult to achieve, than to the Epicureans, who held that the pleasant life is easy to attain. However, as the school developed, the Stoics developed a greater interest in exploring how Stoic principles might be applied by people who are not wise, but merely making progress towards wisdom. Although ordinary Stoics cannot act with the understanding required for wisdom, they can choose actions that are appropriate, and can benefit from advice concerning which actions to choose. The Stoic Panaetius (c.180–c.109 BCE) seems to have shown a particular interest in developing a Stoic ethics for ordinary people, and wrote a treatise offering practical advice. Panaetius played an important role in bringing Stoicism to Rome, and his treatise formed the basis for the first two books of Cicero's work *On Duties*. Seneca shared the view that Stoic principles could be used to generate practical advice for ordinary Stoics (*Letters* 94), and he frequently emphasises that his advice is aimed at those who, like himself, are not wise, but who are trying to make progress towards wisdom.

Seneca on living with wealth

Seneca was well known for his riches, accumulated during his years as tutor and minister to Nero. Unsurprisingly, his wealth provoked accusations of hypocrisy. Tacitus reports that at the trial of Publius Suillius Rufus on charges of extortion and embezzlement (CE 58), Suillius made the accusation with special vehemence: 'What branch of learning, what philosophical school, won Seneca three hundred million sesterces during four years of imperial friendship?' (Tacitus, *Annals* 13.42). We might ask whether Seneca himself thought that his riches were consistent with his Stoic principles.

Seneca's answer to this question seems to vary from work to work. In his treatise *On the Happy Life*, he argues that a philosopher should not be ashamed of being wealthy, and that it is natural to prefer comfort to hardship. Moreover, he points out, a wealthy Stoic will have more scope than a poor one to be generous and diligent in helping others (Seneca, *On the Happy Life* 21.1–23.5). Elsewhere, however, Seneca adopted a rather different position. In his treatise, *On Tranquillity of Mind* (8.9) he states that the wealthy should try to reduce their riches: the best state, he says, is one just short of poverty. Traces of this more austere attitude can be found in his letters to Lucilius. He suggests that poverty is more desirable than wealth, stressing that wealth brings anxieties and responsibilities that hinder progress in philosophy (*Letters* 17.3), and implies that money is generally a corrupting influence (*Letters* 119.9).

However, there is one claim to which Seneca consistently returns. This is the suggestion that a person will not be corrupted by wealth, provided that he or she has the right attitude towards it. In one letter, he develops this idea in an imagined dialogue with Epicurus. Epicurus is represented as saying that those who are rich cannot lead a truly pleasant life, because they will inevitably be tormented by the fear of losing their wealth. Seneca agrees that virtue is compatible with poverty, but goes on:

he also is great-souled, who sees riches heaped up round him and, after wondering long and deeply because they have come into his possession, smiles, and hears rather than feels that they are his. ... he is truly great who is poor amidst riches. 'Yes, but I do not know,' you say, 'how the man you speak of will endure poverty, if he falls into it suddenly.' Nor do I, Epicurus, know whether the poor man you speak of will despise riches, should he suddenly fall into them; accordingly, in the case of both, it is the mind that must be appraised.

(*Letters* 20.10–11)

Seneca's response to Epicurus is that the Stoic can avoid the anxieties produced by wealth by recognising that wealth has no real value, and that it is possible to lead a good life without it.

Moreover, Seneca suggests that there are practical exercises that one can undertake in order to avoid becoming dependent on wealth. He advises Lucilius that he should put aside a few days now and then to practise living in poverty, in order to remind himself that he can get by on very little:

> Let the pallet be a real one, and the coarse cloak; let the bread be hard and grimy. Endure all this for three or four days at a time, sometimes for more, so that it may be a test of yourself instead of a mere hobby. Then, ... you will understand that a man's peace of mind does not depend upon Fortune.
>
> (*Letters* 18.7)

Here Seneca is appealing to a standard Stoic technique – that of helping the mind to cope with a change in fortune by preparing for it in advance. For a truly wise person, who is not tempted to regard wealth as necessary to the good life, such an exercise would be superfluous. But for those who are making progress towards wisdom, the exercise should help to remind them that they need not be dependent on material goods.

Although Seneca emphasises that the exercise should be performed in the right spirit and not as a rich man's amusement, he is still open to the objection that three or four days of physical discomfort and a poor diet are hardly equivalent to many years of deprivation, without hope of relief. More convincing, perhaps, is the advice that Seneca gives in *On Tranquillity of Mind* (9.3), where he suggests that the wealthy should prepare themselves for poverty by permanently adopting a simple style of life. In his letters, Seneca presents himself as having taken this advice: he describes himself as habitually taking cold baths, eating simple food and sleeping on a hard bed (*Letters* 83).

In contrast, Seneca frequently denounces his contemporaries' addiction to luxury, deploring, for example, the fashion for ornate baths (*Letters* 86), gilded furniture and dishes of flamingoes' tongues (*Letters*

110.12). He makes a point of contrasting the ostentatious lifestyles of his contemporaries with the simpler habits of Romans under the republic (*Letters* 86). Seneca's concerns about luxury reflect contemporary anxiety about a decline in traditional values; on this point in particular, he is keen to stress that Stoic principles accord with Roman tradition.

Seneca on the treatment of slaves

As we have seen, the Stoics shared with other ancient philosophical schools the assumption that the fundamental concern of ethics is the individual's own well-being. Yet Stoic philosophers held that reason demands, not only that each individual should choose what will best satisfy his or her own needs, but that each will also treat others with justice, generosity and kindness. Seneca took this to be the special mark of Stoicism: 'no school of philosophers is kinder or more lenient, more philanthropic or attentive to the common good' (Seneca, *On Mercy* 2.5.3). How do these two aspects of Stoicism connect? Seneca explains the point as follows:

> all that you behold, that which comprises both god and man, is one – we are the parts of one great body. Nature produced us related to one another, since she created us from the same source and to the same end ... Let us possess things in common; for birth is ours in common. Our relations with one other are like a stone arch, which would collapse if the stones did not mutually support each other, and which is upheld in this very way.
> (*Letters* 95.52–3)

It is possible to find two distinct claims in this passage. First, Seneca is claiming that we need each other: without the support of others, no individual will able to obtain the things that a wise person will naturally seek. Taken by itself, this is a relatively modest claim. It is consistent with the view that human beings ought ultimately to be concerned with their own interests. It does not imply that we should treat everyone equally: some people – for example, relatives and friends – may be in a better position to help us than others. Nor does it imply that we should treat others as partners: co-operation may not always be the best way of securing the assistance of others. Coercing others, for example by enslaving them, may sometimes be more effective.

However, Seneca also seems to be making a second, stronger claim in this passage. He seems to suggest that all human beings are the same, in some ethically significant sense. We are the same because we are all parts of a greater pattern, shaped by divine reason. It might be thought to follow from this that we should seek the good of others, not for our own sake, but for theirs. For it is possible to argue that, if others are similar to us in an ethically significant way, then any justification that we may have for pursuing our own good will also be a justification for pursuing the good of others. Seneca's argument in this passage is not clear enough for us to be sure that he had this line of thought in mind. But it is known that other Stoics argued that reason demands that we should give equal consideration to all. For example, Hierocles, a Greek Stoic writing at the end of the first century CE, argued that reason requires that we should regard everyone with equal affection and respect. We should not favour someone simply because they come from the same town or because they are related to us (Stobaeus, *Anthologium* 4.671.7–673.11; in Long and Sedley, 1987, pp.349–50).

How far is Seneca committed to this ideal? A test case is provided by one of his letters to Lucilius, in which he discusses the relationship between slave-owner and slave (*Letters* 47). Seneca argues that slave-owners should live on friendly terms with their slaves, eating with them, addressing them in an amiable way, and consulting with them where appropriate. These claims are underpinned by the argument that, because slaves are human beings, they deserve to be treated with as much respect and kindness as any other human being. Slaves, Seneca says, have not become slaves because they deserve slavery; rather, their status is the result of chance. Indeed, it is likely that many slaves are better, wiser people than their owners. Seneca writes:

> Kindly remember that he whom you call your slave sprang from the same stock, is smiled upon by the same skies, and on equal terms with yourself breathes, lives, and dies. It is just as possible for you to see in him a free-born man as for him to see in you a slave.
>
> (*Letters* 47.10–11)

He goes on to argue that a slave-owner's attitude to a slave ought to depend on the slave's character, rather than his or her status in the household: a virtuous mule-driver has more right to eat at his master's table than a steward of dubious character.

Against this, he contrasts the actual behaviour of wealthy Romans towards their slaves, which he describes as arrogant and cruel. In his treatise *On Anger*, he had described how the most trivial transgressions might provoke a Roman slave-owner to violent rage – looking sullen (Seneca, *On Anger* 3.24), slamming a door (3.35) or breaking a cup (3.40). In *Letter* 47, he introduces a new theme, denouncing the way in which his contemporaries' addiction to luxury condemns their slaves to a degrading and futile existence – for example, a life devoted to mopping up the vomit of over-stuffed guests, or to jointing poultry in exactly the right way. It is interesting to contrast Seneca's remarks here with a passage in one of Epictetus' *Discourses* (3.26). Epictetus, himself an ex-slave, excoriates his wealthy pupils for their dependence on the physical ministrations of their slaves: they cannot manage, it seems, without being dressed, undressed, massaged and fed by a troop of attendants. What they want, Epictetus dryly comments, is to live the life of an invalid. Seneca would agree, but in *Letter* 47 he widens his attack on luxury to include its effects, not only on those who consume it, but also on those who are expected to provide it.

In arguing that slaves ought to be treated with respect, Seneca is following in the footsteps of earlier Stoics. Seneca himself reports that Chrysippus held that slaves should be regarded as 'employees for life' (Seneca, *On Favours* 3.22). However, it seems that not all Stoics took this line. According to Cicero, the Greek Stoic Hecato, who lived in the first century BCE, argued that, in a famine, a slave-owner was entitled to allow his slaves to starve, rather than destroying the family's wealth by feeding them at inflated prices (Cicero, *On Duties* 3.89); this suggests that Hecato regarded slaves merely as commodities, on a par with other components of a family's property. Cicero describes Hecato's position as inhumane, and it seems likely that Seneca would have agreed.

As we have seen, Seneca suggests that slaves are slaves only by chance. In contrast, Aristotle had claimed that some people lack the capacity to govern their own lives, and are therefore slaves by nature (Aristotle, *Politics* 1.5). Aristotle's thesis is compatible with the view that most of the people who are actually held as slaves ought to be free, and that some people who are actually free ought to be slaves. So Aristotle need not be understood as denying that, as things are, slaves are slaves by chance. But his argument does imply that the institution of slavery itself can be justified, provided that only those who are incapable of governing their own lives are enslaved. In contrast, Seneca offers no justification of slavery. Indeed, we might wonder whether, as a Stoic, he ought to have argued, not only that the behaviour of Roman slave-owners towards their slaves was wrong, but that the institution of slavery itself was unjust.

Certainly, Seneca was not alone in failing to argue for this conclusion. There is no clear evidence that any ancient thinker suggested that the institution of slavery ought to be abandoned. Bernard Williams argues that the Stoics accepted slavery because they held that being deprived of (legal) freedom was not itself an evil, so that slave-owners were not harming slaves by coercing them – a position that he describes as 'repulsive' (Williams, 1993, pp.115–16). This may well be an accurate account of how individual Stoics managed to avoid confronting the ethical problem of slavery. Nevertheless, it is clear that the suggestion that slaves are not harmed by their situation does not constitute a justification of slavery. If it did, then Seneca ought to argue that, because slaves are not harmed by being harshly treated, slave-owners are entitled to treat their slaves harshly. But

Seneca does not draw this conclusion: as we have seen, he condemns the behaviour of Roman slave-owners as arrogant and cruel. It was open to Seneca and other Stoics to condemn the enslavement of one person by another in just the same terms. The fact that they failed to do so is not explained by their philosophical beliefs.

Seneca on facing up to death

Perhaps the most challenging aspect of Stoic ethical theory is the Stoic attitude to bereavement and death. The Stoics assigned no more value to life than they did to wealth or reputation. According to the Stoics, life itself is not a good: what matters are the choices that you make while you are alive. As Seneca puts it: 'Life is neither a Good nor an Evil; it is simply the place where good and evil exist' (*Letters* 99.12). Conversely, the Stoics held that death is not an evil: what matters is that, when your death comes, you should die with dignity and courage. And so they believed that a wise person would neither fear his or her own death nor mourn the death of others. Stoic literature supplies a wealth of arguments and techniques designed to help Stoics to progress towards a rational attitude to bereavement and death. Seneca's *Consolations* to Marcia and Polybius, and many of his letters to Lucilius, present a range of these arguments and techniques.

What is expected of an ordinary Stoic who has lost a close friend or relative? In a letter to Lucilius, Seneca suggests that those who are making progress toward wisdom ought not to allow themselves to grieve for the dead: 'And if you cry: "One should be allowed a certain amount of grieving, ..." I reply that the "certain amount" can be too long-drawn-out, and that it will refuse to stop short when you so desire' (*Letters* 116.4).

In contrast, he suggests that a wise person who has been bereaved is permitted to weep, because such a person will be able to keep his or her grief under control. Hence, the wise person will grieve with dignity and in moderation. But those who are only making progress towards wisdom are not able to exercise this degree of self-control, and so they should not allow themselves to grieve at all (*Letters* 116.5–8; see also *Letters* 99.16–17).

When addressing those who have actually been bereaved, however, Seneca takes a softer line. He tells a friend Marullus, who has lost his young son, that it is permissible to allow ourselves to grieve, provided that we do not indulge our grief (*Letters* 99). He tells Marcia that moderate grief is permissible, warning her only against excess (Seneca, *To Marcia on Consolation* 4.1; 7.1). Only with Lucilius does he adopt a sterner position: in a letter written after the death of one of Lucilius' friends, Seneca's advice is to move on: 'You have buried one whom you loved; look about for someone to love. It is better to replace your friend than to weep for him'

(*Letters* 63.11). But this is advice that Lucilius, as an Epicurean, should himself endorse.

How, then, should those who are making progress avoid excessive grief? Seneca's method is to challenge the misconceptions that lead us to regard death as an evil. In particular, he is anxious to challenge the idea that the dead and the bereaved have been cheated of something that they had a right to expect. The dead have not been cheated of life, he argues, because they were always fated to die (*Letters* 4.9). Even when someone has died young, it is wrong to think that he or she has been treated unfairly: differences in human lifespan are insignificant when considered against the vastness of time (*Letters* 99.10). Moreover, mere length of life is not itself of any value, since a short life can be better than a long one (*Letters* 99.12–13). Nor have the bereaved been cheated of anything. Bereavement happens to everybody. We have never been given a reason to expect that we will be able to keep our loved ones with us forever. We should make the most of them while they are with us, and then let them go, just as if we are paying back a loan (*To Marcia on Consolation* 10.1–2).

In putting forward these arguments, Seneca is assuming that excessive grief is the product of faulty judgements – for example, that we or our loved ones have been unfairly singled out; that we have been deprived of something that we could expect to keep; that those who have died have lost something of real value. These arguments were not merely of theoretical significance: they were intended to achieve a real practical benefit. Indeed, as Richard Sorabji points out, Seneca sometimes favours practical efficacy over doctrinal precision: in *To Marcia on Consolation* (19.1), Seneca recommends that Marcia should practise self-deception, persuading herself that her son is not dead, but merely absent (Sorabji, 2000, p.223). This recommendation is hardly consistent with the Stoic commitment to honesty. Perhaps it is significant, though, that Seneca is not writing to Marcia as a fellow Stoic, but simply as a fellow human being in need of help.

Similar considerations are brought into play when Seneca offers advice about how to deal with the fear of one's own death. He emphasises the importance of preparing for the inevitable, by reminding ourselves how death can strike at any time, and by remembering that we are constantly in the process of dying. By preparing ourselves, he suggests, we will fortify ourselves against fear when the moment comes, but we will also remind ourselves of the importance of making the most of life while we have it (*Letters* 49). He repeatedly argues that the length of one's life is unimportant: 'At whatever point you leave off living, provided you leave off nobly, your life is a whole' (*Letters* 77.4).

As Seneca recognises, however, the prospect of one's own death raises an additional challenge: anxiety about the process of dying itself. In *Letter*

24, he addresses this issue and, in particular, the fear of meeting a violent death. This was an important ethical problem: no Stoic could claim to be free if he or she could be coerced by the threat of torture and execution. Seneca's technique, once again, is to challenge the false judgements that sustain our fears: 'Remember, ... before all else, to strip things of all that disturbs and confuses, and to see what each is at bottom; you will then comprehend that they contain nothing fearful except the actual fear' (*Letters* 24.12). He urges Lucilius to look past the horrific trappings of the torture chamber – which he compares to a mask used to frighten a child – and to see the threat for what it really is: the threat of pain, which is, after all, something familiar and bearable. Pain, he says, is endured, not only by heroes, but also by ordinary people – and not always for the best of reasons. In addition to other, more admirable examples, he cites the glutton, who braves the agonies of indigestion for the sake of a few more canapés (*Letters* 24.14). Once we accept that we cannot be threatened with anything that we cannot endure, we shall have won our freedom: 'He who has learned to die has unlearned slavery; he is above any external power, or, at any rate, he is beyond it' (*Letters* 26.10).

For Seneca, the ultimate guarantee of freedom, both from anxiety and from external constraint, is the possibility of suicide. This conception of suicide can be traced back to the death of Socrates, as it was presented by Plato in his dialogue *Phaedo*, and it was shared by other Stoics. Epictetus frequently argues that, since any difficulty can be avoided by suicide, we can never be justified in complaining that our situation is unbearable. However, Epictetus also argues that we should not be too ready to make use of this escape route. He imagines his pupils asking him why they should not commit suicide now as a means of avoiding future difficulties: his reply is that this would constitute a dereliction of duty: 'My friends, wait for god, till he shall give the signal, and release you from this service; then depart to him ... Do not depart without reason' (Epictetus, *Discourses* 1.9.16). Seneca, in contrast, rejects the suggestion that Stoic principles imply a presumption against suicide: 'our reasons [for suicide] ... need not be momentous; for neither are the reasons momentous which hold us here' (*Letters* 77.4). He explicitly denies that suicide should be thought of as deserting one's post (*Letters* 77.19–20; see also *Letters* 70.14).

Elsewhere, however, Seneca says that he does not hold that it is permissible to commit suicide for any reason or under any circumstances. He says that to commit suicide simply to avoid pain is cowardly, but that it is right to end your life when pain prevents you from doing the things that are your reasons for living (*Letters* 58.36). In another letter, he explains that he is under an obligation to go on living, despite his ill health, because of the respect he owes to the (admittedly irrational) feelings of his wife Paulina

(*Letters* 104.3). Here, he takes a rather gentler line than Epictetus, who states that, in choosing when to die, one should not take into consideration the irrational emotions of one's friends and relatives (*Discourses* 2.16.40).

In CE 65, Seneca did kill himself, although not because of ill health (Figure 7.2). He had become implicated in a major conspiracy against Nero and was ordered to commit suicide. Tacitus gives a detailed account of Seneca's last hours, and portrays his demeanour as a model of Stoic resolution. He presents Seneca as ordering his friends not to weep, reminding them that they should have been prepared for this turn of events, but as entreating Paulina only to set a term to her grief. He describes the dignity with which Seneca endured a painful and lingering end (*Annals* 15.60–65). As Tacitus presents it, Seneca's death perfectly exemplifies the philosophical principles that he took to govern his life.

Figure 7.2   Luca Giordano (1632–1705), *The Death of Seneca*, oil on canvas. © Bolton Museum and Art Gallery, Lancashire, UK/Bridgeman Art Library.

Further reading

Seneca's philosophical works are accessible and easy to read. Most relevant to the issues discussed here are *On the Happy Life, On the Brevity of Life, On Tranquillity of Mind* and the *Letters*. For an excellent and detailed study of Seneca's life and his views on a range of philosophical issues, see Miriam

Griffin's *Seneca: A Philosopher in Politics* (1992). For an account of Epictetus' life and works, see Anthony Long, *Epictetus: A Stoic and Socratic Guide to Life* (2002). For another attack on the luxurious habits of Romans, see the portrayal of the dinner with Trimalchio in the *Satyricon* by the satirist Petronius: although very different in its approach, Petronius' work introduces similar themes, including the effect on slaves.

There are a number of good introductions to Stoicism and other ancient philosophical schools. John Rist's *Stoic Philosophy* (1969) provides an accessible overview of Stoic theory, while Robert Sharples, *Stoics, Epicureans and Sceptics: An Introduction to Hellenistic Philosophy* (1996) contrasts the views of three different schools in an engaging and illuminating way. More detailed discussions of Stoic philosophy can be found in Julia Annas, *The Morality of Happiness* (1993); Martha Nussbaum, *The Therapy of Desire* (1994); and Gisela Striker, 'Following nature: a study in Stoic ethics', in *Essays on Hellenistic Epistemology and Ethics* (1996).

Bibliography

Ancient sources

Aristotle, *Nicomachean Ethics*, in Ross, D. (trans.) (1925) Aristotle: *Nicomachean Ethics*, Oxford: Oxford University Press.

Aristotle, *Politics*, in Barker, E. and Stalley, R.F. (trans.) (1995) Aristotle: *Politics*, Oxford: Oxford University Press.

Cicero *On Duties*, in Griffin, M. and Atkins, M. (eds) (1991) Cicero: *On Duties*, Cambridge: Cambridge University Press.

Epictetus, *Discourses*, in Gill, C. (ed.) (1995) Epictetus: *Discourses*, translation revised by R. Hard, London: Everyman.

Epicurus, *Letter to Menoeceus*, in O'Connor, E. (trans.) (1993) *The Essential Epicurus: Letters, Principle Doctrines, Vatican Sayings, and Fragments*, New York: Prometheus Books.

Petronius, *Satyricon*, in Walsh, P.G. (trans.) (1999) Petronius: *The Satyricon*, Oxford: Oxford University Press.

Plato, *Phaedo*, in Gallop, D. (trans.) (1999) Plato: *Phaedo*, Oxford: Oxford University Press.

Plutarch, *Brutus*, in Perrin, B. (trans.) (1989) Plutarch: *Lives*, Cambridge, MA: Harvard University Press.

Plutarch, *Cato the Elder*, in Perrin, B. (trans.) (1989) Plutarch: *Lives*, Cambridge, MA: Harvard University Press.

Plutarch, *Cato the Younger*, in Perrin, B. (trans.) (1989) Plutarch: *Lives*, Cambridge, MA: Harvard University Press.

Plutarch, *On Stoic Self-contradictions*, in Cherniss, H. (trans.) (1976) *Moralia XIII, Part 2: Stoic Essays*, Cambridge, MA: Harvard University Press.

Seneca, *Letters to Lucilius*, in Gunmere, R.M. (trans.) (1917) Seneca: *Epistles 1–65*, vol.I, Cambridge, MA: Harvard University Press.

Seneca, *Letters to Lucilius*, in Gunmere, R.M. (trans.) (1920) Seneca: *Epistles 66–92*, vol.II, Cambridge, MA: Harvard University Press.

Seneca, *Letters to Lucilius*, in Gunmere, R.M. (trans.) (1925) Seneca: *Epistles 93–124*, vol.III, Cambridge, MA: Harvard University Press.

Seneca, *On Anger*, in Cooper, J.M. and Procopé, J.F. (trans.) (1995) Seneca: *Moral and Political Essays*, Cambridge: Cambridge University Press.

Seneca, *On the Brevity of Life*, in Basore, J.W. (trans.) (1932) Seneca: *Moral Essays* vol.II, Cambridge, MA: Harvard University Press.

Seneca, *On Favours*, in Cooper, J.M. and Procopé, J.F. (trans.) (1995) Seneca: *Moral and Political Essays*, Cambridge: Cambridge University Press.

Seneca, *On the Happy Life*, in Basore, J.W. (trans.) (1932) Seneca: *Moral Essays*, vol.II, London: Harvard University Press.

Seneca, *On Mercy*, in Cooper, J.M. and Procopé, J.F. (eds) (1995) Seneca: *Moral and Political Essays*, Cambridge: Cambridge University Press.

Seneca, *On Tranquillity of Mind*, in Basore, J.W. (trans.) (1932) Seneca: *Moral Essays*, vol.II, London: Harvard University Press.

Seneca, *To Helvia on Consolation*, in Basore, J.W. (trans.) (1932) Seneca: *Moral Essays*, vol.II, Cambridge, MA: Harvard University Press.

Seneca, *To Marcia on Consolation*, in Basore, J.W. (trans.) (1932) Seneca: *Moral Essays*, vol.II, London: Harvard University Press.

Seneca, *To Polybius on Consolation*, in Basore, J.W. (trans.) (1932) Seneca: *Moral Essays*, vol.II, Cambridge, MA: Harvard University Press.

Sextus Empiricus, *Outlines of Pyrrhonism*, in Long, A.A. and Sedley, D.N. (1987) *The Hellenistic Philosophers*, vol.1, Cambridge: Cambridge University Press.

Stobaeus, *Anthologium*, in Long, A.A. and Sedley, D.N. (1987) *The Hellenistic Philosophers*, vol.1, Cambridge: Cambridge University Press.

Tacitus, *Annals*, in Grant, M. (trans.) (1956) *Tacitus: The Annals of Imperial Rome*, London: Penguin.

Tacitus, *Dialogue on Oratory*, in Hutton, M., Peterson, W., Ogilvie, R.M., Warmington, E.H. and Winterbottom, M. (trans.) (1914) Tacitus: *Agricola. Germania. Dialogue on Oratory*, Cambridge, MA: Harvard University Press.

Modern scholarship

Annas, J. (1993) *The Morality of Happiness*, Oxford: Oxford University Press.

Griffin, M. (1989) 'Philosophy, politics and politicians at Rome', in *Philosophia Togata I: Essays on Philosophy and Roman Society*, Oxford: Oxford University Press, pp.1–37.

Griffin, M. (1992) *Seneca: A Philosopher in Politics*, Oxford: Clarendon Press.

Long, A.A. (2002) *Epictetus: A Stoic and Socratic Guide to Life*, Oxford: Oxford University Press.

Nussbaum, M. (1994) *The Therapy of Desire*, Princeton: Princeton University Press.

Rist, J.M. (1969) *Stoic Philosophy*, Cambridge: Cambridge University Press.

Sharples, R.W. (1996) *Stoics, Epicureans and Sceptics: An Introduction to Hellenistic Philosophy*, London and New York: Routledge.

Sorabji, R. (2000) *Emotion and Peace of Mind: From Stoic Agitation to Christian Temptation*, Oxford: Oxford University Press.

Striker, G. (1996) 'Following nature: a study in Stoic ethics', in *Essays on Hellenistic Epistemology and Ethics*, Cambridge: Cambridge University Press, pp.221–80.

Williams, B. (1993) *Shame and Necessity*, Berkeley: University of California Press.

Essay Eight

The Roman child

Valerie Hope

Introduction

> It is extremely important that children should be brought up properly from the start, although training them is no easy matter ... Freedom that is unrestricted results in a character that is unbearable; total restriction leads to a servile character. A child will be encouraged to gain self-confidence by being praised; on the other hand too much praise makes him over-confident and irascible. We should follow the mean in bringing up children: sometimes the child must be held back, sometimes encouraged. He should not be humiliated or subjected to servile treatment. He must not be allowed to cry and ask for rewards, nor should such behaviour gain him anything; rewards should be given only if he has been good, or promises to be good.
>
> (Seneca, *On Anger* 2.21.1–6; in Gardner and Wiedemann, 1991, n.134)

Seneca wrote his advice in the first century CE, but his comments on childcare would strike a chord with many modern readers accustomed to self-help literature that aims to make them better parents. Some of the issues that Seneca raises, such as the balance between indulgence and discipline (spare the rod and spoil the child) are continuing ones, as is the reality that proffering good advice is easier than following it! The childless Seneca offers guidance, in writing a treatise on self-control and anger, on how to produce a good Roman citizen: how to discipline, socialise and train the (male) child ready for the adult world of the élite and wealthy. The ideal he promotes would not have been accessible or relevant to all Roman children or parents.

This essay aims to explore attitudes towards children and childhood in the Roman world. This is not a straightforward topic, because accessing children through the surviving ancient sources can be difficult. Our perspective is one-sided, providing us with the adult viewpoint of the child and not the child's view of either childhood or adults. This situation is hardly surprising, but it needs to be constantly kept in mind. It is also difficult to distance ourselves from our own cultural assumptions. The modern western world is child oriented. Increasing emphasis is placed on children's rights and the mistreatment and exploitation of children are condemned. Roman attitudes towards children may at times seem similar and familiar when viewed from a modern perspective, yet at others alien, distant and even shocking. This has led some people to highlight a seeming indifference and ambivalence to children in the Roman world. But as this essay will explore, we need to be conscious of the possibility of differing expectations for children and childhood and thus be careful not to make value judgements.

An emperor's childhood

In CE 37, Agrippina the Younger, the great grand-daughter of the first emperor Augustus, gave birth to a baby boy, the future emperor Nero. The breach birth was not easy and was accompanied by ominous portents. Even the baby's father joked that any child born to himself and Agrippina would have an unpleasant nature and be a risk to the public. The child's early years were unstable. Agrippina was banished from Rome by her brother, the emperor Gaius, and not long afterwards her husband died and Nero lost his inheritance and was placed under the care of his aunt, who chose a dancer and a barber to be his tutors. On the succession of the emperor Claudius, Agrippina was recalled from exile and later married the aged emperor. Nero was then educated by two freedmen, and from the age of 12 onwards he was taught oratory by the greatest speaker of the day, Seneca. Over the following years, Nero was prepared for a public career. Despite the existence of a natural son to Claudius, known as Britannicus, Agrippina's son was being groomed and favoured for the succession. Nero was at the centre of his mother's ambitions. On being warned that her son would ultimately murder her, Agrippina responded by saying, 'Let him kill as long as he rules'. Claudius adopted Nero in CE 50 and betrothed him to his daughter Octavia, whom he married in CE 53. In CE 54, the emperor Claudius died, allegedly at the hands of Agrippina. The seventeen-year-old Nero was now emperor. During the early years of his reign, he remained under the influence of his mother and Seneca, and this time was seen as a 'Golden Age'. But as the boy turned into a man he gradually shook off his restraints. Seneca was banished, Agrippina murdered and Britannicus disposed of. Nero's reign degenerated into tyranny and extravagance. There were rumours that he even wandered the streets at night in disguise, mugging his subjects for fun. So much for Seneca's advice on how to bring up a child (see above)! The boy had become an emperor of the worst sort (Suetonius, *Nero*; Tacitus, *Annals* 12–16; Cassius Dio, 60–1).

We could tell numerous other stories of the disjointed early experiences of members of the imperial household. How Julia, the only child of the emperor Augustus, was brought up to be a model of Roman virtue, and then, after being repeatedly married off to beget her father a male heir, was exiled for her immoral behaviour. Or the difficult early years of the future emperor Claudius, who was mocked and ignored because of his physical weakness and deformity. But what does the story of Nero's childhood, and those of other imperial children, reveal about Roman childhood in general? To a modern eye it seems unsurprising that Nero and Julia rebelled: they turned out the way they did because of how they were treated during their childhood and youth. Indeed, the description of the early life of Nero highlights many negative factors in his upbringing such as separation from his parents, a poor choice in early carers and manipulation by his mother. Throughout his youth, Nero was a political pawn to be manoeuvred rather than a child to be loved. However, any close analysis of Nero's childhood soon hits difficulties, since we only know as much or as little as we are told. The main literary sources for Nero's reign are Tacitus, Suetonius and Cassius Dio, all of whom wrote some time after the events they were describing and with their own political agendas in mind. These authors knew the end of Nero's life as well, if not better, than his beginnings; they knew the sort of emperor he would become (or allegedly become) and this hindsight coloured how they represented his youth. Portraits (Figure 8.1) and coin depictions may complement our image of Nero the boy, and capture a sense of innocence lacking in the literary descriptions, but these too were designed with a purpose in mind, that is, to promote and idealise the imperial family. In short, the evidence for Nero's early years suggests some of the factors and influences that affected the childhood of the élite: how children could be manipulated and exploited by adults or be forced to form bonds with their carers rather than their parents. Yet in the end we cannot fully recreate Nero's experiences and feelings as a boy, nor can we equate his childhood to that of the bulk of the population, most of whom were not members of the privileged and powerful élite.

The voice of the child

We do not have the voice of Nero as a child. Indeed, Roman children in general have not left us their voices. The evidence we have is mediated by adults. It is adults who write about children, or commemorate them in inscriptions or make their toys. What we know of children comes from the adult world and, as with much evidence for the Roman period, often reflects the interests and tastes of men rather than women. Many of these men would have had little to do with day-to-day childcare or any extensive interaction with young children, but nevertheless they would have made many fundamental decisions that affected children's lives. Rarely do we gain access to the perspective of mothers, grandmothers and nurses without a male filter. Equally, much of our evidence, especially in terms of literature and art, reflects the narrow social band of the wealthy urban freeborn élite. We learn little of poor children, rural children or slave children and yet we

Essay Eight The Roman child

Figure 8.1 Togate statue of the Young Nero (CE 37–68) Roman, CE c.50 (marble). © The Detroit Institute of Arts, USA, Founders Society Purchase/Bridgeman Art Library.

need to acknowledge that a child's experience of childhood would have been dictated by the socio-economic standing and political status of his or her parents.

Despite these drawbacks, we nevertheless have a range of evidence to draw upon: literature in all its forms; artistic representations such as relief carvings and statues of children; epitaphs and other inscriptions that name children; and material objects such as toys and dolls. All these sources need to be handled with a constant awareness of their original context, purpose and audience. Epitaphs, for example, name thousands of dead children from a comparatively wide social range, but we need to be conscious of who was setting up the epitaphs, who was intended to read them and the extent to which the medium was constrained by convention and chronological and geographic factors. We also need to be aware that the evidence tends to idealise, that it often promotes what was expected rather than what necessarily was. Thus, legal texts may emphasise the extent of a father's powers when these powers were little exercised in reality; funerary portraits of children may exaggerate their maturity to promote the children's potential as the adults they will never become; epitaphs record the poignant deaths of children but use a language of commonplace conventions and clichés. People often said and did what was expected rather than what was actually felt.

The available evidence is in many ways rich and enlightening provided that we are aware of its original purpose and partial and incomplete nature. People rarely wrote explicitly or systematically about matters such as the stages of childhood or details of the education system and thus we often have to piece together a picture by bringing together scattered literary references and material evidence. Inevitably, some questions remain unanswered. There is also a danger, as with much social history, of creating a composite picture, throwing together differing bits and pieces of evidence, from differing places and times, to create an overall impression that has no real chronological specificity. The Roman period spanned several centuries and Roman power spread across a vast area. For the purposes of this essay the focus is limited mainly to the city of Rome during the late republic and the first two centuries of the imperial period, a place and period particularly rich in evidence. Yet we need to remember that both adults and children's experiences of and attitudes towards childhood may not have been static in space and time.

The Roman world is not unique in these problems of evidence and its interpretation. We need to remember that children's rights and legalised protection are relatively recent phenomena in the West. In the pre-modern age, children's voices were rarely audible. For many periods, as for the one we are considering, we only gain access to children through materials created for and by adults, and it can be difficult to reconstruct childhood from this indirect evidence. This lack of evidence and apparent disinterest in children led Philippe Ariès to suggest, in the 1960s, that the very idea of childhood as a separate stage of human life was a modern development (Ariès, 1962). This assertion has been disputed (see below), but it remains true to say that interest in children's history is a relatively recent trend. The rise in interest in the Roman child (and children of other periods) mirrors the rise in concern for the protection, education and rights of the modern child. It also reflects a growing interest in retrieving and reconstructing the history of social groups who, on the surface at least, are not well represented in the surviving evidence: an interest in giving voice to the silent as opposed to always listening to the most vociferous.

Defining the child

In Latin there was no specific word for baby. *Infans*, which literally means 'non-speaking', was not confined in use to infants. The word *liber*, meaning 'freeborn Roman citizen child', could be used for offspring of any age, as could the words for 'son' (*filius*) and 'daughter' (*filia*). The words for 'boys' (*pueri*) and 'girls' (*puellae*) did in general denote children, but beyond this there is a certain linguistic imprecision in describing children and the differing stages of childhood (see Dixon, 1992, p.104; Harlow and Laurence, 2002, pp.36–7). Does this suggest that, in the Roman world, childhood, as has been argued for other periods, was not an acknowledged stage?

Other evidence does suggest that childhood was differentiated from adulthood in ancient Rome, at least for the freeborn. Rites of passage marked the acceptance of the baby into the family and the transition of the adolescent into the adult world. The newborn baby was accepted (or rejected) by its father with the instruction to give it the breast and possibly by being lifted from the ground in a ritual symbolising that the child was to be raised (Suetonius, *Nero* 6; Soranus, *Gynaecology* 10; Corbier, 2001; Dixon, 1988, pp.237–40). Eight days after the birth of a girl and nine days after the birth of a boy a purification rite (*dies lustricus*) was held, with a party for family and friends (Rawson, 2003, pp.110–11). On this occasion, the child was named and given a special protective necklace known as the *bulla* (protective necklace worn during childhood; Figure 8.2). At puberty, a boy underwent a ceremony when he set aside the *bulla* and donned the *toga virilis* ('toga of manhood'). This was usually held before his seventeenth birthday (see, for example, Pliny, *Letters* 1.9). There was no equivalent ceremony for a girl, but her first marriage might be accompanied by a ceremonial putting away of toys.

Literature and imagery also represent children as children, acknowledging their diminutive stature, capturing childish gestures and elements of play. Catullus pictures a young baby in its mother's arms, stretching out its hands and smiling at the father (Catullus 61.209–13). Martial, in remembering the dead child Erotion, recalls her play, chatter and childish lisp (Martial, *Epigrams* 5.34). Cicero and Pliny, in their letters, speak of children with affection (for references see Wiedemann, 1989, pp.84–93). Fronto takes clear delight in watching his young grandson and seeing himself in the child:

> He shows some signs of his grandfather's character as well: he is particularly greedy for grapes. That was the first solid food he sucked

Figure 8.2 Relief of the Servilii family, Rome, 30–20 BCE. The son, Publius Servilius Globulus, is shown separated from his parents by a pillar. His freeborn status is indicated in his name by the letters Q.F, revealing that he is the son (*filius*) of Quintus, and by the *bulla* around his neck. His parents have an L for *libertus/liberta* in their names indicating that they were freed slaves. (Photo: Vatican Museums)

Figure 8.3 Relief from the sarcophagus of Marcus Cornelius Statius depicting scenes from the life of a child (marble), Roman, second century. CE Louvre, Paris, France/Bridgeman Art Library. The relief shows a child being fed at the breast, held by his father, playing with a miniature chariot pulled by a ram, and practising his lessons.

down, and almost for entire days he kept licking at a grape or kissing it with his lips or biting it with his gums or playing with it. He is also particularly keen on little birds: he loves young chicks, pigeons and sparrows. I have often heard from those who were once my own tutors or teachers that right from my earliest childhood, I too was enthralled by these birds.

(Fronto, *Letters to his Friends* 1.12; in Gardner and Wiedemann, 1991, n.129)

Children are described enjoying games, sports, riddles, stories and building sandcastles, and they had dolls, rattles, tops and other toys (for references, see Wiedemann, 1989, pp.145–53; Harlow and Laurence, 2002, pp.46–7; Rawson, 2003, pp.126–30). Images of children show them at play, with toys and pet animals (Figure 8.3) and can emphasise diminutive stature and childish facial features (Figures 8.1–8.4; Bradley, 1998; Rawson, 1997; Rawson, 2003).

The law also sought to define childhood, incorporating age definitions of criminal and financial responsibility. These parameters were often aimed

Figure 8.4 Tombstone of Petronia Grata, first half of the first century CE, Museo Archeologico, Acqui Terme. The relief is an adaptation of the common scene of Aeneas carrying his father and leading his son by the hand. In this case the relief was chosen to express the *pietas* of the deceased and bonds between the living and the dead. Note how the child appears here as a girl, perhaps reflecting the personalisation of the myth by the dedicator Petronia Grata, a freedwoman who set up the stone for herself and her mother. (Used with the permission of the Ministero per i Beni e le Attività Culturali – Archivo della Soprintendenza per i Beni Archeologici del Piemonte)

more at protecting property than the child, but they still give insights into ideas concerning maturity and independence. Most notable is the need for a guardian (*tutor*) if the child's father died. Under seven years of age, a child was too young to deal with matters regarding property and business. As the child grew, it was allowed gradually to assume some responsibility until reaching puberty. After this age a *tutor* was no longer essential for a boy, but the boy was not regarded as fully competent until 25 years of age. Until this time, adult supervision of transactions was still advisable (for discussion of relevant legal texts, see Saller, 1994, pp.181–3). Girls never obtained complete independence, in theory at least, from a male, whether father, husband or *tutor*.

So rituals, literature, art and the law all suggest that in some contexts at least adults did define childhood as a separate status and life stage from adulthood. Childhood was viewed as the period from birth to puberty, the latter was legally defined as 12 for girls and 14 for boys (Gaius, *Institutes* 1.196). In reality the end of childhood was more fluid and staggered. For most girls marriage marked the end of childhood and the girls' departure from the parental home. Some faced marriage in their early teens but others may have remained single and thus at home for longer (Shaw, 1987; Saller, 1987). For a boy childhood moved into adolescence with increasing freedoms and responsibilities, but still with watchful adult supervision since the boy was not regarded as fully adult until his mid-twenties (Saller,1987; Harlow and Laurence, 2002, pp.65–78). Adult control was not easily relinquished: in terms of the law, offspring remained under their father's power and authority (*potestas*) until his death, regardless of their age.

Adult expectations

We can say little about what a child's experience of childhood was like but we can explore an adult's expectations for children, and it is always worth remembering that these adults had themselves once been children. We need to emphasise yet again how socio-economic reality shaped each child's fortune, prospects and experiences. The slave child, the child of the poor urban dweller and the child of the senator would have very different childhood experiences, some may have had little real childhood at all. Our knowledge is mostly coloured by the experiences and expectations of the well to do. Another consideration is time. Across the centuries of the Roman period attitudes, or at least the representation of attitudes, toward children and family life may have changed. This essay mainly draws on evidence from the late republic and early empire, a period which some have characterised as one of increasing sentimental attachment to children and families, at least among the literary élite (Dixon, 1991; Rawson, 2003, pp.4–9). However, the patchy nature of evidence from earlier periods makes it difficult to trace any changes in attitude with certainty, even if we can note that the idealisation of family life was particularly celebrated at certain times.

Many adults may have viewed their children as an investment for the future: a support and comfort in old age, someone to provide and care for them and add to the economic resources of the family. For the rich this was tied to continuity of the family name and family prestige. Children conveyed a sense of posterity and even immortality. On a practical level a child would provide proper burial and commemoration for a parent, and by his or her continuing life a sense of continuity for the individual and the family (Dixon, 1988, pp.23–4). Dio, writing in the second century CE, summarises these 'joys of parenthood' in a speech he attributes to the emperor Augustus, who was attempting to promote the family through legislation:

> How can it be anything but a pleasure to raise up from the ground a child who has been born from the two of you and to feed and educate it, a physical and mental mirror of yourself, so that, as it grows up, another self is created? Is it anything but the greatest blessing to leave behind as our successor when we leave this life an heir both to our family and to our property; one who is our own, born of our own essence, so that only the mortal part of us passes away, while we live on in the child who succeeds us, so that you will not fall into the hands of strangers and suffer an extinction as total as in warfare?
>
> (Cassius Dio 56.3; in Gardner and Wiedemann, 1991, n.110)

Parents cared for children when they were young and helpless. The child was perceived as weak and vulnerable and was characterised as irrational and lacking judgement (Wiedemann, 1989, pp.17–25), hence the need for training and discipline as suggested by Seneca (see above). In return, parents expected respect and obedience and, in addition, that their adult children would care for them when they were elderly. Parents and children were tied by the virtue of *pietas* – a reciprocal relationship of duty and also affection (Saller, 1991; Saller, 1994, pp.102–14). *Pietas* bound both parents and children to care for each other when there was need. It was epitomised by Aeneas, the founder of Rome, and his relationship with his father and son (Virgil, *Aeneid* 2.709–28). As Troy fell, Aeneas carried his elderly father on his back and led his young son by the hand (Figure 8.4).

Children, however, may not always have been viewed as a blessing or a worthwhile future investment. For the poor, a child could represent a substantial drain on resources, and some children may have been abandoned for this reason (see below). To choose to rear the child was a commitment from which the parent (or owner) looked for a return. Part of this return was the prospect that the child would bring future economic security in the parents' old age. However, some children produced income before they reached adulthood. From an early age children may have worked in agriculture or have been apprenticed to a trade. Apprentice contracts from Egypt suggest that children were sent to learn trades in the pre or early teen years (Bradley, 1991, pp.103–24). Even prior to this, more basic unskilled labour or work at home was probably a reality for many (Wiedemann, 1989, pp.154–5), especially slave children. Other children, if not put to work, were exploited to further the political and familial ambitions and connections of their parents; while the most unfortunate were physically and sexually abused at the hands of their masters.

If this suggests that the child was little more than a tool of the parents (or controlling adult) we need to remind ourselves of the harsh realities of the ancient world. Life was tough and short and children had to grow up fast. Adults were in control. In a patriarchal society the rights of the father (and master) were enshrined in the law and there was little state intervention in familial matters. A father had, in theory, absolute control over his children. They remained under his power or *potestas* until his death. Indeed, if the father's own father was alive he was under his control and his children were in the *potestas* of their grandfather. A father could choose to abandon his child, to beat it, to kill it (Dionysius of Halicarnassus, *History of Rome* 2.26). However, the letter of the law was probably rarely followed. Literary and legal evidence suggests that the father's right to execute his child came increasingly to be viewed as unnatural and extreme (Valerius Maximus 5.8; Seneca, *On Clemency* 1.15) and although beatings from parents were expected they were not to be taken to extreme and were intended to discipline rather than to humiliate (Saller, 1991; Saller, 1994, pp.114–30; 133–53; Eyben, 1991). A beating from a teacher may have been more severe (Martial, *Epigrams* 9.68; Suetonius, *Otho* 2.1; Horace, *Letters* 2.1.70).

The father's authority may have been dominant but it was in his and the family's interests for the child to thrive and survive. Adults often praised children for their maturity, for showing adult-like qualities (sometimes called the *puer senex* ('boy–old man') motif; Carp, 1980; Dixon, 1992, p.105). This suggests that parents were eager for their children to grow up, to survive the high mortality of childhood and to exhibit the qualities and skills that were required of them from an early age. Quintilian, an orator of the first century CE, recorded the death of both of his sons and emphasises their maturity. He lost his first son at the age of five, yet the boy was already demonstrating a calm and powerful mind and signs of promise. The second son, 'little Quintilian', who died at the age of nine, displayed talent, application, humanity, generosity, courage, dignity and bravery (Quintilian, *Institutes of Oratory* 6, Prologue 10–12). Pliny the Younger in describing the death of Minicia Marcella, the daughter of his friend Fundanus, praises the girl for both child-like qualities and maturity:

> She had not yet completed her fourteenth year, yet she had the prudence of an old lady; the bearing of a matron, yet kept a girl's sweetness and the modesty of an unmarried woman. How she used to hang from her father's neck! How lovingly and modestly she embraced us as her father's friends! How she used to love her nurses, her child-minders and teachers as was appropriate to the status of each of them! How rarely and with what restraint would she go and play! With how much self-control, patience and constancy did she bear her final illness!
> (Pliny, *Letters* 5.16; in Gardner and Wiedemann, 1991, n.130)[1]

These losses were sharply felt and the children are characterised as not having fulfilled their potential. 'Little Quintilian' had his public career in sight and Minicia Marcella was about to be married. They had almost made it to adulthood and although still children are praised for maturity beyond their years. For the poor, early maturity may have been a necessity rather than a rhetorical parental aspiration. But rich or poor children were expected to learn skills and tasks appropriate to their stations in life, to prepare for their adult roles.

Parents placed their hopes in their children, some of which may have been motivated by self-interest. But for many parents this was not incompatible with the child's own happiness. Further, some may have wished that their child would have a better life than they themselves: investing in the child would bring the child as well as its parents success and prosperity. The poet Horace's father, a freed slave, invested in his son's education at great personal expense and even acted as his son's chaperone. Horace in his poetry provides an idealised view of his father's role:

> Instead he courageously took his boy to Rome, to be taught the accomplishments which any knight or senator would have his own progeny taught. Anyone who noticed my clothes and the servants in attendance (a feature of city life) would have assumed that the money for these items came from the family coffers. My father himself was the most trustworthy guardian imaginable, accompanying me to all my classes.
> (Horace, *Satire* 1.6.77–82; in Rudd, 1973, p.69)

---

[1] An epitaph to a child of the same name suggests that she was not yet 13 years, rather than almost 14 as recorded by Pliny. For Pliny her suggested age serves his rhetorical purpose of emphasising the poignancy of the death of a girl on the point of adulthood and marriage (Bodel, 1995).

The next generation may have had a particular importance for freed slaves. The children of these men and women were born free and represented the beginnings of a new citizen family. Freed slaves often celebrated their new identity and their future hopes as enshrined in their children in grave reliefs, even when the full potential of these hopes had been dashed by death (Figure 8.2).

Indeed, even if many adults did take a pragmatic view of their children's future, we can also find evidence for sentimental attitudes towards children. Children were appreciated for being just children – the cute baby, the charming prattle of the toddler, the joy of play (see above). Children did have toys, they did play games, they did go to school. The ideal existed of the happy family unit, mum, dad and the kids living together happily and lovingly (Dixon, 1991). This ideal may have often been thwarted by the early deaths of both parents and children and complicated by divorce and serial marriage (Bradley, 1991, pp.25–176). Parents did view their children as prospects for the future and when these hopes were dashed they wept for their own loss as well as the child's. Despite high child mortality (see below) it was still seen as a reversal of the laws of nature for a parent to bury a child. Epitaphs might contain standardised expressions such as 'the father did for the son what a son should have done for his father' (Lattimore, 1942, pp.187–92). This may reflect self-interest on the part of the parent, a concern for who will now take care of their burial, but this does not mean that there was no genuine grief. Thousands of other epitaphs, although phrased conventionally and saying what was expected, still suggest heartfelt losses (King, 2000). Maybe relationships were coloured by pragmatism, but did this stop love and affection or genuine delight in parenting?

Caring for the child

A child's world is shaped by adults. In the modern West parents play a pivotal role and that of the mother is especially idealised. But other adults play a part in shaping the child's life; teachers, nannies, childminders, grandparents and other family members have a role to play in influencing, educating and caring for children. In ancient Rome the parental role was also idealised. Cato the Elder, a statesman of the second century BCE, was singled out for the treatment of his son. He was not adverse to changing nappies and bathing the baby and later took responsibility for the boy's education:

> Cato himself says that he did not think it right for his son to be disciplined by a slave, to have his ears pulled by a slave for being tardy at his lessons, or to owe such a valuable asset as education to a slave. Cato himself taught him letters, taught him the laws and taught him

athletics. He instructed him in how to throw a spear, fight in armour, to ride on horseback and to box; he also taught him to endure heat and cold, and to swim through whirlpools and river-rapids. He says that he wrote the book entitled the 'Histories' in his own hand and in large letters to enable his son to learn the laws and customs of Rome at home. And he was as careful to avoid saying anything inappropriate in his son's presence as in that of a vestal virgin.

(Plutarch, *Cato the Elder* 20; in Gardner and Wiedemann, 1991, n.118)

Cato's alleged behaviour is highlighted because it was not the norm in his or in Plutarch's (second century CE) day. The reality was that adults other than the parents were frequently employed in varied childcare roles. Note the various carers and adults that were present during the emperor Nero's childhood. Babies were fed by wet-nurses (*nutrices*, sing. *nutrix*), who often became nannies; male attendants (*paedagogi*, sing. *paedagogus*) tutored and chaperoned young children and teenagers (Bradley, 1991). The child's education was also placed in the hands of others. The responsibility for teaching children rested with the head of the household, the *paterfamilias*. The latter needed to ensure that the child was equipped with the skills required for adult life whether the child was freeborn or slave. For a slave, this would mean work or an apprenticeship; for the well-to-do freeborn male, a sound education in areas relevant to public life, such as oratory; for the freeborn female, preparation for a suitable marriage. Cato taught his son himself, but most fathers probably contented themselves by trying to be positive role models and employing teachers to do the rest. The élite were often educated at home, but schools also existed (for education, see Rawson, 2003, pp.146–209; Wiedemann, 1989, pp.143–75).

So why did parents use these childcarers and teachers, many of whom were slaves? The fact that people were wealthy and could afford carers to do the tasks for which they did not have time or inclination must have been true of many living in a slave society. Early mortality is another factor and left many children bereft of mothers and fathers and in need of alternative care. For the élite and wealthy, divorce and remarriage could also create complex family structures and slave childminders may have provided stability (Bradley, 1991, pp.55–61). Yet the use of childcare was not restricted to the wealthy; for the poor who needed to work, help with children may have been essential. Equally, slave owners might provide childcarers and teachers for their slaves to allow the continuing productivity and usefulness of the parents, plus we should not forget that a well-trained slave child was the property of the master and thus an asset (Bradley, 1991, p.62).

What impact the use of a range of childcarers had upon the child is difficult to gauge and no doubt depended on the quality of care provided by those involved, which in turn must have often been related to the socio-economic status of the child and its parents. Some medically recommended advice, such as not giving colostrum to babies and the use of swaddling clothes, may have done more harm than good, but was well intentioned whether the choice of parent or nurse (Garnsey, 1991, pp.56–8). The use of servile carers did engender debate – was this the best option, should a child be brought up by a slave? Note Cato's alleged comments about servile carers as quoted above and a reference by the doctor Soranus that children drank in some of the character of a nurse with their milk (Soranus, *Gynaecology* 1.19–20). But these musings seem to have made little real impact on practice (Harlow and Laurence, 2002, p.43). The child could develop close relations with its carers, especially the nurse (Figure 8.5). Pliny notes

Figure 8.5   Two sides of what was probably a funeral stele of a professional child-nurse, late third century CE, Römisch-Germanisches Museum, Cologne. The nurse (*nutrix*) named as Anna Severina is depicted nursing and caring for her young charge. The monument may have been set up by the child's family. (There is an alternative theory that Anna Severina was a divinity who protected children.)

how Minicia Marcella was fond of her nurses and other carers (see above). Pliny provided his own nurse with a farm and thus an income (*Letters* 6.3). The emperor Nero's nurses helped to dispose of his body following his suicide and the emperor Domitian's nurse buried his body after he was assassinated (Suetonius, *Nero* 50; *Domitian* 17). The *paedagogus* could also inspire respect and affection, although Martial in tongue-in-cheek fashion complains forcefully about the interference of his into his adolescence, suggesting that the relationship could change as the child matured (Martial, *Epigrams* 11.39; compare Fronto, *Letters* 2.124). Indeed, Cicero suggests, when stressing the social differences between child and carers, that intimacy between the two should be confined to childhood. True friendships are formed by the adult (Cicero, *On Friendship* 1.1.4–5). The carers of one's childhood might be thought of with affection, and even respect, but they were not social equals.

What impact did the use of childcarers have on the parents' relationship with their children? One suggestion is that the use of childcarers could distance parents both physically and emotionally from their young children (for discussion, see Bradley, 1991). Once the child was nearing adulthood, it would demand greater parental attention. Does this suggest that the parents were more interested in the adult child rather than in the young child? Did the emphasis fall solely on training the child in preparation for the benefits it would give its parents as an adult rather than fostering sentimental attachment to young children?

The impact of early death

Were many Roman parents indifferent to their children? Lawrence Stone has argued that parents in earlier pre-modern periods did not invest too heavily emotionally in children who might die (Stone, 1977, p.70). Children may have been distanced from their parents, childhood barely recognised and children treated at best indifferently, at worst cruelly. Arguments for and against this position are often termed the 'indifference debate' (for summaries of this debate, see Dixon, 1992, p.99; Harlow and Laurence, 2002, p.35). For Rome certain factors may suggest that parents could be isolated, indifferent, and at times even cruel, to their children.

Certainly we need to be aware of high mortality and its impact. It is difficult to establish exact demographic figures for life expectancy and mortality rates since there are no conveniently recorded reliable statistics. However, it is possible to make analogies with comparative evidence from other pre-industrial societies. This suggests that average life expectancy was somewhere in the region of 25 years, which means that although many people lived well beyond this age many others died before it (see, in particular, Parkin, 1992; Saller, 1994; Harlow and Laurence, 2002).

Newborn babies and those under one year old must have been particularly vulnerable, and childhood ailments, malnutrition and disease must have killed many before adolescence. The fact was that parents could not presume that their child would live to be an adult. How did this knowledge affect parent–child relations?

It has been argued that the use of childcarers could protect some parents from the full horrors of infant death. Other people were employed to look after vulnerable babies and small children, creating, as noted above, a distance between parent and child. In a world of high infant mortality, this may have given the parent some protection against investing too much emotion in a child that simply might not survive. However, it is difficult to gauge how deliberate, and also how real such distancing was. The social expectations surrounding the deaths of children are more fully documented. We can note that attempts were made to restrict the mourning times allocated to babies and young children (Plutarch, *Numa* 12) and that in terms of how many must have died comparatively few infants were commemorated in surviving epitaphs (Garnsey, 1991, pp.51–2; Rawson, 2003, p.344). For some grieving for young children was an indulgence:

> Is it solace that you look for? Let me give you a scolding instead! You are like a woman in the way you take your son's death; what would you do if you had lost an intimate friend? A son, a little child of unknown promise, is dead; a fragment of time has been lost.
> (Seneca, *Letters* 99.2–3; in Gunmere, 1925, p.131)

These reactions and requirements may seem harsh to a modern reader, but were motivated by practical factors, especially the need to focus on those that survived. Besides, such conventions may not reflect the lived reality. It is doubtful that everyone would have agreed with Seneca, and the very fact that he wrote the letter suggests the existence of other reactions to a child's death apart from those expounded by a wealthy, childless, élite man preoccupied by philosophy. A mother, for example, may still mourn a baby if only in private and not in public (Hopkins, 1983, p.221; King, 2000).

For the poor, infant mortality may have been particularly high and this may have coloured the decision as to whether to rear the child. A baby could be rejected by the father because it was physically weak, deformed, illegitimate or from economic necessity. The baby was exposed or abandoned. It is impossible to gauge how common the practice was. But we can note that exposure was not automatically infanticide since evidence suggests that the babies were often recovered by others and reared as slaves or foundlings (Harris, 1994; Corbier, 2001). Nonetheless, to modern eyes the practice is abhorrent and cruel. Yet the action needs to be viewed in the context of poverty, malnutrition, high infant mortality and inadequate birth control, rather than simply seen as a sign of emotional or moral indifference.

The practice of exposure, high infant mortality, the lack of mourning times for infants, coupled with the overarching power of *patria potestas* and widespread employment of wet-nurses and carers could all be used to imply that Roman children were abused and that parents were indifferent about their care and survival. However, this would take an inadequate view of the evidence and would apply modern value judgements. The evidence must be viewed in its socio-economic context, where people made decisions according to cultural requirements. In other words, people probably did the best that they could when faced with tough choices in an often harsh environment. Besides, we could also marshal plenty of evidence to show that parents loved their children and mourned their premature deaths. To be sure we can no more take this evidence out of context and isolate it from other material than the negative evidence, but it does remind us that we cannot generalise or judge in simple polarised terms.

Conclusion

It would be misleading to make bold assertions about how people felt and acted towards children in most societies and periods. For the Roman world, as for many times and places, the evidence is often ambivalent and inconsistent. We can note, for example, that a single author such as Cicero or Pliny can be both detached from children and sentimental towards them in his written work (Harlow and Laurence, 2002, p.34). On the one hand, unwanted children could be abandoned, while, on the other hand, children could be viewed as sweet and endearing. On the one hand, children needed to be trained, tamed and civilised, while, on the other hand, children were viewed as individuals with adult-like qualities. Children could be neglected, sent out to work and beaten. Simultaneously, children could be loved, cherished and grieved for. We cannot compress this varied evidence into one general experience of childhood, either positive or negative. For some, childhood was harsh; for others, it was joyous, both from the perspective of the adult and of the child.

The evidence from the world of Roman adults does suggest that children were often wanted and cared for, even if this was partly motivated by adult self-interest. The high infant mortality rate and harsh economic realities do not mean that parents were emotionally detached from their children. Children were the future. A child was an asset that needed nurture and protection but also discipline and training. If the child was not brought up properly and failed as an adult this reflected on the parents. Children needed to be shaped and trained for the future – a future as adults, but children were still regarded as children.

Further reading

A useful entry-point to the range of primary sources relevant to Roman childhood is the source book by Jane Gardner and Thomas Wiedemann (1991), especially pages 96–116. The most comprehensive scholarly study of Roman childhood is the book by Beryl Rawson (2003) which covers all the key topics such as birth, education, family and public life as well as death. The collection of papers edited by Suzanne Dixon (2001) includes much that is of interest while a book on the Roman life course by Mary Harlow and Ray Laurence (2002) addresses key issues relating to growing up in ancient Rome.

Bibliography

Ancient sources

Cassius Dio, *Roman History*, in Gardner, J. and Wiedemann, T. (1991) *The Roman Household: A Sourcebook*, London: Routledge.

Fronto, *Letters to his Friends*, in Gardner, J. and Wiedemann, T. (1991) *The Roman Household: A Sourcebook*, London: Routledge.

Horace, *Satire*, in Rudd, N. (trans.) (1973) *The Satires of Horace and Perseus*, London: Penguin.

Pliny, *Letters*, in Gardner, J. and Wiedemann, T. (1991) *The Roman Household: A Sourcebook*, London: Routledge.

Plutarch, *Cato the Elder*, in Gardner, J. and Wiedemann, T. (1991) *The Roman Household: A Sourcebook*, London: Routledge.

Seneca, *Letters*, in Gunmere, R.M. (trans.) (1971) *Seneca in Ten Volumes*, London: Heinemann and Cambridge, MA: Harvard University Press.

Seneca, *On Anger*, in Gardner, J. and Wiedemann, T. (1991) *The Roman Household: A Sourcebook*, London: Routledge.

Modern scholarship

Ariès, P. (1962) *Centuries of Childhood: A Social History of Family Life*, trans. R. Baldiek, London: Vintage Books (first published Paris: Plon, 1960).

Bodel, J. (1995) 'Minicia Marcella: taken before her time', *American Journal of Philology*, vol.116.3, pp.453–60.

Bradley, K. (1991) *Discovering the Roman Family*, Oxford: Oxford University Press.

Bradley, K. (1998) 'The sentimental education of the Roman child: the role of pet-keeping', *Latomus*, vol.57, pp.523–57.

Carp, T. (1980) '*Puer senex* in Roman and medieval thought', *Latomus*, vol.39, pp.736–9.

Corbier, M. (2001) 'Child exposure and abandonment', in Dixon, 2001, pp.52–73.

Dixon, S. (1988) *The Roman Mother*, London and Sydney: Croom Helm.

Dixon, S. (1991) 'The sentimental ideal of the Roman family', in Rawson, 1991, pp.99–113.

Dixon, S. (1992) *The Roman Family*, Baltimore: Johns Hopkins University Press.

Dixon, S. (ed.) (2001) *Childhood, Class and Kin in the Roman World*, London: Routledge.

Eyben, E. (1991) 'Fathers and sons', in Rawson, 1991, pp.114–43.

Garnsey, P. (1991) 'Child rearing in ancient Italy', in D. Kertzer and R. Saller (eds) *The Family in Italy: From Antiquity to the Present*, New Haven and London: Yale University Press, pp.48–65.

Harlow, M. and Laurence, R. (2002) *Growing Up and Growing Old in Ancient Rome: A Life Course Approach*, London: Routledge.

Harris, W.V. (1994) 'Child exposure in the Roman empire', *Journal of Roman Studies*, vol.84, pp.1–22.

Hopkins, K. (1983) *Death and Renewal*, Sociological Studies in Roman History, vol.2, Cambridge: Cambridge University Press.

King, M. (2000) 'Commemoration of infants on Roman funerary inscriptions', in G. Oliver (ed.) *The Epigraphy of Death: Studies in the History and Society of Greece and Rome*, Liverpool: Liverpool University Press, pp.117–54.

Lattimore, R. (1942) *Themes in Greek and Latin Epitaphs*, Champaign: University of Illinois Press.

Parkin, T. (1992) *Demography and Roman Society*, Baltimore: Johns Hopkins University Press.

Rawson, B. (ed.) (1991) *Marriage, Divorce and Children in Ancient Rome*, Oxford: Oxford University Press.

Rawson, B. (1997) 'The iconography of Roman childhood', in B. Rawson and P. Weaver (eds) *The Roman Family in Italy: Status, Sentiment, Space*, Oxford: Clarendon Press, pp.205–32.

Rawson, B. (2003) *Children and Childhood in Roman Italy*, Oxford: Oxford University Press.

Saller, R. (1987) 'Men's age at marriage and its consequences in the Roman family', *Classical Philology*, vol.82, pp.21–34.

Saller, R. (1991) 'Corporal punishment, authority and obedience in the Roman household', in Rawson, 1991, pp.144–65.

Saller, R. (1994) *Patriarchy, Property and Death in the Roman Family*, Cambridge: Cambridge University Press.

Shaw, B. (1987) 'The age of Roman girls at marriage: some reconsiderations', *Journal of Roman Studies*, vol.77, pp.30–46.

Stone, L. (1977) *The Family, Sex and Marriage in England, 1500–1800*, London: Weidenfeld & Nicolson.

Wiedemann, T. (1989) *Adults and Children in the Roman Empire*, London: Routledge.

Essay Nine

The voice of a Roman audience

Valerie Hope

Introduction

> Suppose applause to be a trivial matter, which it is not, since it is given to all the best citizens; but if it is trivial, it is so only to a man of character, but to those who depend upon the merest trifles, who are controlled and governed by rumour and, as they themselves put it, by the favour of the People, applause must seem immortality, and hissing death.
>
> (Cicero, *Pro Sestio* 106; in Gardner, 1958, p.193)

Cicero, writing at the end of the republic, captures the power of public reactions, how a crowd's positive or negative response could make or break people's spirit. The applauding or hissing audience is both empowered and empowering. Cicero knew this all too well; he may have regarded himself as 'a man of character', but he still cared intensely about the public reactions of others (see below). But who does Cicero mean by the 'People'? And where did they have opportunity to express opinions by clapping or hissing?

The intention in this essay is to evaluate the role of the theatre, amphitheatre and circus in Roman life, concentrating in particular on the expectations and responses of the spectators. The focus will fall not on the buildings themselves or the types of entertainment provided, but on why people attended and the relationship between the audience and the benefactor(s). The essay outlines the social and political dimensions of the popular entertainments held in Rome during the late republic and early empire and how the audience at these events could find a common voice.

Reconstructing the experience

The Colosseum, Circus Maximus and Theatre of Marcellus are among the most striking remains of ancient Rome (Figures 9.1 and 9.2). The sheer scale of the structures serves as a potent reminder of the might of Rome and the wealth and manpower at its disposal. Across the empire similar buildings associated with mass entertainment survive, symbolising the extent and success of Romanisation. But beyond the architectural wonders

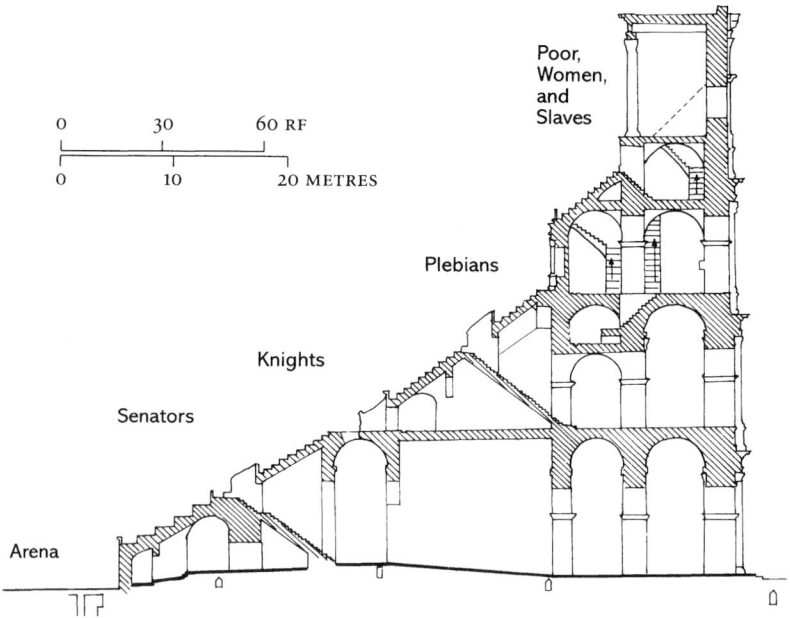

Figure 9.1 Colosseum, schematic reconstruction of main seating zones. (Reproduced from A. Claridge, *Rome – An Oxford Archaeological Guide*, Oxford: Oxford University Press, 1998, p.279, figure 133; adapted from M.L Conforto and A.M. Reggiani, *Anfiteatro Flavio*, Rome: Edizioni Quasar, 1988)

Figure 9.2 Theatre of Marcellus, Rome. (© 2000. Photo: Scala, Florence)

of these structures is it possible to access the people that used them? Thousands were present at the spectacles held in these buildings and in the temporary wooden versions that predated them. Can we gauge their responses and reactions to what they experienced? The largest obstacle in this quest is that the individual voices of 'ordinary people' are rarely recorded in the ancient sources. What we have comes through a filter that is predominantly male and of the wealthy élite classes. These authors, and it is mainly literary evidence we are drawing upon here, commented on the audience's reactions and behaviour when it suited them, often in connection with analysis of the political climate. In these descriptions, authors tend to mass the people (*plebs sordida*) together and rarely acknowledge the inherent variations within the group created by such factors as legal status, employment, wealth, age and gender (Horsfall, 2003, pp.26–8; Yavetz, 1988, pp.141–55). It is difficult to judge who was present at a particular event and the real dynamics of the reactions and interactions of the audience. The spectators become an indiscriminate crowd of people, at times a loutish and brutish mob, whose behaviour is analysed according to the perspective of the author and his political agenda. The only distinction commonly made is between the mass of people on the one hand and the élite (senators, *equites* and the emperor) on the other. This perspective must simplify the whole experience and often isolates the reactions of the audience from the fuller context of the venue and the show. That is to say, the commentators are interested in the audience for any political statements and reactions that might be forthcoming, and not in the details of what 'the day out' fully entailed to those attending. We struggle to reconstruct the entirety of the experience for those sitting in the back rows and instead have to make do with an élite interpretation of only some elements.

There is a certain irony in this one-sided perspective, since the theatre, amphitheatre and circus were places that united the people. Here the Roman populace was brought together in unity and the pursuit of common goals. However, simultaneously the divisions of Roman society were displayed for all to see. The social hierarchy was visibly expressed through the physical structure of the venues and the seating arrangements (Figures 9.1 and 9.3). In the arena and on the stage were society's outcasts – criminals, prisoners and lowly slaves – who were 'selling' their bodies for the entertainment of others (Wiedemann, 1992, pp.28–30; Edwards, 1993, pp.123–8). By contrast, the seats were occupied by members of the accepted social order, graded by their importance. The senators, *equites* and people were seated in separate areas, emphasising the major distinctions present in society. In some venues there may have been further divisions, with men and women seated separately, or people from the same trade

Figure 9.3 Reverse of a coin issued after the death of Titus (CE 81), view of the Colosseum showing both the interior and the exterior. The seating is divided into horizontal and vertical bands, with the emperor's box visible in the centre. The heads of the spectators are represented as dots. (© American Numismatic Society, New York)

guilds or differing towns and provinces sitting together (Edmondson, 1996, pp.100–1; Roueché, 1993, pp.83–128). The impact of this arrangement is perhaps best emphasised when we consider dress and the bands of colour present in the banks of seating: the purple of the emperor; the white toga with a broad purple band of the senators; the narrow purple stripe on the togas of the *equites*; the white togas of the citizens; and the darker cloaks of the poor (Edmondson, 1996, p.85; Parker, 1999).

The exact workings of the seating arrangements are, in fact, difficult to ascertain and we have to acknowledge that they operated in slightly differing ways for the differing venues, but from the late republic and throughout the empire legislation sought to impose status distinctions (Edmondson, 1996, pp.86–93; Futrell, 1997, pp.161–6; Rawson, 1987). This also suggests that the rules were not always followed. People could try to pass themselves off as something that they were not and sit in the reserved seats (Martial, *Epode* 5.8; Horace, *Epode* 4.15–16; Reinhold, 1971). Martial tells of a man who during the reign of Domitian, when the seating rules were strictly enforced, wishes to be seen as a knight and tries to sit in their special seats:

> Dislodged from there too, the wretch moves to the gangway and, half-supported by the end of a bench, where he is ill received, he pretends to the knights with one knee that he is sitting and to Leitus [an usher] with the other that he is standing.
>
> (Martial, *Epode* 5.14.8–11; in Shackleton Bailey, 1993, p.367)

On the one hand, such behaviour suggests that the distinctions mattered; on the other hand, it indicates that there was fluidity in their interpretation and application. The whole issue of who sat where reminds us that these events brought together many differing social groups, and the events had an important role to play in shaping Roman social structure and social norms (Edmondson, 1996, p.82). There was both unity and diversity in the Roman audience.

To attend the theatre, amphitheatre or circus must have been an experience that appealed to all the senses – it was simultaneously crowded, noisy, smelly and eye-catching. We can easily imagine the tightly packed bodies, the shouts and catcalls, the smell and taste of food, sweat, excitement and blood, the costumes, the colours and gestures of the entertainers and the grandeur and scale of the buildings. All these things mattered to those attending and contributed to the experience. But the exact way in which people's senses were stimulated, what they saw and heard and thus what they felt and experienced, would not have been the same. The élite experience, about which we hear the most, may have been a comparatively sanitised one; from the late republic the élite had special reserved seats (see above) and they arrived at the venues, through separate uncrowded entrances, after the masses had taken their places. Nevertheless, they were still sensitive to the audience that surrounded them, conscious of how it reacted to them as well as the entertainments offered. The republican élite and later the emperor wanted to be perceived as separate from the mass of the audience but also part of it. This is reflected in how the events of stage, circus and arena are recorded; the view is from the reserved seats of the élite but they look back to the people behind them as much as to the spectacular entertainments unfolding in front of them.

The theatre, amphitheatre and circus were above all public venues, what happened there was highly visible and audible. The audience could shout and make its voice heard, it watched and studied the élite and the élite watched and studied it. As one scholar has recently noted, the Roman theatre was 'a perfect venue for self-display and self-fashioning' (Parker, 1999, p.163). In these public venues reputations were made and broken, not just those of charioteers, gladiators and actors, but of republican politicians and to a lesser extent the later emperors.

Pleasure

Major festivals filled the Roman year. These events were centred on religion, they were the community's way of honouring the gods. The traditional spectacles were *ludi*, ceremonial processions followed by chariot races held in the Circus Maximus or on the open space of the Circus Flaminius. With time, theatrical shows (*ludi scaenici*) also became associated with these *ludi*. The traditional public ceremonies did not include gladiatorial games (*munera*). The latter developed from combats held after the funerals of wealthy and prominent individuals (Auguet, 1972, pp.19–25; Futrell, 1997, pp.11–44; Hopkins, 1983, pp.3–7). It is difficult to know exactly how many days were occupied by shows of the various kinds. By the time of Augustus, the seven annual state *ludi* involved 13 days for chariot races and 48 days for stage shows. On top of this would have been gladiatorial contests and other spectacles such as those associated with military victories (Wiedemann, 1992, p.12). The number of festival days increased during the first century CE, and in the second century the emperor Marcus Aurelius allegedly reduced the number of days to 135 (*Lives of the Later Caesars. Marcus Aurelius* 10.10). What is clear is that the populace of Rome was accustomed to regular entertainment, which took various forms. We need to remember that who was putting on a show, what it was being held for (e.g. religious festival or funeral games), when it was held and where it was held would all have affected the ambience and atmosphere.

The theatre, amphitheatre and circus were not the only opportunities for gatherings, celebrations and entertainment. We can also note the scale and grandeur of triumphal processions, while other venues, such as fora (public squares), stadia (for athletics) and baths, allowed for interaction on a more limited scale. But it was at the circus, theatre and amphitheatre that people came together en masse on a regular basis. It is worth remembering when we picture impressive stone structures such as the Colosseum (Figure 9.3) that these were relatively late introductions to Rome. Wooden theatres and amphitheatres, generally of a temporary nature, were originally erected for theatrical and gladiatorial spectacles. These were often located in the Roman forum, drawing on this historical backdrop, and their construction, décor and associated novelties became part of the entertainment (Wiles, 2003, pp.98–104). We can note, for example, the extravagant theatre built by Aemilius Scaurus in 58 BCE, for a few days' temporary use and described by Pliny the Elder the following century:

> As aedile he constructed the greatest of all the works ever made by man, a work that surpassed not merely those erected for a limited period but even those intended to last for ever. This was his theatre, which had a stage arranged in three storeys with 360 columns; ... The lowest storey of the stage was of marble and the middle one of glass (an extravagance unparalleled even in later times), while the top storey was made of gilded planks.
>
> (Pliny, *Natural History* 36.114; in Eichholz, 1962, p.89)

The prime reason for attending the theatre, amphitheatre and circus must have been pleasure and entertainment. At these venues the people of Rome could witness extravagance and novelty, humour and horrors. It is not my intention here to focus on the nature of the entertainments, and indeed reconstructing exactly what went on can be challenging. As we have noted,

Essay Nine The voice of a Roman audience

ancient authors comment more on the audience's reaction than on the details of the shows themselves. For the theatre, few plays and dramas survive; for the amphitheatre and circus, the fights, executions, beast hunts and chariot races can often only be listed in the broadest of terms. This is not to say that the content of the shows and races did not matter, but sometimes élite authors found it beneath themselves to provide all the details of what appealed to the masses (Livy 41.28.11; Tacitus, *Annals* 13.31; Cassius Dio, *Histories* 72.18.3). It was the unusual and the extravagant which could draw comment, often because it was intended to draw a reaction from the people. The surprising and the innovative, especially in the amphitheatre, could add to the 'wow' factor and make the events more memorable. Exotic beasts, fantastic contraptions and the flooding of arenas might draw particular comment. In his imperial biographies, Suetonius generally notes the types, scale and quality of entertainments provided by each emperor, and these become a factor in how the reign is evaluated (see below).

For a modern reader the catalogues of slaughtered animals and people make for grim reading and it is impossible to see any pleasure in the pain and humiliation of others. The idea of pleasure and how it is derived is culturally defined. What happened in the Roman amphitheatre in particular is at odds with many modern views on animal rights, persecution of minorities and capital punishment. Yet in the modern world there can be ambivalence and conflicting practices; after all, capital punishment is still widely practised. It is perhaps the element of spectacle that we find most disturbing. The Roman public not only witnessed, but also enjoyed the destruction of its victims, those it regarded as outcasts, criminals and enemies (Figure 9.4). The punishments served to alienate the condemned and to distance them from the rest of Roman society. The arena audience may have found unity and solidarity as it watched the destruction of those it had cast aside. However, there were some dissenting voices in antiquity. Cicero notes the brutish nature of the spectacles put on by Pompey in 55 BCE and recalls that the audience even felt sympathy for some elephants destined to die (Cicero, *Letters to his Friends* 7.1). Seneca, a Stoic philosopher of the first century CE, and later Augustine, writing in the late fourth or early fifth centuries, also had reservations about blood letting and mindless death in the arena (Seneca, *Letters* 7; Augustine, *Confessions* 6.9). However, both were more concerned about the negative impact on the spectators: how the crowd mentality took over and people displayed all their baser instincts. There was little concern, compassion or mercy for the victims, just the usual comments from the élite about the mobish and brutish nature of the common rabble.

Figure 9.4 Mosaic from the Villa di Dar Buc Ammera, Zliten, Libya, depicting a hunt, executions and gladiators, with musical accompaniment. Images which drew on the events of the arena were common decorative motifs in the domestic sphere, often commemorating in visual form the shows provided, at great personal expense, by the owner of the house. (German Archaeological Institute, Rome, negative nos 61.1891/1892. Photos: Koppermann)

Roman spectators may have become numb to death; they may have viewed those killed as hardened criminals deserving of their punishment and felt distanced from them. But we need to remember that the amphitheatre was not just about death and destruction. For those watching trained gladiators, the ethos of noble combat was more important than blood and gore. Gladiators were despised for their debasement but admired for their fighting prowess (Wiedemann, 1992; Barton, 1993; Kyle, 1998, pp.80–1). They could gain fame and fortune and ardent admirers. Graffiti from Pompeii recall gladiators as heartthrobs: Celadus, a Thracian gladiator, made all the girls sigh, while Crescens, who fought with a trident and net, held the hearts of all the girls (*Corpus Inscriptionum Latinarum*, vol.IV, 4397; 4356). These simple texts scratched by anonymous hands provide a differing perspective on the voice of the audience. For élite commentators, the reputations of politicians and emperors were gauged at these public venues (see below). For many of the spectators, the entertainers probably inspired more passion and devotion than the shows' benefactors. Some people supported individual gladiators or types of combatants, others were devotees of certain actors and pantomimes. The circus with its chariot races could in particular divide the city between supporters of the differing teams, which were denoted by colours (Pliny, *Letters* 9.6). Supporting 'your team' or 'your gladiator' would have created differing voices in the audience and simultaneously created a sense of identity and solidarity between people with shared interests.

The level of passion and solidarity that could be stirred up is suggested by an incident that occurred in Pompeii in CE 59, when a riot broke out in the amphitheatre between the people of Pompeii and some visitors from the neighbouring town of Nuceria (Tacitus, *Annals* 14.17; Figure 9.5). The fight had its origins in local rivalries and suggests the potential existence of

Figure 9.5 Fresco from Pompeii depicting the riot of CE 59 in the town's amphitheatre. (© Alinari Archives/Bridgeman)

divisions, resentments and opposing views within an audience. Clearly, for the spectators, Roman entertainment was not just about death and inflicting suffering and nor should we underestimate the differences between the types of 'shows'. In this essay, for simplicity and convenience, I often speak in general terms of the 'Roman audience', but there is danger of isolating this audience from what it was actually watching and experiencing, especially when our main sources are so biased towards the élite political perspective. As we have already seen, a Roman audience was far from homogenous, and equally the venues and types of spectacle would have appealed to differing people in differing ways and would have thus impacted upon the group dynamics of those present.

Entertainment, with a political dimension to be sure (see below), was what the races, contests, mock battles, beast hunts and plays were primarily about, but there were other factors that encouraged people to attend. We should not forget the religious associations of many of these spectacles; they were not acts of worship, but religious fervour may have played a part for the crowd (Beacham, 1999, p.32). The shows could also give the audience an opportunity to experience the exotica of empire and learn about its extent and thus be reminded of the might of Rome. Historical themes to plays and mock battles promoted Rome's glorious past. Fights and contests encouraged a competitive ethos, promoting military supremacy and the virtues of courage and bravery. The punishment of criminals in the arena, often through humiliating and painful deaths, brought retribution to the public eye and acted as a deterrent to would be criminals and dissenters (Coleman, 1990). But any of these messages would be lost unless the spectacles held the gaze and attention of the audience. People went because it was free entertainment, and no doubt gambling and the distribution of gifts made it even more exciting. The shows regularly broke up the monotony and toil of life. At these venues you could have fun, lose yourself in the crowd, become momentarily anonymous, while still part of a vociferous group, and thus gain a new confidence to express opinions about both the show and the political regime (Yavetz, 1988, pp.18–20).

Power

So who was responsible for providing the people of Rome with so much spectacle and entertainment? In the republic, the *ludi* were an offering to the gods by the community. These *ludi* were paid for by the state treasury, but the presiding magistrate was expected to top up the funds and thus took the credit for a good show. By the late republic, impressing the people in the circus or the theatre was a way to gain popular success and to enhance your pool of votes at the next election. Gladiatorial shows were not state funded. They were the responsibility of the relatives and heirs of wealthy individuals who used the death to promote familial and individual power by entertaining the people of Rome. But through both *ludi* and *munera* the wealthy ruling élite gave entertainment to the poor inhabitants of Rome and in return hoped to receive their support. During the late republic, shows became increasingly extravagant. Cicero records people providing exceptional *munera* at great personal expense in order to improve their chances of election: for example, the shows organised by Milo in the 50s BCE, which allegedly cost more than Milo could afford (Cicero, *Letters to his brother Quintus* 3.6(8).6; *Pro Milo* 95; *Pro Murena* 38; *Pro Sestio* 54.116). In the Rome of the emperors, *ludi* and *munera* continued to be held but were increasingly controlled by the emperor to prevent competitive displays among the élite (see below). We can note as well that under the emperors stone structures gradually replaced the construction of less permanent wooden theatres and amphitheatres. But in the imperial period there was still a distinction between state religious occasions, financed by grants from the public treasury, and privately funded *munera*. This distinction was perhaps more apparent outside Rome where the local magistrates and the wealthy were still expected to fund shows, whereas display in Rome was increasingly monopolised by the emperor (Hopkins, 1983, pp.12–14).

During the republic at least, the circus, amphitheatre and theatre were foci for the competitive display of power in front of a captive audience. The leading lights could advertise wealth and popular support by the construction of an impressive venue and the scale and grandeur of their shows. These were places to advertise and to gain popular support, both for those funding the events and for other competing politicians who attended. The privileged seating in the theatre, in particular, visually underlined senatorial superiority, but there were additional ways to get yourself noticed by the people and to make sure that you stood out. Office holders could wear the symbols of office and be attended by lictors (Suetonius, *Julius Caesar* 80); military victors could wear their decorations (Livy 10.47); retinues of slaves and attendants could create an impressive, eye-catching entry. The leading politicians of the republic were honoured by being allowed to wear striking symbols at shows. In 45 BCE, Julius Caesar was allowed to wear triumphal dress at all games, a laurel wreath at all times and had a special seat in the orchestra of the theatre (Cassius Dio 42.19.3; Suetonius, *Julius Caesar* 76).

The enhanced visibility of the élite brought them many advantages in terms of prestige, power and popular support, but there could be disadvantages too. Visibility could bring vulnerability to attack and ridicule. This was especially the case in the theatre of the late republic where privileged seating was first introduced. At the circus and amphitheatre of the time it was still possible to surround yourself with your followers and supporters regardless of status; not so at the theatre with its allotted seats for the élite. Here you could find yourself vilified by both the audience and the actors when you may have been desperate to blend into the background rather than to stand out (Parker, 1999, p.168).

Republican reactions

During the late republic, the relationship between audience and benefactor was not just about giving entertainment to gain votes. How the people reacted to the shows, to the benefactor and to others present became crucial. As an audience people gained a voice and a confidence that they did not have elsewhere – they expressed opinions. They could clap, cheer, boo, hiss and insult. The audience provided a barometer of the political climate and who was in and out of favour. The presiding magistrate or benefactor of the show might not be the only one to get a reaction. Rival factions in the audience could take the opportunity to express support for their favourites and hurl abuse at the opposition. Politicians might pay people to cheer in their favour and boo their opponents. The audience became performers adding to the drama of the events (Edmondson, 1996, p.82). Indeed, sponsoring a show did not guarantee you a good reaction. Cicero notes that in 59 BCE, Gabinius, a candidate for the consulship, was hissed at while attending gladiatorial shows he had organised (Cicero, *Letters to Atticus* 2.19.3).

Cicero's works contain many references to public spectacles and events, especially those held at the theatre. He takes pleasure in being greeted by loud and steady applause as he enters the theatre (*Letters to Atticus* 4.15.6). He notes when Julius Caesar received little applause (*Letters to Atticus* 2.19.3) and how others were received with boos and hisses (*Letters to his Friends* 8.2.1). Cicero was very aware that the theatre was 'a microcosm of Rome' (Parker, 1999, p.170). In a speech given in support of Sestius, Cicero observes the political role of recent spectacles (Beacham, 1999, p.57). He notes that during his exile one of his supporters, when attending a gladiatorial show, received great applause. By contrast, the brother of Cicero's opponent Clodius tried to creep into the arena unnoticed, but when the crowd spotted him hissing ensued (Cicero, *Pro Sestio* 59.126).

In the theatre the audience could also react to plays and actors. The actors could make political comments by twisting or altering the words of the script to praise or ridicule politicians, and the audience responded with appropriate cheers and boos. An injection of topicality could bring a vibrancy and contemporary relevance to the plays and encourage interaction between audience and actors. Once more in the *Pro Sestio*, Cicero includes examples of this, noting the ability of actors to work the audience and give new meaning to old lines, twisting them to make reference to Cicero and his exile (Bartsch, 1994, pp.72–5): 'What shouts of applause greeted his performance of this passage, when they took no notice of the acting, but applauded the words of the poet, the earnestness of the actor and the hope of my recall' (Cicero, *Pro Sestio* 56.121; in Gardner, 1958, p.199).

In one play, a reference to Tullius, a sixth-century BCE king, was interpreted as a reference to Cicero (whose middle name was Tullius) and the crowd encored a thousand times (Cicero, *Pro Sestio* 58.123). By contrast, when Clodius attended a play he was not only insulted by the crowd but by the actors as well (Cicero, *Pro Sestio* 55.118). Thus, the politicians could find themselves surrounded by praise or vilification – generated from behind them by the audience and in front of them by the actors (Parker, 1999, pp.171–2).

The spectacles given at the circus, theatre and amphitheatre of the late republic allowed the sponsors to display their wealth and generosity, allowed other leading politicians to make claims on popularity and allowed the people to express opinions en masse and in a forceful manner. In the factional politics of the late republic, there were no doubt times when the spectators were manipulated and stirred up by organised ringleaders to act and react in a certain way. The audience did not necessarily shout and cheer with one voice. The élite gauged the reactions of the crowd and may have sought to control it by encouraging their supporters to act positively.

In the final analysis, what we are left with is élite interpretations of how the people acted and the significance of their behaviour. It suits Cicero to interpret the crowd as being favourable to him and less favourable to his opponents. What the people actually felt and did is more elusive. Nevertheless, the popularity, or impression of popularity, conferred by the people did seem to matter. Politicians were not just chasing votes but also a more general sense of popular support; they thrived on the applause and large-scale adulation of the Roman crowd (Veyne, 1990).

Emperor and people

Under Augustus and the emperors, claims to prestige and popular support by anyone other than members of the imperial family could be seen as a challenge to the emperor's authority. It was in an emperor's interests to control the ambitions of the élite. Augustus sought to bring greater organisation and control to the *ludi* and *munera* by, for example, requiring that all *munera* receive senatorial authorisation, thereby restricting the senators freedom to put on such shows at will (Cassius Dio 54.2). Further restrictions were imposed by Tiberius, and from the time of Domitian gladiatorial games could no longer be held in Rome except by the emperor, a relative of the emperor or a magistrate on the emperor's behalf. The applause, cheers and support of the people were to become the emperor's prerogative. He became the ultimate benefactor of the people. The political power of both senate and people was gradually curtailed. The emperor did not seek the people's votes by entertaining them, but he still needed, or at least desired, that his position was affirmed by popular support expressed en masse in the traditional venues of theatre, circus and amphitheatre. It was this change in the crowd's role from one interested in politics (in principle at least) to one only interested in entertainment and free handouts that led the satirist Juvenal to make the following cutting comment at the beginning of the second century CE:

> But nowadays, with no vote to sell, their motto
> Is 'Couldn't care less'. Time was when their plebiscite elected
> Generals, Heads of State, commanders of legions: but now
> They've pulled in their horns, there's only two things that concern them:
> Bread and Games.
>
> (Juvenal, *Satires* 10.78–81; in Green, 1974, p.207)

But despite Juvenal's dismissive view the people did retain their voice and their ability to react favourably (and sometimes unfavourably) to the political regime. Besides, to many people food and entertainment may have always mattered more than the political identity of the provider.

Putting on a good show was a central way in which the emperor curried favour with the masses. An emperor aimed to impress and to match or to outdo the shows of his predecessors. In his self-composed epitaph, the *Res Gestae Divi Augusti*, Augustus lists the shows and spectacles that he gave to the Roman people. He notes that 10,000 gladiators took part and 3,500 beasts were killed (*Res Gestae* 22). A splendid naval battle receives particular attention:

> I produced a naval battle as a show for the people at the place across the Tiber now occupied by the grove of the Caesars, where a site 1,800 feet long and 1,200 broad was excavated. There thirty beaked triremes or biremes and still more smaller vessels were joined in battle. About 3,000 men, besides the rowers, fought in these fleets.
>
> (Augustus, *Res Gestae Divi Augusti* 23; in Brunt and Moore, 1967, p.31)

The scale and frequency of these events were a factor in how Augustus wished his rule to be remembered and may be exaggerated accordingly. Those emperors who provided little of note at the spectacles were often perceived, at least so we are told by the élite sources, as unpopular, distant and uninterested in the people.

A good emperor put on a good show to hear the applause of the people and would gain an even more positive response if he appeared to be interested and accessible. An emperor needed to be present, to be attentive, to enjoy the show, basically to become like the people and enter into the spirit of the event. As one modern commentator puts it, 'the emperor himself was part of the show, both as provider and participant in the spectacles' (Beacham, 1999, p.ix). Those emperors who did not interact with the people were criticised. Augustus was careful to pay attention at shows, all too aware that Julius Caesar had gained a bad reputation for doing his paperwork while attending performances (Suetonius, *Augustus* 45). Similarly, Marcus Aurelius was ridiculed for reading and signing documents in the circus (*Lives of the Later Caesars. Marcus Aurelius* 15). The emperor needed to interact with the audience, to listen to its requests and appear to respond to them. Many of these requests centred on the entertainment itself – should an actor be freed, a gladiator spared? The emperor Tiberius did not enjoy this crowd pressure and, after being forced to free an actor, avoided the theatre and rarely gave shows (Suetonius, *Tiberius* 47). Titus, on the other hand, got the balance right, entering into the banter with the people without losing his dignity (Suetonius, *Titus* 8). Indeed, despite his need to impress the audience and be accessible to it, the emperor also needed to keep a respectable distance – to overstep the mark would compromise his dignity and reputation. The emperor was a senator and was expected to behave with the decorum fitting his rank. He might wish to align himself with the common people, but he could not afford to alienate the senate.

Dialogue between emperor and people was not always restricted to the show and its events. The people could give voice to other concerns, especially those that affected their physical well-being, such as the food supply. Under Augustus, the people complained, presumably at a show of some description, about the cost of wine, and demanded gifts of cash (Suetonius, *Augustus* 42). Augustus always answered such queries without always giving into the demands (Millar, 1992, p.372). An audience could also wilfully misinterpret the words and actions of performers, especially actors, to pass comment on the regime. Under the empire, writers and actors were more wary of overtly criticising the political situation: they risked punishment if they mocked the emperor. Gaius is said to have burned to death a poet who wrote an ambiguous verse in a play (Suetonius, *Gaius* 27.4). However, the audience's reaction could turn a line or statement into a slur or protest even if the writer or actor had not intended it as such (Bartsch, 1994, pp.75–80).

An audience could affirm whether it was happy or unhappy with the emperor, his character, the shows he gave or the food supply that he was ultimately responsible for. If the people were unhappy, the public arena gave the emperor the opportunity to respond to, or at least to acknowledge their desires and wishes. The key was for the emperor to act concerned (Yavetz, 1988, pp.100–2), and if he played his part well he could turn the boos into cheers. The theatre, circus and amphitheatre may not have altered the course of imperial policy or even have made or broken emperors directly, but they were powerful and very public venues for the negotiation of roles, status and popularity. The people may not have wanted a revolution, but at least they could make it plain that they wanted a better emperor (Yavetz, 1988, p.105).

The reactions of the audience also impacted on the long-term reputation of the emperor and the literary definition of good and bad rule as defined by the élite authors. A good emperor got the balance right; he entertained the people splendidly, received due adulation, but in the process did not compromise his or the senate's role and dignity. A bad emperor either ignored the people and did not cater for their entertainment adequately or worse still tried to become too much like the crowd, wanting ever more applause, enjoying the shows too much and humiliating the élite. We can note, for example, that among the many failings of Nero, according to the sources, were the nature of his shows and his behaviour at them. Nero loved spectacle and pandered to the crowds' demands with great extravagances. He humiliated senators and knights by making them perform, and even wished to be a performer himself and thus receive even more applause from the people (Suetonius, *Nero* 11–12; Bartsch,1994, pp.1–62; Beacham, 1999, 197–254). These things are interpreted as failings in the surviving sources, but may not have been so viewed by the Roman plebs.

Conclusion

The inhabitants of the city of Rome regularly attended the circus, theatre and amphitheatre. They liked to be entertained on a grand scale and their leaders, whether senators of the late republic or the emperors, liked entertaining them. The benefits were mutual. The people received free entertainment, and their leaders support and mass popularity. Reconstructing what it was really like to attend these events may always elude us. The experience must have differed according to who you were, your legal status, age, gender and other factors that dictated where you sat and who sat next to you (Figure 9.6). It would be a mistake always to lump everyone together and assume that they automatically shouted, applauded, hissed or booed with one voice, even if the élite sources would sometimes have us believe this. Yet en masse the ordinary inhabitants of Rome did gain a certain power and strength that they simply did not have elsewhere.

This essay has explored aspects of the mass entertainments held in Rome and has aimed to highlight some of the complexities and inherent

Figure 9.6 Relief from the tomb of Caius Lusius Storax, Chieti, early first century CE, Museo Nazionale, Chieti. The relief is a rare depiction of spectators watching a gladiatorial show. Among the audience, flanked by musicians, are presumably Storax and other leading officials of the community. The gladiators fight in a frieze below. (Photo: Hutzel, German Archaeological Institute, Rome, negative no. 62.1068)

difficulties in considering crowd reactions and dynamics. There are many areas that it has not been possible to cover in detail, such as the contents of the spectacles and shows, the structure of the buildings and their relationship to power, politics and religion and also issues of exploitation and cruelty for the sake of pleasure. It is also worth remembering that the circus, amphitheatre and theatre were not the only centres for social interaction and entertainment. Other places and events also brought people together and turned the Roman populace, or chosen elements of it, into an 'audience'. For example, triumphal processions, funerals, the morning *salutatio* (visit, or greeting between patron and client) and private dinner parties could all encompass spectacle and display. The relationship between pleasure and entertainment on the one hand and power and politics on the other pervaded many aspects of Roman society.

Further reading

The large and beautifully illustrated book *The Art of Ancient Spectacle* edited by Bettina Ann Bergmann and Christine Kondoleon (1999) contains several papers that address spectacle and audience. Thomas Wiedemann's book (1992) remains a useful introduction to the ways of the amphitheatre while the more recent work by Richard Beacham (1999) addresses a range of spectacle entertainments. The relevant primary sources are diverse. Cicero's *Pro Sestio* and Suetonius, *Lives of the Twelve Caesars* would be useful starting points. An alternative approach would be to look at the selection of texts found in Jo-Ann Shelton's source book, especially pages 329–58.

Bibliography

Ancient sources

Augustus, *Res Gestae Divi Augusti*, in Brunt, P.A. and Moore, J.M. (trans.) (1967) *Res Gestae Divi Augusti*, Oxford: Oxford University Press.

Cicero, *Pro Sestio*, in Gardner, R. (trans.) (1958) *Cicero: The Speeches. Pro Sestio and In Vatinium*, Cambridge, MA: Harvard University Press (first published 1958).

Corpus Inscriptionum Latinarum (1863–present) ed. T. Mommsen *et al.*, Berlin (vol.IV ed. R. Schoene and C.Zangemeister, 1871).

Juvenal, *Satires*, in Green, P. (trans.) (1974) *The Sixteen Satires*, London: Penguin (first published 1967).

Martial, *Epode*, in Shackleton Bailey, D. (trans.) (1993) Martial: *Epigrams*, vol.1, Cambridge, MA: Harvard University Press (first published 1917).

Pliny, *Natural History*, in Eichholz, D.E. (trans.) (1962) Pliny: *Natural History*, vol.10, books 36 and 37, Cambridge, MA: Harvard University Press (first published 1912).

Suetonius, *Lives of the Twelve Caesars*, in Graves, R. (2003) Suetonius: *Lives of the Twelve Caesars*, London: Penguin (first published 1957).

Modern scholarship

Auguet, R. (1972) *Cruelty and Civilization: The Roman Games*, London: George Allen & Unwin (first published Paris: Flammarion, 1970).

Barton, C. (1993) *The Sorrows of the Ancient Romans: The Gladiator and the Monster*, Princeton: Princeton University Press.

Bartsch, S. (1994) *Actors in the Audience: Theatricality and Doublespeak from Nero to Hadrian*, Cambridge, MA: Harvard University Press.

Beacham, R. (1999) *Spectacle Entertainments of Early Imperial Rome*, New Haven and London: Yale University Press.

Bergmann, B.A. and Kondoleon, C. (1999) *The Art of Ancient Spectacle*, Washington, DC: National Gallery of Art and New Haven and London: Yale University Press.

Coleman, K.M. (1990) 'Fatal charades: Roman executions staged as mythological enactments', *Journal of Roman Studies*, vol.80, pp.44–73.

Edmondson, J. C. (1996) 'Dynamic arenas: gladiatorial presentations in the city of Rome and the construction of Roman society during the early empire', in W. Slater (ed.) *Roman Theater and Society: E. Togo Salmon Papers 1*, Ann Arbor: University of Michigan Press, pp.69–112.

Edwards, C. (1993) *The Politics of Immorality in Ancient Rome*, Cambridge: Cambridge University Press.

Futrell, A. (1997) *Blood in the Arena*, Austin: University of Texas Press.

Hopkins, K. (1983) *Death and Renewal*, Sociological Studies in Roman History Volume 2, Cambridge: Cambridge University Press.

Horsfall N. (2003) *The Culture of the Roman Plebs*, London: Duckworth.

Kyle, D. (1998) *Spectacles of Death in Ancient Rome*, London and New York: Routledge.

Millar, F. (1992) *The Emperor in the Roman World*, London: Duckworth.

Parker, H. (1999) 'The observed of all observers: spectacle, applause, and cultural poetics in the Roman theatre audience', in Bergmann and Kondoleon, 1999, pp.163–79.

Rawson, E. (1987) 'Discrimina Ordinum: the lex Julia theatralis', *Papers of the British School at Rome*, vol.55, pp.83–114.

Reinhold, M. (1971) 'Usurpation of status and status symbols in the Roman Empire', *Historia*, vol.20, pp.275–302.

Roueché, C. (1993) *Performers and Partisans at Aphrodisias, Journal of Roman Studies Monograph 6*, London: Society for the Promotion of Roman Studies.

Shelton, J. (1998) *As the Romans Did*, Oxford: Oxford University Press.

Veyne, P. (1990) *Bread and Circuses: Historical Sociology and Political Pluralism*, trans. B. Pearce (first published in French as *Le Pain et le cirque*, Paris: Éditions du Seuil, 1976).

Wiedemann, T. (1992) *Emperors and Gladiators*, London and New York: Routledge.

Wiles, D. (2003) *A Short History of Western Performance Space*, Cambridge: Cambridge University Press.

Yavetz, Z. (1988) *Plebs and Princeps*, Oxford: Clarendon Press (first published 1969).

Glossary

Note on Roman names: Roman males are listed either by, first, the common English version of their name or by the second part of their full Roman name (the *cognomen*) unless a subsequent part is commonly used. The full Roman name is give in parentheses.

Academy The oldest of the Greek philosophical schools, the Academy was founded by Plato in Athens early in the fourth century BCE.

Achaeans A Homeric name for the various Greek peoples who united in the expedition to Troy.

Achilles The central hero of Homer's *Iliad*, the Greeks' greatest warrior at Troy, king of Phthia and son of Peleus and Thetis. Achilles kills the Trojan hero Hector in revenge for the death of his friend/lover Patroclus, and eventually dies himself at the hands of Paris (Alexander).

Aedui A tribe in Gaul, settled in Burgundy, France.

Aemilius Scaurus (Marcus Aemilius Scaurus) (first century BCE) Politician who spent vast sums of money on extravagant games.

Aeneas The principal character of Virgil's Latin epic, the *Aeneid*; a Trojan, he escapes from the captured city of Troy and, after many adventures, arrives in Italy to become the founder of the Roman people.

Aeneid *See* Aeneas.

Aeon Roman God of eternal time.

Aeschylus (*c.*525/4–404/3 BCE) One of the three major Athenian writers of tragedy in the fifth century BCE. His most famous work, the *Oresteia* trilogy, tells of the return home of Agamemnon from Troy, his murder by his wife Clytemnestra and her lover Aegisthus, and the revenge of Agamemnon's son, Orestes.

Agamemnon One of the main characters of Homer's *Iliad*, leader of the Greek expedition to Troy. His quarrel with fellow-Greek Achilles has serious consequences, which drive the plot of the poem.

***agon* (pl. *agones*)** Greek competition, contest.

Agrippa (Marcus Vipsanius Agrippa) (*c.*62–12 BCE) Roman military leader and friend of the emperor Augustus, responsible for many building projects in Rome.

Agrippina the Younger (CE *c.*15–59)   Niece and fourth wife of the Roman emperor Claudius. Mother, by an earlier marriage, of the emperor Nero and great granddaughter of the emperor Augustus.

Ajax   Important character in the *Iliad*, renowned for his strength. Following the fall of Troy, he is defeated in a dispute with Odysseus over the armour of Achilles and commits suicide.

Alcaeus (late seventh to sixth century BCE)   Poet from Mytilene on the island of Lesbos, contemporary of Sappho.

Alcibiades (*c.*451–404/3 BCE)   Athenian general and politician, brought up in the house of his guardian Pericles. Exiled from Athens, he intrigued with Sparta and Persia, and was eventually murdered while under Persian protection.

Alexander the Great (356–323 BCE)   Macedonian leader; led an expedition that conquered most of south-eastern Asia.

Amazons   Mythical race of female warriors from the Black Sea coast of Asia Minor. In myth and art, the eastern matriarchal Amazons are often found in conflict with (and worsted by) Greek male fighters.

Amphidamas   King of Chalcis in Euboea, said to have died in the war between Chalcis and the neighbouring Eretria in the late eighth century BCE.

amphora (pl. amphorae)   Large pottery jar used for storage and transport of oil, wine and other foodstuffs in the Greek and Roman worlds.

Andromache   Wife of Trojan warrior Hector and mother of Astyanax. After Hector's death and the fall of Troy, her son is killed by the Greeks and she becomes the concubine of Neoptolemus, who is the son of Achilles, her husband's slayer.

Aphrodite   Greek goddess of love whose Roman equivalent was Venus. Central to Aphrodite's cult is her sexuality and seductiveness but she is also a deity concerned with such diverse areas as seafaring and civic harmony.

Apollo   God of healing, prophecy and music. An appeal to him from one of his priests in *Iliad* 1 leads to a plague in the Greek camp before Troy.

apostrophe   Rhetorical device in which an author directly addresses a person or thing, either present or absent.

Apuleius (other names uncertain) (CE *c.*125–*c.*170)   African-born orator and writer of various works: philosophical, forensic, short descriptive pieces on a variety of topics and a famous novel, *The Golden Ass*.

arche Athenian power or indirect rule, exercised through an 'alliance' of Greek states (sometimes described as 'empire' but not in the modern sense of the term).

archons Annually appointed ruling magistrates in Athens.

Argives Another Homeric name for Greeks (*see* Achaeans).

Argolid District of Greece, south-west of Athens; contains the citadels of Mycenae and Argos.

Argonauts Group of mythical heroes who went on an expedition, led by Jason, to the eastern coast of the Black Sea in quest of the Golden Fleece.

Ariovistus Leader of the Suebi, a Germanic tribe that reached the Rhine in its expansion south-west.

Aristophanes Athenian comic playwright and foremost exponent of 'Old Comedy', whose theatrical career dated from the early 420s BCE to his death in the mid-380s. Eleven of Aristophanes' plays survive, *Birds*, *Lysistrata* and *Frogs* being among the most famous.

Aristotle (384–322 BCE) Greek philosopher and literary critic, a pupil of Plato, who later founded his own philosophical school at the Lyceum in Athens. His followers were known as Peripatetics. Aristotle wrote numerous philosophical works, including the *Nicomachean Ethics* and the *Politics*.

Athena Greek goddess of war, wisdom and craft, whose Roman equivalent was Minerva. Athena was both a protectress of warriors and of many cities (including Athens, Sparta and Troy). She is the supporter of the Greek heroes, especially Odysseus, in the Homeric poems.

Attica The city state and territory of Athens, taking in some 2,400 square kilometres. Aside from Athens, other settlements in Attica included Brauron, Eleuis, Sunium and Rhamnous.

Augustine (Aurelius Augustinus) (CE 354–430) Christian author, priest and bishop.

Augustus (Gaius Julius Caesar Octavianus Augustus) (63 BCE to CE 14) Son of a senator but not of a noble family, he ruled the empire from 27 BCE (at the age of 36) until his death. At nineteen, he inherited the cash, cachet and military might of his great-uncle Julius Caesar, who had adopted him, and not only survived political turmoil but manipulated the warring factions at Rome and beyond in his favour.

bard (*aidos*) Modern name for the ancient Greek performer (and in Homer's case, the composer) of epic poems.

Black figure   Name for a technique of vase painting in the seventh and sixth centuries BCE in which a black silhouette was painted onto an orange background and after firing incised anatomical and decorative details were added.

Brutus (Marcus Junius Brutus) (*c*.85–42 BCE)   Leader of Julius Caesar's assassins, who fell at the battle of Philippi. Portrayed as noble by Shakespeare because of his devotion to senatorial rule, he was also notorious in his own time for extorting 48 per cent interest on his loan to the city of Salamis in the Roman province of Cyprus.

bulla   Protective necklace given to Roman children.

Burrus (Sextus Afranius Burrus) (died CE 62)   Roman soldier who became tutor and later adviser to the emperor Nero.

Caelius (Marcus Caelius Rufus) (*c*.88–48 BCE)   Known as an eloquent correspondent and friend of Cicero's, a lover of Clodia, sister of Clodius, and subject of a famous trial, he was later a supporter of a radical programme and died in southern Italy in a rebellion against Julius Caesar.

Caesar (Gaius Julius Caesar) (100–44 BCE)   Born near the Subura in Rome, notable commander and conqueror of Gaul who effectively dismantled the power nexus of the ruling class in Rome and became permanent dictator of the city and empire until his assassination.

Calypso   Goddess who detains Odysseus for several years on his way home from Troy.

Cassius Dio (Cassius Dio Cocceianus) (CE 155–230)   Roman of Greek descent from Nicaea in Bithynia. He wrote a vast *Roman History* (in Greek) covering a period from the earliest times to CE 229.

Catalogue of Ships   Modern conventional name for the long detailed list, in *Iliad* 2, of the Greek and Trojan forces fighting at Troy.

Cato the Elder (Marcius Porcius Cato) (234–149 BCE)   Roman Republican statesman, remembered for his rigid moral principles.

Cato the Younger (Marcus Porcius Cato) (95–46 BCE)   Great grandson of Cato the Elder, Cato the Younger was a Roman republican statesman and an adherent of Stoic philosophy. His opposition to Julius Caesar in the civil war led him to commit suicide, and he came to be regarded as the ideal Roman Stoic.

Catullus (Gaius Valerius Catullus) (*c*.84–*c*.54 BCE) Born in Verona, flourishing as a poet in the 50s and 60s BCE, he provides information on a number of key and lesser-known political figures but is most famous for his love poems to 'Lesbia' and some striking (in literary terms) longer poems with mythological themes.

Celer (Quintus Caecilius Metellus Celer) (*c*.102–59 BCE) Husband of Clodia, sister of Clodius.

censors Pair of Roman magistrates, elected by the *comitia centuriata* for a finite period (how long varied by the late republic) as conductors of the citizen census but also traditionally supervisors of public morals; they could exclude people from their voting tribes and from the senate. They also had responsibility for leasing land and buildings, farming out tax contracts, etc.

centaurs Mythical creatures that were half-man, half-horse, often associated with lustful and violent behaviour as well as a love of alcohol. Conflicts between humans and centaurs were particularly popular in Archaic Greek art.

choregos (**pl.** *choregoi*) Rich sponsor of the training of the Chorus in the Athenian drama festivals; this role was seen as a public service or *liturgy*.

Chrysippus (*c*.280–*c*.206 BCE) Greek philosopher who was the third head of the Stoic school and an important influence on later Stoic thought.

Cicero (Marcus Tullius Cicero) (106–43 BCE) Roman republican orator, author and statesman. His life and character are known in detail from his official writings and his personal correspondence. Cicero had an abiding interest in philosophy and wrote many philosophical works, including *On Duties*, which was based, in part, on an earlier work by the Greek Stoic Panaetius of Rhodes. He was forced to commit suicide by a powerful triumvirate comprising Mark Antony, Lepidus and Octavian.

Circe Goddess with magical powers who hosts Odysseus and his crew for a year on their way home from Troy.

city state (*polis*) Typical Greek form of politically and economically independent state in the Classical period.

Claudius (Tiberius Claudius Nero Caesar Drusus) (10 BCE to CE 54) Emperor of Rome CE 41–54.

Cleisthenes Athenian politician who rose to power in Athens after playing a key role in the overthrow of the city's tyranny. Cleisthenes instigated a series of populist reforms, including the reorganisation of the citizen body into a new series of tribes, which lay the foundations of Athens' radical democracy.

Cleopatra (69–30 BCE)   Ruler of Egypt, lover of Julius Caesar and Mark Antony. She was part of the Ptolemaic dynasty, Macedonian Greeks put into power in Egypt by Alexander the Great.

client, *cliens* (*see also* patron)   Roman free man in a reciprocal relationship with (usually) someone of a higher social status than himself. Freed slaves were assumed to be obliged to their former masters while enjoying their patronage and protection.

Clodia   One of the aristocratic Claudii family whose brother Clodius relinquished aristocratic status to become a tribune of the people. All the sisters are called 'Clodia'. One was the lover of Catullus and one (the wife of Quintus Caecilius Metellus Celer) was involved with Caelius and a witness for the prosecution at his trial; these two may or may not be the same 'Clodia'.

Clodius (Publius Clodius Pulcher) (*c.*92–52 BCE)   Tribune of the people, a powerful force in Rome in the 50s BCE. He was at first nurtured by the first triumvirate (Julius Caesar, Crassus and Pompey) but later turned on them. Killed in a confrontation with Milo and his armed entourage.

comitia centuriata **(century-based assembly)**   Wealth-based assembly at Rome empowered to enact laws, elect senior magistrates, declare war and inflict the death penalty.

consul   One of the two chief magistrates elected annually to oversee the running of Rome and the military campaigns throughout the empire.

Corinna   Female lyric poet, probably from Tanagra in Boeotia, traditionally thought to have been working in the late sixth or early fifth century BCE.

Crassus (Marcus Licinius Crassus) (*c.*112–53 BCE)   Consul in 70 and 55 BCE, he was immensely rich, a great deal of the wealth accumulated through the Sullan proscriptions. He made an uneasy alliance with Pompey and Julius Caesar (the first triumvirate) but his political ambitions were usually served by competition and conflict with his peers rather than co-operation. He was killed in battle (at Carrhae) while on his glory campaigns in Parthia.

crater   Large vessel for mixing together water and wine during a banquet.

curia   Hall, often used to refer specifically to the hall where the Roman senate met.

Cyclopes   In Greek legend, a group of mythical giants said to have used their great strength to build the citadels of Mycenae and elsewhere.

Darius (*c*.550–486 BCE)   King of Persia and father of Xerxes whose various attempts to invade mainland Greece were all thwarted, one of the largest setbacks being the Athenian victory at the Battle of Marathon in 490 BCE.

Dark Age   Modern name conventionally given to the period in Greek history from the twelfth to the eighth centuries BCE, so called because Greek culture at this time appears to have been at a low level and we know little about it.

demagogue   Populist politician or 'crowd-pleaser'.

Demodocus   In Homer's *Odyssey* (8 and 13), a blind bard at the court of king Alcinous of the Phaeacians, where Odysseus receives hospitality.

demos   The people or ordinary (male) citizens in Greece.

dictator   Roman office with supreme power but for a specified time and for a specified task when the city or its empire was in crisis.

didaskalia (**pl.** *didaskaliai*)   Greek public records (i.e. records of winners in the drama competitions).

Diomedes   In the *Iliad*, a Greek fighter prominent in the first part of the poem.

Dionysius of Halicarnassus (first century BCE)   Greek rhetorician and historian.

Epictetus (CE *c*.55–*c*.135)   Stoic philosopher, who began life as a slave. His teachings are preserved in two works, the *Discourses* and the *Handbook*.

Epicurean School   The philosophical school founded by Epicurus in the fourth century BCE.

Epicurus (341–271 BCE)   Greek philosopher who established a school in Athens at the end of the fourth century BCE. His doctrines are preserved in several letters and many fragments.

epideixis   Decorative or 'display' oratory, speeches delivered in public as an art form and/or to advertise the expertise of the sophists.

equites (**singular** *eques*)   Historically those Roman citizens wealthy enough to serve in the cavalry, defined by the property qualification of 400,000 sesterces.

eudaimonia   Greek term, which can be translated as 'well-being' or 'flourishing'. Ancient philosophers assume that every individual acts for the sake of his or her own *eudaimonia*, although they disagree about what constitutes *eudaimonia*.

Eumaeus Odysseus' faithful swineherd in the *Odyssey*.

Euripides (*c*.480–405/6 BCE) Youngest of the three major fifth-century BCE tragedians; he took the Trojan War and its aftermath as the theme of several of his plays.

Finnish Kalevala National Finnish epic compiled from traditional sources by the nineteenth-century CE Finnish scholar Elias Lönnrot.

focaliser Person from whose point of view a particular event or experience is perceived or interpreted in a story.

forensic oratory Speeches delivered in the courts to impress juries.

Fronto (Marcus Cornelius Fronto) (CE *c*.100–*c*.166) Orator and senator. Friend of the emperor Marcus Aurelius, his correspondence with whom survives.

Furies Also known as Erinyes. Ancient goddesses of retribution, one of whose roles is to punish wrongs, especially murder, done to blood relations.

Gallio *See* Novatus.

Gorgon Mythical female monster with the power to turn to stone anyone who looked at her.

Gracchi brothers (Tiberius Sempronius Gracchus) (CE 163–133), **(Gaius Sempronius Gracchus)** (CE 154–121) Tribunes of the people in the second century BCE, they put forward a programme of agrarian reform and also supported enfranchisement of the non-Roman population of Italy. Both were designated enemies of the state by the senate and met violent ends.

Great Dionysia Main Athenian festival, including dramatic competitions, celebrated at the end of March when the city was again full of visitors after the winter.

Hadrian (Publius Aelius Traianus Hadrianus) (CE 76–138) Roman emperor CE 115–138, particularly known for his interest in and promotion of Greek culture (philhellenism).

Hecato (first century BCE) Greek Stoic philosopher.

Hecuba Wife of the Trojan king Priam.

Hector Leader of the fighting opposition to the Greeks at Troy; killed by Achilles in *Iliad* 22.

Helen Wife of the Greek Menelaus; her abduction by the Trojan Paris (Alexander) causes the Trojan War.

Helios Sun god.

Helvia (first century CE) Wife of Lucius Annaeus Seneca the Elder and mother of Lucius Annaeus Seneca the Younger.

Hera Goddess, wife of Zeus, the king of the gods. In Homer's *Iliad*, she is fiercely partisan on the Greek side.

Heracles Demi-god, son of Zeus and a mortal woman Alcmene, famous for heroic exploits and labours.

Hermione Daughter of Menelaus and Helen of Sparta and wife of Achilles' son Neoptolemus.

Herodotus (fifth century BCE) The earliest Greek historian whose work survives, he was from Halicarnassus on the east coast of Asia Minor. Herodotus' *Historia* ('History' or 'Enquiry') was the first narrative of its kind: it is a wide-ranging history of the Greek world and its neighbours, whose central topic is the Persian Wars of the 490s and 480s BCE.

Hesiod (eighth/early seventh century BCE) Poet, composing in the Homeric style on themes of agriculture and the generations and characteristics of gods.

hetairai Courtesans in Athens.

Hierocles (end of first century CE) Greek Stoic philosopher.

Hittites A people living in central Asia Minor in the second half of the second millennium BCE, who probably had relations with Troy and maybe Greece.

Horace (Quintus Horatius Flaccus) (65–8 BCE) Roman poet who was born in Venusia to a father who was an ex-slave. He became part of Augustus' literary circle.

imperator Originally a title conferred upon a highly successful general, later a routine title of the emperor.

Iphitos Friend of Odysseus and the giver of his great bow, murdered by Heracles.

Isocrates (436–338 BCE) Athenian orator whose speeches engage with some of the most central political issues of the fourth century BCE and whose stylistic influence was profound. Isocrates' most famous works include his public speeches advocating unity among the Greek states.

Ithaca Island in the Ionian sea, off the west coast of Greece, Odysseus' home.

Jason *See* Argonauts.

Julia (39 BCE to CE 14)   Only child of the emperor Augustus, she was married three times in an attempt to secure the succession. Augustus exiled her in 2 BCE due to allegations of adultery.

Julio-Claudians   The dynasty established by Augustus and including the emperors Tiberius, Gaius (Caligula), Claudius and Nero.

Justinian (CE 527–65)   Emperor in the eastern and parts of the western Roman empire, ruled from Byzantium.

Juvenal (Decimus Iunius Iuvenalis) (CE c.65–130)   Roman satirist who wrote in the early decades of the second century CE on the decadence and immorality of life in Rome.

kouros   Statue of a nude male standing upright.

Laertes   Odysseus' father.

Lapiths   Tribe from Thessaly in northern Greece, whose mythical king, Perithoos, made the mistake of inviting centaurs to his wedding. In the drunken fight that broke out, the centaurs assaulted Perithoos' bride, Hippodame.

lays   Name given by modern commentators to legendary stories, thought by some scholars to be the precursors of formal epic poems.

Lepidus (Marcus Aemilius Lepidus) (c.88–12 BCE)   Consul in 46 BCE and triumvir (with Mark Antony and Octavian) 43–36 BCE. He had inherited influence in Cisalpine Gaul (Gaul the Italian side of the Alps) and acquired powers in Spanish provinces. Outmanoeuvred by his fellow triumvirs (his troops eventually deserted to Octavian) he retired from public life and died of natural causes in 12 BCE.

Lesbia   Pseudonym of Catullus' mistress Clodia. *See* Clodia.

libertas   'Freedom'. Denoted the rights of Roman citizens but also a watchword of those who wished to retain or restore republican government and their privileges and powers when one-man rule was on the agenda.

libertus/a   Roman freed slave.

Lucilius (Gaius Lucilius Junior) (first century CE)   Friend of Lucius Annaeus Seneca the Younger, to whom Seneca addresses a set of letters on philosophical questions.

Lucretius (Titus Lucretius Carus) (CE c.99–c.55)   Roman Epicurean philosopher, author of the poem *On the Nature of Things* in which he set out and argued for the doctrines of Epicurean philosophy.

ludi   Public shows or spectacles.

ludi scaenici   Theatrical shows.

lyric poetry   Poetry originally composed to be sung to the lyre, in a variety of metres other than hexameter which is used for epic.

Lysias   Attic orator who worked in the late fifth and early fourth century BCE, whose main activity comprised writing speeches for litigants to deliver in court. He was acclaimed as a master of the naturalistic 'Attic' style of speech writing (as opposed to the more florid 'Asiatic' style).

Mamurra (other names uncertain)   Julius Caesar's chief of engineers and allegedly a partner in his sexual and financial ventures.

manumission   The formal freeing of slaves in Rome.

Marcia (first century CE)   Roman woman to whom Seneca the Younger addressed a consolation on the death of her son.

Marius (Gaius Marius) (*c.*157–85 BCE)   Consul at the end of the second century BCE, he was famous for his campaigns in Africa. He changed the composition of the army from conscripted to professional.

Mark Antony (Marcus Antonius) (*c.*83–30 BCE)   Consul, triumvir, a close ally of Julius Caesar, famous for his relationship with Cleopatra. Finally lost the battle for power to Octavian when defeated along with Cleopatra's Egyptian forces at Actium in 31 BCE.

Martial (Marcus Valerius Martialis) (CE *c.*40–102)   Roman poet, originally from Spain, who wrote topical poems reflecting the social life of his day.

Marullus (other names uncertain) (first century CE)   Mutual friend of Seneca the Younger and Lucilius Junior. Reproved by Seneca for grieving excessively over the death of his young son.

Megalensian Games   Inaugurated in 204 BCE to mark the introduction of the Great Mother Cybele, a deity who was imported into Rome from Asia and established near the Temple of Victory on the Palatine hill.

Menelaus   Red-haired king of Sparta and brother of Agamemnon. It is the abduction of Menelaus' beautiful wife, Helen, by Paris/Alexander that is the cause of the Trojan War.

metic (*metoikoi*)   The Greek translates as 'those who live with'. Resident foreigners in Athens who often played a key role economically as craftsmen and traders. Unlike citizens, however, metics and their families did not enjoy any political rights such as the right to vote or hold office.

Milo (*c*.87–48 BCE)   A protégé of Pompey, he engineered Cicero's recall from exile and organised rival street gangs in opposition to Clodius. Cicero attempted to defend him when he killed Clodius in 52 BCE but Pompey had withdrawn all support and intimidated Cicero into silence. Milo was exiled but later died in an abortive rebellion against Caesar in south Italy in 48 BCE.

munus **(pl. *munera*)**   Roman gladiatorial games.

Muses   Goddesses of poetry, song and art and hence patrons of poets. Their home was thought to be the region of Pieria in Thessaly (or sometimes nearby Olympus). Homer and Hesiod both invoke the Muse(s) and ask for help in the creation of their poems.

narratology   Theory of narrative, which aims to describe how the narrative production, such as in literature, works using analytical methods derived from Russian Formalism and French Structuralism.

Neoptolemus   Son of Achilles and the slayer of the Trojan king Priam. On his return to Greece, Neoptolemus married Hermione, the daughter of Menelaus and Helen, having already taken Hector's wife Andromache as a concubine.

Nero (Nero Claudius Caesar Augustus Germanicus) (CE 37–68)   Emperor of Rome CE 54–68.

Nicias (*c*.470–413 BCE)   Athenian general and politician known for his great wealth. He opposed aggressive imperialism but was made to lead the Sicilian expedition and was defeated and killed in Sicily.

nobiles   Literally meaning 'known' and referring to the most prestigious ruling-class families, it came to refer in the later republic to men descended from holders of the consulship.

Novatus (Lucius Annaeus Novatus), also known as **Gallio** (*c*.5 BCE to CE 65)   Elder brother of Seneca the Younger. Roman senator who eventually became governor of Achaea.

nutrix **(pl. *nutrices*)**   Nurse.

Octavian *See* Augustus.

Odysseus   One of the greatest Greek heroes in Homer's *Iliad*, as well as the eponymous hero of the *Odyssey*, which means the 'song of Odysseus'. His adventures and return home from Troy form the theme of the *Odyssey*.

Oedipus   Son of King Laius of Thebes, who killed his father and married his mother, Jocasta. Following the discovery of his guilt, Oedipus wandered, blind, accompanied by his daughter, Antigone.

oikos The Greek word for 'house' or 'household' which, as in English, can also refer to the people who make up the household, that is, the extended family. The *oikos* played a key role in ancient Greek society, serving as an important focus of loyalty and the basic unit of social organisation.

Olympus High mountain in northern Greece, traditionally the home of the gods.

Orestes Son of Agamemnon, he avenges his father's murder (*see* Aeschylus).

Ovid (Publius Ovidius Naso) (43 BCE to CE 17) Leading Latin poet at the time of Augustus. Particularly known for love poetry, mythological poetry and a poetic calendar.

paedagogus Person in charge of young children.

Panaetius of Rhodes (*c*.180–*c*.109 BCE) Greek Stoic philosopher. Head of the Stoic school from *c*.129 BCE. Author of a book offering moral advice to those who had not achieved wisdom. Panaetius was instrumental in bringing Stoic philosophy to Rome and his book was the model for the first two books of Cicero's *On Duties*.

Panathenaic festival Major Athenian festival which was held every four years; in the sixth century BCE, the occasion for the recitation of the Homeric poems.

pancratium Contest in the athletic games, literally 'trial of strength', including wrestling, judo and boxing, but with no holds barred.

paterfamilias Male head of a family who had *potestas* over others.

patria potestas The power of the *paterfamilias*.

Patroclus One of the main characters in Homer's *Iliad*, Achilles' henchman and close friend, whose death in battle causes Achilles to return to the fight and kill Patroclus' killer, the Trojan Hector.

patron, *patronus* (*see also* client) In Rome, someone of sufficient wealth, standing and influence to have others beholden to him in some way. All citizens with freed (manumitted) slaves were patrons with ready-made clients.

Paulina (Pompeia Paulina) (first century CE) Wife of Seneca the Younger.

Peleus Elderly father of Achilles.

Penelope Wife of Odysseus; courted by oppressive suitors in Ithaca on the assumption that Odysseus is dead, she nevertheless holds out and is eventually reunited with him.

Pericles (*c*.495–429 BCE) Athenian general and politician. Aristocrat member of the Alcmaeonidae family, but became a leader of the developed democracy. *Choregos* for Aeschylus *Persians* (472 BCE), leader of the Athenian public building programme in the 440s and 430s, and leader of the Athenians in the war against Sparta (in which his defensive policy was admired by Thucydides). He died in the plague.

Peripatetic School The philosophical school founded by Aristotle in Athens during the fourth century BCE.

Perses Hesiod's brother, named in Hesiod's *Works and Days*.

Petronius (Petronius Arbiter) (first century CE) Roman satirist, author of the *Satyricon*, who is thought by many to be identical with Titus (or Gaius) Petronius, a Roman of senatorial rank who was forced to commit suicide by Nero in CE 66.

Phaeacians The people who give Odysseus hospitality when he is shipwrecked on his way home.

Pharius (first century CE) Slave of Seneca the Younger.

Phemius In Homer's *Odyssey*, a bard in Odysseus' home in Ithaca.

Philoctetes Greek hero at Troy whose festering wound in his foot leads the Greeks to abandon him on a deserted island; the principal character of a play by the fifth-century BCE tragedian Sophocles.

Philostratus (Lucius Flavius Philostratus) (CE *c*.170–*c*.244) From the island of Lemnos; wrote the *Lives of the Sophists*, our major source for the 'Second Sophistic', the Greek literary movement of the second and third centuries CE.

pietas Duty, loyalty and their observance.

Pindar (*c*.518–438 BCE) Boeotian poet, best known for the composition of Victory Odes.

Pisistratus Ruler of Athens in the second half of the sixth century BCE.

Plato (*c*.429–347 BCE) Greek philosopher and follower of Socrates, author of numerous philosophical works on contemporary ethical themes, mostly written in dialogue form, in which Socrates typically appears as a character. He wrote dialogues critical of Homer and other Greek poets and was the founder of the oldest philosophical school, known as the Academy.

plebs The people; the common people of Rome; the general body of Roman citizens. This came to mean those who were not senators or *equites*, that is, the lower orders.

Pliny the Elder (Gaius Plinius Secundus) (CE 23–79)   Scholar with wide interests. His surviving work, the *Natural History*, is an encyclopaedic compilation. It surveys all aspects of 'scientific' knowledge of the time and includes information about Roman social and economic life, political institutions and art.

Pliny the Younger (Gaius Plinius Caecilius Secundus) (CE *c.*61–*c.*112)   Born at Como of a wealthy family, he was brought up by his uncle, Pliny the Elder. He was a successful lawyer and administrator who followed a senatorial career culminating in governing Bithynia-Pontus under the emperor Trajan. Nine books of his literary letters survive, and a collection of correspondence with Trajan from his time in Bithynia.

Plutarch (CE *c.*50–*c.*120)   Greek scholar and author who wrote a collection of paired biographies of eminent Greeks and Romans known as the *Parallel Lives*.

Polybius (first century CE)   Freedman of the emperor Claudius, to whom Seneca addressed a consolation on the death of his brother.

Polyxena   Trojan daughter of Priam and Hecuba; following the fall of Troy, ritually sacrificed to the dead Achilles.

Pompey (Gnaeus Pompeius Magnus Felix) (106–48 BCE)   Dominating military leader who raised a private army and joined with Sulla, achieving a triumph at the age of 25. With his collection of client kings across the East he was for many years an unassailable force at Rome.

porticus   Rectangular building with colonnades on the interior of each side, often associated with theatres or temples.

Poseidon   God of the sea and horses; brother of Zeus.

potestas   Roman legal authority over someone or something.

praefectus fabrum   In Rome, chief of engineers: *praefectus* refers to one placed in charge. *Praefecti* might be officers in the army, state and judicial officials, etc.

Priam   Elderly king of Troy; in *Iliad* 24, he secretly ransoms from Achilles the body of his son Hector.

Ptolomy (Claudius Ptolemaeus) (second century CE)   Wrote books on astronomy, geography, astrology and harmonics; lived in Alexandria, Egypt.

Quintilian (Marcus Fabius Quintilianus) (CE *c*.35–*c*.95)   Roman orator and writer on rhetoric, originally from Spain. He wrote a textbook on the training of an orator.

rhapsode   Performer (not creator) of epic poetry, for example at festivals such as the Panathenaia.

Romulus Augustulus (fifth century CE)   Last emperor in the Roman West, deposed in CE 476.

Rubicon   A little river that separated Cisalpine Gaul (Gaul the Italian side of the Alps) from Italy. In crossing the Rubicon and advancing from Ravenna to Rimini, Julius Caesar was 'invading' the territory of Rome with his army.

salutatio   In Rome, ceremonial morning visit of a client to his patron.

Sappho (late seventh to sixth century BCE)   Female lyric poet from Mytilene on the island of Lesbos, contemporary of Alcaeus. Her poems, a number of fragments of which survive, have given rise to the English word 'Lesbian', since many refer to love between women or girls.

senate   The ruling body in Rome composed of senior ex-magistrates and additional members chosen by the censors on the basis of their ability to finance equipment of a horse for military service (*see equites*).

Seneca the Elder (Lucius Annaeus Seneca) (*c*.55 BCE to CE *c*.40) Roman rhetorician and writer. Father of Seneca the Younger.

Seneca the Younger (Lucius Annaeus Seneca) (*c*.4 BCE to CE 65) Roman statesman, writer and philosopher. Seneca was tutor and later adviser to the emperor Nero and a prominent Stoic philosopher. He wrote a number of treatises on Stoic ethics and a set of philosophical letters addressed to his friend Lucilius Junior.

Sequani   Gallic tribe centred at modern Besançon, France.

shaft grave   Deep rectangular pit found in, for example, Mycenae, used as a burial chamber.

Socrates (*c*.470–399 BCE)   Greek philosopher who produced no philosophical writings, but his philosophical concerns and methods were represented by his pupil Plato in a number of dialogues. Socrates eventually committed suicide, having been convicted by an Athenian court on charges of impiety related to his unorthodox beliefs and of corrupting the young.

Sophocles (*c*.495–406 BCE)   Middle of the three major fifth-century BCE tragedians; like Aeschylus and Euripides, he wrote plays on the Trojan War theme.

Soranus (second century CE)   Greek physician who practised in Rome under the emperors Trajan and Hadrian. He wrote on medical matters including midwifery.

stasis   In Greece, civil conflict.

Stoic School   Philosophical school founded by Zeno of Citium in Athens at the end of the fourth century BCE. The school was named after its meeting place, the Stoa Poikile ('Painted Colonnade'). Notable heads of the school included Chrysippus and Panaetius of Rhodes.

Stoicism   Greek philosophical movement or school, which Roman followers tended to present more as an attitude or way of life, especially regarding how to survive adversity with equanimity and be guided by reason not emotion.

strategos (**pl.** *strategoi*)   In Greece, an elected general.

Suetonius (Gaius Suetonius Tranquillus) (CE *c.*70–*c.*130)   Biographer writing in the first century CE. North African, with the status of *eques*. We have an incomplete version of his book *The Twelve Caesars*.

Suillius (Publius Suillius Rufus) (*c.*15 BCE to CE *c.*58)   Roman senator, prosecuted for extortion in CE 58.

Sulla (Lucius Cornelius Sulla Felix) (*c.*138–79 BCE)   Succeeded Marius as a highly effective commander in Africa and later campaigned in Gaul and Asia Minor. Like Julius Caesar, he marched on Rome and ruled the roost in two spurts of punitive government (his enemies were killed and his methods generally unorthodox).

Sulpicius (Servius Sulpicius Rufus) (*c.*104–43 BCE)   Friend and correspondent of Cicero, he was consul in 51 BCE but more of a jurist than a politician. Cicero procured a commemorative statue in the forum on his death.

symposium   Drinking party, sometimes used as the subject for vase paintings.

Tacitus (Publius Cornelius Tacitus) (CE *c.*55–*c.*117)   Roman historian. Author of the *Annals* and the *Histories*. He was a prominent orator and pursued a political career which began under the emperor Vespasian and culminated in the governorship of Asia under the emperor Trajan.

Telemachus   Son of Odysseus; he plays a major part in the *Odyssey*, especially the first four books.

Thetis   Divine mother of Achilles; her appeal to Zeus on her son's behalf provides the initial impetus of the plot of the *Iliad*.

Thucydides (*c*.460–400 BCE)   Athenian historian and general.

Timaeus (*c*.350–260 BCE)   Greek writer of a history of Sicily.

toga   The formal and official dress of a Roman citizen. It was a gown made of a single piece of heavy white woollen material. The *toga virilis* ('gown of manhood') was a toga assumed by young male Romans when they came of age.

tribunes, tribuneship (*tribuni plebis*)   In Rome, officers of the people (their number seemed to vary) whose area of jurisdiction grew and whose person was supposed to be inviolate. They had the right to veto legislative acts and decisions across the board.

tribute   Money paid by a subservient city/state to an imperial overlord (e.g. in the Athenian or Roman empire).

triglyph   Panels carved with three vertical sections found on the entablature of a Greek temple (i.e. the section above the columns but beneath the cornice) that separated other panels (metopes) that were often sculpted.

triumvirate (*triumviri*)   Panel of three Roman officials. The name was also given to a powerful alliance of three men who took over the reins of government and divided the Roman provinces among themselves. Significant senatorial enemies suffered property confiscation or even death during their hegemony.

Trojan Cycle   Series of epic poems that together tell the story of the Trojan War and its aftermath. Most of the poems, attributed to various authors, including Homer, are lost and available only in later summaries (the *Iliad* and *Odyssey* are the exceptions).

Trojan Horse   Wooden horse built by the Greeks to trick the Trojans into admitting them into Troy and so leading to the fall of the city.

Trojan War   War between a coalition of Greeks against Troy, arising from the abduction of Helen.

Troy VI and Troy VIIa   Successive phases of occupation of the site of the city of Troy, thought to be associated with an attack by Greeks in the thirteenth century BCE, in which may lie the origin of the legend of the Trojan War.

Tullia (*c*.79–57 BCE)   Cicero's beloved daughter who died in childbirth. She was married three times, her last husband, Publius Cornelius Dolabella, being her own choice and not as politically advantageous to

Cicero (in fact more of an embarrassment) as her previous marriage alliances. In their very brief marriage she bore Dolabella two sons, both of whom died in infancy.

Tutela Roman goddess protective of cities and combining aspects of other deities including Fortuna.

tutor In Rome, a legal guardian.

Ulysses Latin name for Odysseus.

Virgil (Publius Vergilius Maro) (70–19 BCE) Author of the Latin epic, the *Aeneid*. *See* Aeneas.

Xerxes (*c.*520–465 BCE) King of Persia, who continued to pursue the ambitions of his father, Darius, to conquer mainland Greece after the latter's death in 486 BCE. Xerxes' plans were also thwarted by the Greeks, who scored significant victories over the Persians at Salamis (480 BCE), Platea and Mycale (479 BCE).

Zeno of Citium (334–262 BCE) Greek philosopher who founded the Stoic philosophical school in Athens at the end of the fourth century BCE. None of his works have survived.

Zeus King of the Greek gods.

Index

the Academy (school of philosophy) 153
Achilles
    alleged tomb of 49
    in Homer's *Iliad* 34, 47, 52, 58, 59, 119
        as a Homeric hero 48–9, 62–3
        and the poet's narrative 74
Aemilius Scaurus 198
Aeneas 16, 49, *179*, 181
Aeon, god of eternal time *27*
Aeschines 120
Aeschylus 49, 62
    and Aristophanes' *Frogs* 126
    Eumenides 102, 124
    Oresteia 63
    Persians 93–4, 95, 106, 118, 120, 124
    Suppliants 124
Agamemnon 49, 53, 63
    gold death-mask at Mycenae 53, *54*
agōn
    different meanings of 120
    in drama 125, 126
    in rhetorical debate 122
Agrippina, wife of Claudius 154
Agrippina the Younger 173
Alcaeus 83
Alcibiades, speech in the Athenian Assembly (415 BCE) 117–18, 122
Alexander the Great 32, 49
alphabetical writing, and the Homeric poems 56–7, 62, 64
America, Classical period of the Lowland Maya 11
Amphidamas, King 80
amphitheatres *see* theatre, amphitheatre and circus audiences
Andromache
    in Euripedes 104–6
    in Homeric poetry 49
Anna Severina (nurse) *186*
Anonymus Valesii 22

anthropology 11
anxiety, Seneca on death and freedom from 166–7
Aphrodite, goddess, in Sappho's poetry 81–3
Apollo of Tenea statue 33–4, *35*
'apostrophe' device, in Homeric poems 72–3
apprenticeships, and Roman children 182
archaeology, and Classical Studies 8, 9, 12, 18
Archaic period 31, 35, 40, 43
    and the Hallstatt D period 40, 41, 42–3
    and sculpture 33–4, *35*
    and tyranny 37
architecture, and Classical Studies 9, 18
Ariès, Philippe 176
Ariovistus, Suebi tribe leader 146–7
Aristophanes
    Clouds 87, 90, 121, 122, 126
    Frogs 125
        Nathan Lane adaptation *127*
    Lysistrata 126
    Peace 87
    Wasps 87, 126
Aristotle 9, 153
    Nicomachean Ethics 157
    Poetics 62
    Politics 164
    and Stoicism 157
art
    and Classical Studies 12
    history of 8, 9
    and periodisation 38
astrology 29–31
Athena, goddess 16, 52, 58, 82
    in Homer's *Odyssey* 114–15
    and the Parthenon 98, 99–101
        Parthenos statue 99–100
        Promachos statue 100
        temple of Athena Nike *99*, 100–1, *101*
Athens 19, 98–106
    Archaic and Classical periods in 40

city state (Attica) 89–92
and the Delian League 98
dramatic festivals 122–5, 129
and the 'Fifty Years' 98
and Hellenism 92–8
oratory in 119–20, 119–22
Panathenaic festival 57
the Parthenon 98–101, *99, 100, 101*
performance culture in 112, 122–5
sack of (480 BCE) 37, 93
schools of philosophy 153–4
self-identity in 86–92
victory and Athenian democracy 117–19

athletics 112, 128
in Homer's *Odyssey* 113–15
scenes from Black-figure Panathenaic amphorae *117*

Atticus 16

audiences 193–209
and Athenian dramatic festivals 124–5
and oratory 120–2
see also theatre, amphitheatre and circus audiences

Augustine, *Confessions* 199

Augustus, emperor (formerly Octavian) 30, 38, 133, 173, 181
and festivals 198
shows and spectacles given by 205, 206, 207
silver coin of *30*

Aulus Gellius 10

authorial voices, in early Greek poetry 69–84

babies 177, 186, 188–9
exposed or abandoned 188–9
infant deaths 188

Badian, Ernst 143

barbarians
and Greek identity 86, 93–6, 97–8, 106–7
in Greek tragedy 104–6

BC/AD and BCE/CE systems 23–4

bereavement, Seneca on 165–8

Blegen, Carl 55

boys (Roman children)
babies 177
deaths of 182–3
and the law 180
rites of passage 177

Britannicus, natural son of Claudius 173

Bronze Age (*c.*2500–1100 BCE), and the Trojan War 54, 59

bulla (childhood protective necklace) 177, *178*

Burrus, Roman military officer 154

Byron, George Gordon, Lord 53

Byzantine empire 22

Caelius, trial of 143–5

Caesar
title of 133
see also Julius Caesar

Caius Lusius Storax, relief from the tomb of *209*

calendars, Roman 25–6

Cambridge Illustrated History of Ancient Greece 112–13

cannibalism, and Stoicism 159

Carthage
earliest archaeological finds at 22
foundation of 21

Cartledge, Paul 123

Cato the Elder 153, 184–5

Cato the Younger 154, 159

Catullus 8, 134–5
and children 177
poems 135, 141–2, 143, 146
relationship with Lesbia/Clodia 143–4, 145
and Roman politics 135, 141–2
and the trial of Caelius 143–5

Celadus, gladiator 200

Central Europe, table of periods 31

children *see* Roman children

choice, and Stoicism 159

Chrysippus, Stoic philosopher 159, 164
Cicero, Marcus Tullius 9–10, 16, 133–4, 135, 189
    on audiences 193, 203, 204–5
    Brutus 38
    bust of *134*
    character 145–6
    correspondence with Sulpicius 136–9
    Letters to Atticus 204
    Letters to his brother Quintus 203
    Letters to his Friends 199, 204
    On Duties 160, 164
    On Friendship 187
    oratory skills 140
    and philosophy 153
    Pro Milo 203
    Pro Murena 203
    Pro Sestio 193, 203, 204–5
    and Roman politics 134, 136–9, 140, 142
    and the trial of Caelius 144–5
circus *see* theatre, amphitheatre and circus audiences
Circus Maximus, Rome 193, 197
citizens
    Roman citizens and voting 140, 148
    and self-identity in Classical Athens 89–90
citizenship 37
city states (Greek *polis*) 62
    Athens 89–92
        and dramatic festivals 124–5
        and barbarians 96–8
'Classical', meaning of in English 10
Classical civilisations/periods 10–11
Classical period (fifth to fourth centuries BCE) 10, 31, 33–9, 40, 43
    and democracy 36–7
    and Hellenism 92–8
    and sculpture 33–7, *36*
    and self-identity 86–92
    and Troy 49
Classical Studies 11–12, 39
    interdisciplinary approach to 12–19

Claudius, emperor 154, 173–4
Cleon, and the Mytilene debate 121, 122
Clodia Metelli 144–5
Clodius 143–4, 145, 204, 205
Coarelli, Filippo 16
Colosseum 193, *194*, *196*, 198
comparative literature 11
Constantinople, Ottoman conquest of 22
context, and periodisation 39–40
Corinna 91
the cosmos, and time 25–9
Crescens, gladiator 200
Darius, Persian king 92
'Dark Age' (Greek) 59
Dark Ages (Western Europe) 10
David, Jacques Louis 9
death
    and amphitheatre audiences 198–200, 202
    of Roman children 182–3, 187–9
        epitaphs 175–6, 184, 188
        grave reliefs *178*, 184
        infants 188–9
    Seneca on 154, 165–8, 188
Delian League 98
Delphi, Pythian Games 116
Delphi Charioteer, bronze sculpture *115*, 115–16
demagogues 122
demes, and the Athenian city-state 89–90
democracy 10
    Athenian
        and drama 126
        and oratory 119–22
        performance culture in 112, 122–5, 129
        and self-identity 91–2, 103–4
        and victory 111, 117–19
        and the Classical period 36–7

and the Roman republic 140–1, 148, 149

Demodocus (bard in the *Odyssey*) 59, 76, 113

Demosthenes 120

diachronic study 39

Dio Cassius 173, 174, 181, 199, 203, 205

Diomedes 60

Dionysus, god 16

Dionysius of Halicarnassus 182

Dionysus, play festivals of 123

display oratory 119

Domitian, emperor 187, 196, 205

the *Doryphoros* (spear-bearer) statue 34–5, *36*, 37

drama 8
- *agōn* in 125, 126
- and Athenian identity 101–6
- Chorus in 125–6
- comic plays and the trial of Caelius 145
- contests and debates in 125–6
- depiction of barbarians in 93–5
- dramatic festivals in Athens 122–5, 129
- and Homeric poetry 49
- and performance 112, 128–9
- self-identity in 86–7
- *stichomythia* in 125

Drusus Caesar 24

eastern Mediterranean, and the ending of the Classical world 22

eudaimonia (well-being), and Stoicism 156–60

education
- and Roman children 184–5
- study of the classics 9

Egypt
- Herodotus on Egyptian priests 5–6
- horoscope plaque *29*

embedded focalisation, in Homeric poems 74

epic poetry 10, 82
- and the celebration of victory 116
- *see also* Homer/Homeric poems

Epictetus, Stoic philosopher 156, 163–4

Discouses 167, 168

Epicureanism 154
- and Stoicism 156, 157–8

Epicurus 153, 154
- *Letter to Menoeceus* 158
- and wealth 160–1

epideictic oratory 119

epideixis 120

epigraphy, and the assassination of Julius Caesar 15, 18

epitaphs, for Roman children 175–6, 184, 188

equites, in the Roman republic 140, 195, 196

ethics
- and Stoicism 156–60
- and death 166–8
- and the treatment of slaves 162–5

Euripides
- *Andromache* 104–6
- and Aristophanes' *Frogs* 126
- *Children of Heracles* 102
- *Hecuba* 64
- *Helen* 60–1, 104
- *Iphigenia in Tauris* 104
- *Medea* 102, 103
- *Orestes* 94–5
- *Suppliant Women* 102, 103–4, 124
- *Trojan Women* 104, 105

Euripides 49

excellence, and Homeric heroes 47–8, 63–4

'experiencing' the Classical world 5–7

fame
- in Homeric poetry 112–15
- and victory 115–16

famine, and slaves 164

fathers
- of Roman children 174, 183
- and childcare 184–5
- and infant deaths 188
- legal rights of 176, 182
- and rites of passage 177

fear of death, Seneca on 166–7

'folk poetry', and the Homeric poems 57–8

foreigners, and self-identity in Classical Athens 88–9

forensic oratory 120

freedmen
    children of 183, 184, 185
    grave reliefs *178*, 184
    in the Roman republic 149

freedom, Seneca on death and 156

freedom of speech 37

Fronto, *Letters to his Friends* 177–9, 187

funerals 197, 209

Gabinius 204

Gaius, emperor 173, 207

Gaius Norbanus Flaccus 24

Gallio, brother of Seneca 154

Gaul, Caesar and wars in 142, 146–7

Geertz, Clifford 112

gender
    and Homeric poems 49, 83
    and lyric poetry 83
    and Roman children 174, 177, 180, 182–3
    and victory in Classical Rome 16
    see also women

gender studies 11

geography, and the Classical world 11, 12, 21

Gildenhard, Ingo 27–8

Giordano, Luca, *The Death of Seneca* 168

girls (Roman children) 177
    babies 177
    deaths of 183
    and the law 180
    and marriage 177, 180, 183, 185

gladiatorial games (*munera*) 148–9, 197, 199–201, *200*, 202–3, 205, *209*

god, Stoic conception of 158–9

Goldhill, Simon 112

Gorgias, sophist 121–2

Gracchi brothers 142, 143

Grand Tour 9

grave reliefs
    and Roman children *178*, 184
    tomb of Caius Lusius Storax *209*
    see also tombstones

Greece, table of periods 31

Greek cultural influence, time span of 12

Greek language
    and barbarians 96, 97
    and Classical Studies 11, 12
    translations of 7

Griffin, Miriam 154

Hadrian, emperor 49

Hall, Edith
    Inventing the Barbarian 93
    on performance in ancient Greece 112–13, 114, 128

Hall, Jonathan, *Hellenicity* 96

Hammond, Kate 142

head lice, and the Classical world 5–7

Hecato, Greek Stoic 164

Hector
    alleged tomb of 49
    in Homer's *Iliad* 47, 51, 52, 58, 63

Helen of Troy
    in Euripides 60–1, 94–5
    in Homeric poetry 49, 51, 56

Helios, sun god 76

Hellenism
    and fame 113
    and Greek identity 92–8

Hellenistic period 31, 32, 38

Hera, goddess *48*, 48

Heracles (Hercules) 52

Herculaneum, discovery of 9

Hercules 16

Herodotus 97–8, 120
    on the Heraclid dynasty 29
    on lice 5–6, 7
    on the Persian Wars 97

heroism 10

Hesiod 69, 78–81, 83
    Theogony 60, 78–9, 81, 82
    Works and Days 26, 33, 60, 78, 79–80

Hierocles, Stoic philosopher 163

Hippias of Elis 89

Hissarlik, and the site of Troy 53–6

history
    and the Classical period 10
    study of ancient 8–9

Homer/Homeric poems 10, 19, 47–65
    and current Homeric scholarship 64
    female characters in 49
    and Greek 'folk poetry' 57–8
    and the Greek oral tradition 58–9, 60, 62
    and the Greek/Roman gods and goddesses 49, 52
    heroes of 47, 51–2, 62–4
    and the identity of Homer 51
    Iliad 8, 47, 52, 57, 58, 59, 61, 64
        'Catalogue of Ships' 52, 72
        and the Greek oral tradition 60
        narrative voice in 52, 69, 71, 72, 73–4
        oratory in 119
        and Sappho's poetry 82
        and Troy 55
        victory in 116
        weakness of heroes in 62–3
    narrative voice of 69, 71–8
        'apostrophe' device 72–3
        characters speaking through the poet 75–7
        and the Muses 52, 71–2, 73–4, 76–7, 119
        poet speaking for 'himself' 73
        poet's narrative 74
    Odyssey 16–18, 47, 52, 57, 58, 59, 64, 75–9
        and the Greek oral tradition 60
        narrative voice in 69, 71, 72, 73, 74, 75–9
        tensions in 63
        victory and fame in 113–15
    and other Greek legendary material 60–4
    and philology 83–4
    and popular drama 49
    'portraits' of Homer 69, *70*
    and the Trojan War 49, 52–6, 57, 59–60
    and Troy 49–51
    victory and fame in 112–15
    and the Wolf hypothesis 56–7, 59

Horace
    Letters 182
    Satire 183

horoscopes *29*, 29–31

Horsfall, Nicholas, *The Culture of the Roman Plebs* 148–9

human geography 11

Hymn to Delian Apollo 60

Iliad see Homer/Homeric poems

incest, and Stoicism 159

India, 'Classical' civilisation in 11

'indifference debate', and Roman children 187–9

infant mortality, and Roman children 188–9

Ingres, Jean-Auguste-Dominique, *The Apotheosis of Homer 70*

interdisciplinary approach 12–19

Iron Age 31, 33
    Hallstatt D period 40, 41–3

Islamic conquest, and the ending of the Classical world 22

Isocrates, Athenian orator 98

Italy, table of periods 31

Jason and the Argonauts legend 60

Joffroy, R. 40

Jong, Irene de 71

Julia, daughter of Augustus 173, 174

Julius Caesar 133, 134, 144
    assassination of 13–15, 18
    and Catullus 134, 135
    The Conquest of Gaul 146–7
    dramatisations of 135
    and gladitorial games 149

and the Julian calendar 23
reform strategy 143
and republican values 136, 138
reputation for corruption and sexual
    excess 141, 142
and Roman politics 140
silver denarius of *143*
and the theatre 203, 207

Juno, goddess 16

Justinian, emperor 22

Juvenal, *Satires* 206

Korfmann, Manfred 56

kouros statues 34, *38*

language, and Classical Studies 12

Latin language
    and Classical Studies 11, 12
    translations of 7

'lays' (short poems), and Homeric poetry 57–8

lekythoi 128

libertas, Roman concept of 140

liberty 10, 37

life expectancy, and Roman children 187–8

literature
    and the assassination of Julius Caesar
        15, 18
    and Classical Studies 12
    comparative 11
    textual criticism 8, 9

Livy 199, 203

Lucilius Junior, Seneca's letters to 154, 155, 159, 160, 161, 163, 165–6, 167

Lucretius 153, 154
    The Nature of the Universe 33

ludi (festivals) 197, 198, 202, 203, 205

luxury, Seneca on 161–2, 163–4

lyric poetry 82, 83
    and the celebration of victory 116

Lysias 120
    On the Murder of Eratosthenes 91

MacKendrick, Paul 145

Marathon, battle of (490 BCE) 93, 101

Marcia, Seneca's consolations to 154, 165, 166

Marcus Aurelius, emperor 198

Marcus Junius, silver denarius of *149*

Martial 13
    Epigrams 177, 182, 187
    Epode 196

Maya civilisation 11

Megalensian Games 145

methodology, and interdisciplinary approaches 18

metics (non-Athenians), and self-identity in Classical Athens 88–9

Middle Ages, and ancient philosophy 9

Milo, murderer of Clodius 144, 203

Minerva/Athena *see* Athena, goddess

Minicia Marcella, death of 183, 187

Moisson, M. 40

mosaics, personifications of time featured on *27*, 28–9

Mouritsen, Henrik 148

the Muses
    and Hesiod 78–9, 79–80, 81
    in Homeric poetry 52, 71–2, 73–4, 76–7, 119

museums 8, 9

Mycenae 49, 51, 57
    Bronze Age palaces 59
    gold death-mask excavated from 53, *54*
    Lion Gate *50*
    pottery 55

mythology, and the assassination of Julius Caesar 15, 18

Mytilene debate 121–2

names, and self-identity in Classical Athens 86–92

nannies/nurses, and Roman children 185, *186*, 186–7

narratology 71–84
    in Hesiod 69, 78–81

in Homeric poetry 71–8
nationalism (nineteenth-century), and the Homeric poems 57–8
Nero, emperor 154, 155, 160, 168
    early years 173, 174, 185
    nurses 187
    and shows and spectacles 208
    togate statue of *175*
Nestor's Cup 63
Nicias, speech in the Athenian Assembly (415 BCE) 117–18, 122
Ober, Josiah 125
Octavia, daughter of Claudius 173
Odysseus 16–18, 63–4
    in Homer's *Odyssey* 52, 57, 62, 75–6, 77, 78, 113–15
    representation on a vase *17*
Odyssey see Homer/Homeric poems
Olympic Games 21, 24, 111, 116, 118
oral dissemination
    Caesar's *Conquest of Gaul* 147
    Homeric poems 58–9, 60, 62
oratory, in Athens 119–22
Orientalising period 31, 33
Orpheus 16
Ottoman empire 22
Ovid, *Metamorphoses* 26–8
pain, Seneca on fear of 167
Panaetius, Stoic philosopher 160
Parenti, Michael 133, 142
parents
    of Roman children 180–4
        and the 'indifference debate' 187–9
    see also fathers
Parry, Milman 58
the Parthenon 98–101, *99*, *100*, *101*
    Acropolis gate *99*, 100
    temple of Athena Nike *99*, 100–1, *101*
Patroclus 47

patronage, and victory in Greek culture 115–16
patronyms, in Classical Athens 90
Paulina, wife of Seneca 155, 167–8
Peloponnesian War (431–404 BCE) 98, 106–7
Penelope, in Homer's *Odyssey* 63, 77–8
'people power', in the Roman republic 149–50
performance
    and Athenian democracy 112, 122–5, 129
    different meanings of the word 111–12
    and oratory 120–2
    victory and fame in Homeric poetry 112–15
    victory and patronage 115–16
Pericles 107, 118
    Funeral Speech 119, 122
periodisation 31–43
    and context 39–40
    defining boundaries between periods 32–3, 37, 39, 43
    hindsight and periods 33
    precision in 32
    table of periods 31
    and the Vix female burial 40–3, *41*, *42*
Peripatetic School of philosophy 153, 156
    and Stoicism 157, 158, 159
Persian Wars
    and Athens 98, 101, 106
    and Hellenism 92–6, 97–8
Persians, as barbarians 93–6, 97–8, 106–7
Petronia Grata, tombstone *179*
Phaeton, son of Pheobus the sun god 26–7
Pharius, slave of Seneca 155
Philocleia, Attic tombstone of *88*
philology 83–4
philosophy 8, 9, 12, 153–69
    Greek philosophers in Rome 153
    schools of 153–4, 156
    see also Seneca the Younger; Stoicism
Philostratus, *Lives of the Sophists* 51

pietas (parent-child relationships) 181
Pindar
    Nemean Eight 116
    Nemean Two 116
    Pythian Seven 116
Pisistratus, Athenian ruler 57, 64
Plato 54, 153
    Apology 47
    Euthyphro 87
    Lysis 87
    Phaedo 167
    Protagoras 87
    Republic 87
    on time and the cosmos 26
pleasure
    and spectacle 198–202
    and Stoicism 157–8
Pliny the Elder
    on lice 6–7
    Natural History 16, 198
Pliny the Younger 189
    Letters 177, 182–3, 186–7, 201
Plutarch
    Brutus 153
    Cato the Elder 153, 185
    Cato the Younger 153
    Numa 188
    On Stoic Self-contradictions 159
poetry 10
    see also Hesiod; Homer/Homeric poems; Sappho
Polemarchus, son of Cephalus 89
political oratory 120
politics
    and periods 36–7
    in the Roman republic 140–3
    and Stoicism 154
    and theatre audiences 205, 206, 209
Polybius, Seneca's consolations to 154, 165
Polyclitus 38
    'The Canon' 34
Polyxena, sacrifice of *61*
Polyzelus, tyrant of Gela 116

Pompeii 6, 9, 200
    amphitheatre riot (59 CE) *201*, 201–2
Pompey the Great 13, 15, 133, 141, 144
    and gladiatorial games 149, 199
    statue of in the *porticus* of Pompey 13, *15*, 16–18
poverty
    and Roman children 181–2
    and Stoicism 159, 160–2
prehistory 10, 21
    'Three Age' system of 33
Priam, Trojan King 51, 53
Procopius, *History of the Wars* 22
Ptolomy, *Tetrabiblos* 31
punishment, and amphitheatre audiences 199–200, 202
Quintilian, *Institutes of Oratory* 182
race, and barbarians 96–7
rationality 10
reason
    and Stoicism 156–60
        and the treatment of slaves 162–5
religion
    Greek religion and barbarians 96, 97
    women and religious rituals 128
rhetoric 114, 120–2
    and Athenian dramatic festivals 124
Roman Catholic church 11
Roman children 19, 172–89
    adolescents 177, 180, 187
    adult expectations of 180–4
    artistic representations of 175–6
    babies 177, 186, 188–9
    bulla (protective necklace) 177, *178*
    and childcare 184–7, 188
    deaths of 139
    and differentiation of childhood 177
    education of 185–6
    imperial 173–4
    and the 'indifference debate' 187–9
    language describing 177
    legal definitions of childhood 179–80

literature and imagery representing
  177–9
and *pietas* (parent-child
  relationships) 181
reliefs depicting children and
  childhood *178*
rites of passage 177
Roman attitudes to 172–3
Seneca on childrearing 172
sentimental attachments to 180–1, 184
voices of 174–7
and work 182

Roman cultural influence, time span of 12

Roman empire
  dating the end of the 22
  the emperor and theatre audiences
    195, 203, 205–8
  and historical works 135–6
  imperial children 173–4
  Julio-Claudian dynasty 133
  and Stoicism 153–4
  and Troy 49–51

Roman republic 133–50
  comitia centuriata 140
  and democracy 140–1, 148, 149
  equites 140, 148
  famous figures 133–5
  and modern scholarship 147–8
  and 'people power' 149–50
  and philosophy 153
  politics 140–3
  and republican values 136–9
  statue of Roman general from
    Tivoli *139*
  and theatre audiences 204–5
  veiled head of old republican *137*

Roman system of identifying years 24

Romantic movement, and Greek antiquity 53

Rome (city) 19
  Capitoline Annals *25*
  Circus Flaminus 197
  Circus Maximus 193, 197
  Colesseum 193, *194*, *196*, 198
  festival days 197–8
  Forma Urbis Marmorea 13, *14*
  forum 198

Greek philosphers in 153
population of 135
porticus of Pompey 13–18, *14*
Theatre of Marcellus 193, *194*
time measurement in 24
traditional date of founding of 24

Romulus Augustulus, emperor 22

Salamis, battle of (480 BCE) 93–4, 100

Sappho 69, 81–3, 91

satire, and Catullus 141–2

Sauron, Gilles 16

Schliemann, Heinrich 53–4, 64

sculpture 10
  Delphi Charioteer *115*, 115–16
  grave reliefs *178*, 184, *209*
  Greek sculpture and periodisation
    33–7, *35*, *36*
  and the Parthenon 99–101, *100*, *101*
  reliefs depicting children and
    childhood *178*
  statues in the *porticus* of Pompey *15*,
    16–18
  see also tombstones

self-identity in Athens 86–92

Seneca the Elder 154

Seneca the Younger 154–68
  on childrearing 172, 181
  Consolations 154, 165, 166
  on death 154, 165–8
    of young children 188
  on gladitorial games 199
  herm of *155*
  Letters 154–5, 157, 159, 160–2, 163,
    164, 165, 166–8, 188, 199
  life 154
  on living with wealth 160–2
  and Nero 173
  On Anger 154, 163, 172
  On Clemency 182
  On Favours 164
  On the Happy Life 154, 160
  On Mercy 154, 162
  On Tranquillity of Mind 154, 160, 161–2
  suicide of *168*, 168

tragedies 154
treatises 154
on the treatment of slaves 162–5
on well-being (*eudaimonia*) 159

Septimius Severus, emperor *114*

Seveilii family relief *178*

Sextus Empiricus, *Outlines of Pyrrhonism* 159

Shelley, Percy Bysshe 53

slaves
abandoned babies reared as 188
as childminders 185–7
children 182, 185
freed 149
naming of 88, 91
Seneca on the treatment of 162–5

social stratification, and self-identity in Classical Athens 86–92

sociology 11

Socrates 47–8, 87, 159

sophists 120, 121–2

Sophocles 49
Ajax 64
Antigone 126
Oedipus at Colonus 102
Philoctetes 61, 64

Sorabji, Richard 166

Soranus, *Gynaecology* 177

Sparta
and Athens 98, 101, 105–6, 117
and the Peloponnesian War 106–7

statues *see* sculpture

Stobaeus, *Anthologium* 163

Stoicism 138, 153–4
and death 165–8
and Seneca's everyday conduct 155–6
and Seneca's *Letters* 154–5, 160
and the treatment of slaves 162–5
and wealth 160–2
and well-being, reason and choice 156–50
see also Seneca the Younger

Stone, Lawrence 187

Suetonius 8, 199
Augustus 30, 207
Domitian 187
Julius Caesar 13, 141, 203
Nero 173, 177, 187, 208
and Nero 173, 174
Otho 82
The Twelve Caesars 133, 136, 142
Tiberius 207
Titus 207

suicide, Seneca on 167–8

Suillius, trial of 160

Sulpicius, correspondence with Cicero 136–9

sundials, Roman 28

synchronic study 39

Tacitus
Annals 154, 160, 168, 173, 199, 201
Dialogue on Oratory 153
and Nero 173, 174

Telemachos 58

textual criticism 8, 9

theatre, amphitheatre and circus audiences 193–209
crowd reactions and dynamics 208–9
and the emperor 195, 203, 205–8
equites 195, 196
experiences of 197
and festival days 197–8
and gladitorial games 148–9, 197, 199–201, *200*, 202–3, 205, *209*
in the late republic 204–5
and the people 193, 195
and pleasure and entertainment 198–202
power of 193, 203–4, 206
seating arrangements *194*, 195–7, *196*, 203, 208
senators 195, 196, 208
visibility of the élite 203–4

Theatre of Marcellus, Rome 193, *194*

Thebes 57, 60

Theseus, mythical king of Athens 103

Thomas Aquinas, St 9

Thucydides, *History of Peloponnesian War* 117–18, 118–19, 120–2

Tiberius, emperor 142, 205, 207

Timaeus 21

time 12, 18–19, 21–44
    and the beginning and end of the Classical world 21–3
    and the cosmos 25–9
    dating the Trojan War 53–6
    local measurement of 24
    organisation of 23–5
    and people 29–31
    and periodisation 31–43
    and written records 21–2

Timodemus of Acharnae 116

Titus, emperor 196

tombstones
    identity and inscriptions on 87–8, *88*, 89, 91
    Petronia Grata *179*
    see also grave reliefs

torture, Seneca on fear of death and 167

tragedy, and Athenian identity 101–6

translations
    of ancient Greek and Latin 7
    and textual studies 8

trittyes, and the Athenian city-state 89, 91–2

Trojan War 16, 24
    and Homeric poetry 49, 52–6, 57, 59–60

Troy
    and Aeneas *179*, 181
    alleged site of Homer's Troy 49–51
    excavations at 53–6, *55*

Tullia, daughter of Cicero 136, 138

Tullius 205

Turner, Victor 112

Tutela, statuette of the goddess *28*

tyranny, and the Archaic period 37

the underworld, and the *porticus* of Pompey 16–18

Venus, goddess 16

Vesuvius, Mount, eruption of 6, 32

victory
    in Homeric poetry 112–15
    and patronage in Greek culture 115–16

Virgil 10
    Aeneid 7, 49, 64, 181

Vitruvius, *On Architecture* 13

Vix female burial 40–3
    crater 40, *41*, *42*, 43

voting, and Roman citizens 140, 148, 149

wealth, Seneca on living with 160–2

Wedgwood, Josiah 9

well-being (*eudaimonia*), Stoicism on 156–60

western Mediterranean, ending of the Classical world 22

Williams, Bernard 164

wisdom
    and Stoicism 157–60
    and death 165–8

Wiseman, Peter 141–2, 146, 147

Wolf, F.A., on the Homeric poems 56–7, 59, 64

Woman at Tomb (*lekythoi*) *128*

women
    and self-identity in Classical Athens 90–1
    statues of in the *porticus* of Pompey 16, 18

Xenocrateia, Attic tombstone of *88*

Xerxes, Persian king 49, 92

years, systems of identifying 23–4

Zeno of Citium 153

Zeus, god *48*, 48
    in Hesiod's *Works and Days* 79–80
    in Homeric poems 52, 74, 76

Zissos, Andrew 27–8

Acknowledgements

Grateful acknowledgement is made to the following sources for permission to reproduce material within this book:

Page 81: Sappho, 'Fragment 1', in M.L. West (trans.) (1994) *Greek Lyric Poetry*, Oxford: Oxford University Press.

Page 135: Catullus, 'Poem 5', in J. Michie (trans.) (1998) *Catullus – Poems*, Ware: Wordsworth Editions.